LITTLE RICHARD
Send Me Some Lovin'

Spencer Leigh

McNIDDER & GRACE

Published by McNidder & Grace
21 Bridge Street
Carmarthen SA31 3JS
Wales, United Kingdom

www.mcnidderandgrace.com

First published in 2024

A catalogue record for this work is available from the British Library.

ISBN 9780857162441 paperback
ISBN 9780857162458 ebook

Designed by JS Typesetting Ltd, Porthcawl
Cover designer Tabitha Palmer

About the Author

The journalist, acclaimed author and BBC broadcaster Spencer Leigh is an authority on popular music, especially the Beatles. He has written many music biographies including, most recently, Bob Dylan, Simon & Garfunkel, Elvis Presley, Frank Sinatra and Buddy Holly. Collect the set!

Spencer Leigh has been broadcasting his weekly show, On the Beat, on BBC Radio Merseyside for over 30 years and he has interviewed thousands of musicians. He has written over twenty-five books, hundreds of album sleeve notes and obituaries of musicians for the *Guardian*, the *Independent* and the *Oxford Dictionary of National Biography*.

Spencer is an Honoured Friend at Sir Paul McCartney's Liverpool Institute of Performing Arts (LIPA) and has a Gold Badge of Merit from the British Academy of Composers and Songwriters

‘Only those who will risk going too far can possibly find out how far one can go.’

T. S Eliot

‘I wouldn’t say I started it all, but I don’t remember anyone else before me playing that stuff.’

Little Richard

‘Great people follow their own path.’

Bob Dylan

‘You do somethin’ no one else can.’

Little Richard (‘Miss Ann’)

‘You do somethin’ no one else can.’
(**Everybody else**)

Foreword

Little Richard to me is a timeless genius and as important as Elvis Presley. We think of his rock'n'roll power songs as having been around forever, but 'Tutti Frutti', 'Long Tall Sally', 'Lucille' and 'Good Golly Miss Molly' all appeared in an incredible creative burst between 1955 and 1958. He was a timeless genius but got sidelined in the 1960s, possibly because of the rich plethora of talent around like Sam Cooke, Otis Redding and James Brown.

This book tells us so much about Little Richard – a man who was always happy in his shoes and in what he was doing in a time where people were overtly judgemental (as opposed to the covertly judgemental masses who stalk social media today).

With his inimitable gender-crossing style, he must surely have been the main inspiration for Prince and many others – a black man wearing make-up and flamboyantly gender-neutral clothes, talking about religion and singing his lungs out … it must have been beautiful to watch.

Wish I'd seen in him in Liverpool in 1963, just casually strutting the stage holding a chair in his teeth (as you do).

I thought we'd had some pretty wild times in The Christians but reading Spencer's depictions of Little Richard's times with Larry Williams and Esquerita, I feel like our nights were pretty tame.

This book is an excellent read from a time when music led the way.

Garry Christian of the Christians, Liverpool 2023

Contents

Introduction

At five minutes to midnight on New Year's Eve 1999, I said to my wife Anne that we must start the Millennium by playing something joyous, optimistic and full of life, and she said, 'Well, that rules out Leonard Cohen.' I began with the war cry of rock'n'roll – Little Richard's 'Tutti Frutti', released in the UK in 1956 and a record that told you that life would never be the same again.

Little Richard recorded some of rock'n'roll's biggest hits, including 'Long Tall Sally', 'Rip It Up', 'Lucille' and 'Good Golly Miss Molly'. Many other rockers including Elvis Presley, Eddie Cochran, Buddy Holly, Jerry Lee Lewis and the Everly Brothers recorded his songs, but Little Richard has not left a large legacy of tracks known to the general public – perhaps 12 as a generous assessment. That's only half an hour's music and his first album, *Here's Little Richard*, contained half of them.

The discography I've compiled took me by surprise because I kept coming across excellent records which didn't sell. Little Richard's approach was set in aspic, and nobody wanted anything different from him. 'I Don't Know What You've Got (But It's Got Me)', made with Jimi Hendrix in 1965, is a wonderful example of deep soul music, but it has been ignored. Even by Richard himself – he doesn't even mention it in his autobiography.

Bill Medley of the Righteous Brothers told me that when he was growing up, 'I would put my ear to the speaker for a Little Richard record and I could sing along with it pretty good. Soon I could do exactly what he was doing.'

He's not the only one. Little Richard was a prime influence on the beat groups of the British Invasion, and the Beatles included 'Long Tall Sally' in nearly all their stage shows. Indeed, Paul McCartney said, 'The first song I ever sang in public was 'Long Tall Sally' at a holiday camp.' It was the Beatles' most performed song and they also wrote songs which aped Little Richard, notably 'I'm Down'. What is the *Whoo!* in 'From Me to You' but 100% Richard? Then in the 1970s, Little Richard influenced Elton John, David Bowie and Michael Jackson. Glam was a reboot of Little Richard. In the '80s, Prince updated Richard's look, style and general mischievousness when writing about sex.

The so-called rock'n'roll lifestyle starts with Little Richard, and the link between sexuality and religion is a key component of both Little Richard's and Leonard Cohen's work, admittedly in very different ways.

I've followed Little Richard from the time I heard 'Tutti Frutti' and 'Long Tall Sally' in 1956. I've bulky files of press cuttings but, outside of his autobiography and a *Rolling Stone* interview, Richard avoided conversations with the media and, like a seasoned politician, had set responses. There was little of the antagonism associated with his compadres, Chuck Berry and Jerry Lee Lewis, but it was often nonsense accompanied by an enormous smile.

My good friend, Chas White, collaborated with him on that book, published in 1984 – a masterful work to be sure, one of the best -ever rock books, but he had to accept Little Richard on Little Richard's own assessment. Chas' book doesn't question his outlandish claims, but it is a fabulous work, akin to David Niven's outrageous Hollywood memoir, *The Moon's a Balloon* (1971).

Chas described Little Richard to me as 'a totally fascinating human being' and I can buy into that. It has been enormous fun to research this book and then write about him. Where I part company with Chas is that I believe the key to Little Richard is that he was acting the entire time, and I would say the same of David Bowie, although Bowie was always expanding on what he had created.

Comparing Little Richard to an opera singer, Chas says that Little Richard makes Pavarotti sound like 'a squeaky mouse'. Maybe with appropriate training, Richard could have sung opera, but the key difference between opera and rock voices is in interpretation. Bob Dylan, Neil Young and Tom Waits have shown that not being able to carry a tune perfectly is no drawback. It is the ability to convey the meaning of the words that counts, and some performers are more like actors than professional singers in that regard.

Little Richard's influences are discussed in some detail. When he burst open the UK scene, no one had witnessed anything like it, but as *Send Me Some Lovin'* shows he had taken a bit from this and a bit from that and certainly his songwriting was a patchwork quilt. I don't, however, think that this diminishes his achievements. The way he brought it together was unique – and Little Richard showed that there was something new under the sun.

Furthermore, Little Richard was a Black, bisexual man in an era of segregation. His outlandish clothes, his pompadour and his make-up challenged the norm, so maybe he was a protest singer. His songs changed society as much as Bob Dylan's.

Little Richard's ego was monstrous. I thought before writing this book that he was funny and entertaining. I still think that but find him even more of a comedian than I expected, and, primarily, this is a book about a man who always wanted to be the centre of attention. Little Richard is an absolute gift for a writer and one thing is certain: neither I nor anyone else could have invented him. Little Richard is unique – and then some. Some books are a hard slog, but this one has been total entertainment.

By a quirk of fate, Little Richard was precisely in the right place at the right time to match the absurdity of his personality with the ridiculousness of rock'n'roll.

Obviously, in a book about a little richard, you're going to get penis jokes. There's the first one. Enjoy the book.

CHAPTER 1
Georgia on My Mind

I. Peach Pickin' Time down in Georgia

Georgia in the south-east of America is an average-sized state, smaller than the UK and with a population of 10 million. The official state song is the truly exceptional 'Georgia on My Mind', written by two friends Hoagy Carmichael and Stuart Gorrell, who both came from Indiana. At a party in 1930, Carmichael played his new melody, and Gorrell asked if he could write a lyric, even though he had never written one before. It was a cold night in Indiana and the lyric was full of warmth and sunshine.

Hoagy Carmichael sensed it was a wonderful song, but although it was published in 1930, it didn't find fame until 1941 when it was recorded by both Anita O'Day and Billie Holiday. In 1960 there was a brilliant interpretation by Ray Charles for his album *The Genius Hits the Road*, and it became a million-selling single. Actually, Charles hadn't hit the road at all: he was born in Albany, Georgia, about 160 km (100 miles) from Macon where Little Richard was raised.

In 1968 the song was jokingly referenced by the Beatles in 'Back in the USSR' when John Lennon and Paul McCartney used its title to refer to the country in the Soviet Union. In 1978 'Georgia On My Mind' was a key track on Willie Nelson's album of standards, *Stardust,* the title song also being a Hoagy Carmichael tune.

Despite his exceptional lyric, Stuart Gorrell didn't consider himself a songwriter. He became a banker and never published another song. When people asked him if 'Georgia on My Mind' was about a girl or about the state, he would answer, 'What do you think?' Clever move: the mystery endures to this day. Although there are hundreds of versions, Little Richard never recorded it, but he didn't often record standards and his views about Georgia were mixed: he loved the state but there was danger all around him as he was growing up. This was a region where Black men were lynched.

In 1987 Ray Charles told the American writer, Joe Smith. "The biggest thing that ever happened to me was when 'Georgia on My Mind' became the state song. That really touched me. This state used to lynch people like me."

Little Richard sometimes called himself the Georgia Peach because the state has the perfect climate for growing fruit and vegetables. Just off the coast are St. Simons Island and Cumberland Island, and in the sixteenth century Franciscan monks introduced peaches to the area. The sweetness of Georgia's peaches is renowned.

Richard Penniman was born in Macon, Georgia, 80 miles south-east of Atlanta. The city was established in 1823 as a cotton port on the Ocmulgee River. As a transport hub, Macon was crucial. Its elegant train station from 1916 was designed by Alfred T. Fellheimer, whose CV included Grand Central Station, New York in 1903. Old photographs feature the prominent sign, 'Colored Waiting Rooms'.

Many of the antebellum houses have been preserved and there is a cherry blossom festival every March. The city now has a population of 150,000 and is aware of its musical heritage with statues of James Brown and Otis Redding and talk of one for Little Richard.

The Georgia Music Hall of Fame opened on Martin Luther King Boulevard in 1996 and represented over 400 artists from Georgia, including REM. It displayed a photograph of James Brown meeting Pope John Paul II. Unfortunately, we don't know what the two leaders were discussing. The museum closed in 2011, due to a lack of visitors – an indication that music tourism doesn't always work.

Still, there is an Allman Brothers Museum, and Duane Allman was inspired to write 'Little Martha' by the statue of Martha Ellis in Rose Hill Cemetery. It's on their 1972 album *Eat a Peach*, the title being another reference to Georgia's produce.

Although there isn't a Little Richard statue yet, you can travel along Little Richard Penniman Boulevard to Mercer University. The university was established in 1833 and named after a Baptist minister and community leader. There's no connection with the Georgian songwriter Johnny Mercer, who was born 160km (100 miles) away in the coastal city of Savannah, his tribute to the area being 'Moon River' for Audrey Hepburn in the film *Breakfast at Tiffany's* (1961). There was a Moon River close to Savannah and 'my huckleberry friend' presumably means that it was blue: again, another mysterious phrase that the songwriter didn't explain.

The Little Richard House Resource Center is situated in Little Richard's childhood home in Craft Street. It is opposite Jefferson Park, and stages social and musical events. The single-storey house isn't where it used to be on Pleasant Hill. For a time, it was going to be demolished to make way for a highway, but then the whole premises was transported a mile away. Considering it is about a hundred years old, it has endured very well, especially as the small building had been a home to the Penniman family with their 12 children.

The Center is not a Little Richard museum, offering information about health, literacy and employment, how to fill in a job application, and how to learn about modern technology. It does, however, pay tribute to Little Richard's life and when Richard heard about the Center in 2019, he said, 'Thank you for everything you've ever done for my old house. That old house has a lot of tutti frutti, aw rutti.'

So too does the Greyhound bus station. It was there that Little Richard washed dishes and dreamt of being a star, though he was worried that constant dishwashing might ruin his pretty hands.

II. Open the Door, Richard

In the liner notes for his first LP, *Here's Little Richard* (1956), Richard gave his date of birth as Christmas Day, 1935, a date that, though much repeated, is wrong. Choosing Christ's birthday and making himself three years younger is narcissism on both counts and the key to Little Richard's life.

Richard Wayne Penniman was born in the Pleasant Hill neighbourhood of Macon on Monday, 5 December 1932. This was to be his home, although he often lived away from it, until he had a major hit single with 'Tutti Frutti' at the start of 1956.

His grandfather, his uncle and a cousin were all preachers, and worship was to play a major role in Little Richard's life.

For most of his adult years, Little Richard was attracted to the Seventh-day Adventists, and was an evangelist for them from the early 1960s.

Although Little Richard's comments on religion can be inconsistent, he was accepted into the ministry of the Seventh-day Adventists. They have modified their beliefs in recent decades and are now part of the Christian family of churches. They have Observer status at the World Council of Churches and are on good terms with the evangelical wing. They differ from Jehovah's Witnesses who are still something of an outpost in Christian belief.

Seventh-day Adventists practise strict temperance and as the name suggests, they observe the Sabbath from sunset on Friday to sunset on Saturday – that is, the same as the Jewish Sabbath. They have 20,000 pastors but Little Richard was never responsible for a congregation.

Hopefully, I report Little Richard's thoughts about religion accurately in this book, but by and large, I will not be commenting further. The whole study of rock and religion and what various performers have believed merits a book in itself and would involve Elvis Presley, Little Richard, George Harrison, Pete Townshend, Bob Dylan, Leonard Cohen, Al Green, Sinéad O'Connor, Cliff Richard and the Singing Nun. I've got a title: *I Say a Little Prayer.*

When I saw Little Richard in Liverpool in 2000, he asked the Jewish people in the audience to raise their hands. At the time, I thought, 'This is interesting. They've come to see a rock'n'roll legend and now they'll be told to turn to Christ.' But no, once the hands were raised, he said: 'I'm Jewish myself' and continued on his rockin' way.

The rock musician and writer Sid Griffin had the same experience as he told me, 'Richard stopped the show, acknowledged the applause and then said, "How many Jewish people do we have in the audience tonight?" It was a weird tangent but it was as entertaining as the rest of the show.' And that's it precisely – no matter what he is doing, Richard is mesmerising.

Little Richard had religion in his family. His grandfather, Walter Penniman, was a pastor for the African Methodist Episcopal Church. Walter had six sons and four daughters and his first son, Charles, known as Bud, was Little Richard's father. His life was built around more worldly pursuits: raising a large family and working hard to provide. He was a skilled bricklayer and stonemason who developed a profitable sideline in moonshine – that is, illegal whiskey usually made at night (hence the name) which flaunted the strict Prohibition laws of the 1920s. He did go to church and help with the services, but his real interest was in his family and selling bootleg booze. Indeed, he opened his own Tip-in Inn.

Richard's mother, Leva Mae Stewart, was the youngest in a family of eight. Richard would say that there was American Indian blood in the family, basing this on his grandmother's long silver hair and high cheekbones. Leva Mae was deeply religious and in Macon, she was an active member of the New Hope Baptist Church. Her brother, Louis, became a Baptist pastor in Philadelphia.

Bud met Leva at a church meeting, and they married when she was only 14, something that was common at that time in the Deep South. Their first child Elnora was born the following year: the name was chosen by Bud's mother, but everybody called her Peggie. Then there was Charles, named after his father and sometimes called Bobby, followed by Richard Wayne. He was going to be Ricardo Wayne Penniman, after Leva's father, but the clerk made a mistake and wrote 'Richard Wayne'.

It is often reported that Richard was born with the right leg shorter than the other, maybe by as much as three inches. However, there is plenty of footage of Richard walking over the years and only occasionally is there a noticeable limp. Also, he appears to be wearing standard shoes with no built-up heel on one foot. Richard has said that this imbalance gave him a feminine walk when he was young and he was mocked for it, but again you should take a lot of what Richard says with 20 pinches of salt. Indeed, he sometimes joked that he invented hip-hop.

There is colour footage of Richard performing 'Rip It Up' on TV in 1963 and he is obliged to walk up and down a staircase – looks perfectly okay to me. Similarly, he goes down a staircase to a lower deck in the film, *Catalina Caper* (1967), again without difficulty.

After Richard, there were nine more children, the later ones being Marquette de Lafayette, Walter Maurice (named after Bud's father), Horace Dearcy (known as Tony), Robert Realdo, Leva La Leda (known as Silvia), Artis Elaine, (Deanie), Gail June, Freka Diedra (known as Peaches) and Peyton Larry. Leva said of her last daughter, 'I wanted a name that I'd never heard before.'

They lived on Pleasant Hill in a Black neighbourhood in this single-storeyed house near the railway track, so the children had to take care. They had electricity and running water, but their home was on a dirt road. The white families lived a couple of roads away on paved streets.

Bud built swings and slides for his growing family and they had such fun that white kids would come over to find out what was going on. Black families were not allowed in the white shops, and neither Richard nor his siblings dared venture into their territory.

Leva took her children to the New Hope Baptist Church on Third Avenue in Macon on Sunday mornings and some of her children, including Richard, sang as the Tiny Tots or the Penniman Singers.

The Pennimans had a piano which had belonged to Leva's father, and Richard taught himself the rudiments. That, he thought, was all he needed and he never seriously studied the instrument, although he did assimilate some techniques along the way. By and large, he adapted the songs to his abilities and took it from there.

Richard would sometimes go with his grandmother to the Fountain Tempa, an African Methodist Episcopal church on Sunday evenings. He enjoyed the loud and lively gospel music at their services.

Richard said, 'When Black people go to church, they want to shout. They are the shoutingest people I have ever seen in my life. I've seen an old lady do a James Brown right across the floor. Black people are very emotional.'

Right from the get-go, Richard was mischievous, often in trouble with his family, the church and the authorities. His brother Charles thought that it was part of his nature: Richard always wanted attention.

Richard had fun with his waste products. He said, 'I pooped in a jelly jar, and I closed up the jar and put it in the cabinet with mother's preserves.' Another time he wrapped a turd and gave it as a peace offering to a neighbour who had criticised him. Leva once threw a bottle at him which accidentally hit his head and drew blood.

Richard was encouraged by his cousin Bertha May, known as Boodlum. They once locked up a grocer in his own store. When Bud got a Model T Ford, they pushed it down a hill.

Charles was taught to box by his father and sometimes defended Richard from his detractors, but he didn't recognise his early musical ability. 'He would beat on tin cans and I thought he couldn't sing at the time. It was just a noise.' Nevertheless, Richard sang in the church choir and as a young teenager, he was putting his flamboyance to good use, getting ready to perform as Little Richard.

Richard attended both Methodist and Baptist services in Macon, but one of his sisters,

Peggie, went to hear a Seventh-day Adventist preacher, Elder Ward. Richard recalled, 'His wife was playing the piano, and the girls was going to the tent because Elder Ward was a very good-looking guy. They were all going to the meeting, trying to get this woman's husband, He was just smiling at them – then he hit them with the truth, so he was a very good preacher.'

This led to some family trouble. Even though Bud's father was an Adventist minister, that brand of religion was not for him. Richard recalled, 'Peggie became an Adventist. She threw the pork chops in the backyard as she had read that God didn't want us to eat that kind of food. The Bible tells us what is clean and what is not clean. My daddy was mad with her and at the time I was mad with her too as I wanted my pork chops.'

Richard attended Macon's Ballard-Hudson High School but he had little application and was a below-average student. He did learn a little saxophone, joining his school's marching band.

As a teenager, Richard sang in the Macon Sanctified church. Often associated with Black communities, this branch of Christianity offered an energetic form of worship: believers reliving their experience and everybody singing with great fervour. Even by these standards, Little Richard was seen as too enthusiastic and was nicknamed the War Hawk. Richard said in 1959, 'Religion is essentially a happy thing and something you should enjoy. That also showed up in my piano playing. One day in church I was enjoying myself so much that I added a boogie woogie rhythm to the hymns. That didn't please the minister and at the age of 14, I was sacked for it.'

At the same show, Richard sang with Dr Hudson's Medicine Show, its main function being to sell snake oil in sideshows at carnivals. Dr Hudson was from Macon and Richard sometimes travelled with him. The snake oil was $2 a bottle and said to be good for anything. Well, good for nothing really.

Bud didn't object to Richard going away for a few days: an exhibitionistic child in a small house takes up a lot of space. He told Leva, 'He doesn't want to go to school, so let him go. He has our phone number.' The Ballard-Hudson High School made no attempt to retain him, although a board outside the school today proudly acknowledges that Little Richard and Otis Redding were former pupils.

If only Richard had paid attention in the maths classes, he would have handled his contracts better in the mid-50s. He did, however, love music by musicians such as Cecil Gant, and he heard what he could in clubs and on the radio.

* * *

When Private Cecil Gant returned to Los Angeles in 1944 after war service, he recorded 'I Wonder' for the small Gilt-Edge label. Not many copies were pressed because of a shortage of shellac, but everybody wanted this song which captured the mood of the times. Secret deals were made for shellac and the record sold a million copies. Entrepreneurs realised that there was a market for R & B. Gant himself became depressed and died in 1951 but 'I Wonder' had kick-started the independent record business. As Little Richard reached his teenage years, there was a great array of wonderful records on the radio.

Even if Little Richard hadn't mentioned his influences, we could guess them. Outside of gospel music, Richard's prime influence was Louis Jordan and His Tympany Five. Their R & B hits were often humorous. Jordan was fond of rolling his eyes and pulling comic faces: see, for example, the YouTube clips of 'Beware Brother Beware' and 'Deacon Jones'.

The first secular song that Richard performed in public was 'Caledonia', a No.1 R & B record for Jordan in the summer of 1945. Louis Jordan, Jack McVea, Dusty Fletcher, the Three Flames and the Count Basie Orchestra all recorded hit versions of 'Open the Door, Richard', a novelty R & B hit from 1947. Richard loved its rhythm, its words and naturally, its title.

Louis Jordan spent a record-breaking 113 weeks at the top of *Billboard*'s R & B charts and his classic 'Saturday Night Fish Fry' from 1949 has a repeated refrain, 'It was rockin', it was rockin''. As well as Jordan's showmanship influencing Little Richard, his band line-up was copied by Fats Domino, his arrangements by Bill Haley, his sly humour by Ray Charles, and his lyrical style by Chuck Berry.

Although a Black artist, Louis Jordan even made the US country charts with 'Ration Blues' (a truly topical song from 1944) and 'Is You Is or Is You Ain't My Baby?' (1947).

Little Richard's debt to Jordan is obvious: his explosive but repetitive 'Keep-a Knockin'' sounds as though it was written on the spot, but its origin lies in a 1928 piano blues by Bert Mays, '(No use a-knockin' 'cause) You Can't Come In', which went into Louis Jordan's repertoire. Jordan, an audacious, pop-eyed dancer, also pioneered jump music, which was wilder than swing. He was among the first to make music videos and he made a Western in which he is playing a saxophone while riding a horse.

More recently, Louis Jordan's music was celebrated in the theatrical success, *Five Guys Named Moe.* Jordan had it all – and he knew it: he said, 'Rock'n'roll was not a marriage of rhythm and blues and country and western. That's white publicity. Rock'n'roll was just a white imitation of what we did.' Louis Jordan was inducted into the Rock and Roll Hall of Fame in 1987.

As for Jordan himself, his prime influence was the jazz singer and trumpeter Louis Armstrong. In 1926, while Armstrong was recording a hectic novelty, 'Heebie Jeebies', the sheet music fell to the floor and rather than stop singing, Louis improvised his vocal. His nonsense syllables have come to be known as 'scat', a style copied by Ella Fitzgerald, Little Richard and Van Morrison, to name but three. The song itself has a nonsense title but there are numerous examples of silly titles in rock'n'roll. Richard's own 'Heeby-Jeebies' is a different song with the same title.

Fats Domino was also listening to Louis Armstrong's wonderful 'Blueberry Hill' (1949), one of Richard's favourite songs.

Slim Gaillard was a marvellous entertainer, mixing jazz and comedy in a very personal way. Like a hip Stanley Unwin, he invented his own jive talk, called Vout-o-Reenee, which ended words with 'o-reenee' or 'o-roonie'. One record, 'Flat Foot Floogie (with a Floy Floy)', was about a prostitute with gonorrhoea. His double act with bassist Slam Stewart was a radio success and they had a pop hit as Slim & Sam with a piece of nonsense based on the Italian phrase for chopped fruit, 'Tutti Frutti'. Most likely, this developed into a dirty song which, in turn, was cleaned up by Little Richard for his first hit single in 1955. Gaillard performed well into the 1980s, being the subject of a BBC-TV documentary and a host for the Wigan Jazz Festival.

In 1943 Carmen Miranda, with a greengrocer's store on her head, sang 'The Lady in the Tutti Frutti Hat' for the Busby Berkeley musical *The Gang's All Here.*

Then there's 'Be-baba-leba' by Helen Humes from 1945. The high-pitched vocalist made this record with the Bill Doggett Octet, and Bill went on to make a memorable rock'n'roll instrumental, 'Honky Tonk', which you will know even if you don't recognise the title. Helen had been one of Count Basie's vocalists – and lovers – but had to leave when his wife found out about their affair. The nonsense song, a development of the phrase 'be bop' was an inspiration for Little Richard ('Awopbopaloobop Alopbamboom') and Joe 'Mr Piano' Henderson ('Hey! Ba Ba Re Bop').

'The House of Blue Lights' by Freddie Slack and his Orchestra from 1946 is an early example of white folk singing R & B. Freddie Slack was a pianist and arranger whose vocalist was Ella Mae Morse. She refers to him as 'Daddy-O' during the song, the first time that the term was put on record. The song itself was a variation of 'Pinetop's Boogie Woogie' (1929), and it was subsequently associated with the singing pianist Merrill E Moore, a strong influence on Jerry Lee Lewis. Little Richard, you'll remember, saw Miss Molly dancing at the House of Blue Light.

Joe Lutcher, brother of Nellie, sang with Nat King Cole. His energetic big band music was influential, notably 'Rockin' Boogie' (1947) and the fast-moving R & B number 'Rockola' (1948), which was in praise of the famous jukebox: 'Rock, rock, rock, Rockola'. David Rockola, who gave the company his perfect name, died in 1993 at age of 96. Joe Lutcher left music to join the church – and, in time would encourage Little Richard to do the same.

Art Rupe, the owner of Specialty Records recalled, 'Joe Lutcher was one of our early artists and he had become a minister. His mission was to convert pop singers to the church with his old superstition that it is evil to sing pop. He got to Little Richard, and Little Richard began to believe the idea.'

Willie Lee Perryman from Hampton, Georgia, better known as Piano Red, released 'Rockin' with Red' on RCA in 1950 – just before Little Richard joined the label. It is full of sexual innuendo: 'She knows how to rock, If you've even been rocked, you'll know just what I mean.' The words and melody are almost identical to Richard's 1957 hit, 'She Knows How to Rock', now listed with Richard as the composer.

There were many songs packed with innuendo like Wynonie Harris' 'I Like My Baby's Pudding' which was used, possibly without appreciating its implications, in *The Great British Bake-Off* on Channel 4.

Wynonie Harris' repertoire was high on sexual content – 'Lollipop Mama', 'I Want My Fanny Brown' and even his most famous record, 'Good Rockin' Tonight' in 1948. It was no act, either: he was foul-mouthed and would record his one-night liaisons and play them on the tour bus the following day. He put up a sign outside his house, 'This is where the greatest blues singer in the world lives', until the authorities made him remove it.

Harris added a dance beat to the blues, but straight-down-the-line, undiluted blues were also popular. One of the biggest R & B records of 1952 was 'Dust My Broom' by Elmore James with Sonny Boy Williamson on harmonica.

Chris Smither, a contemporary blues performer who writes for Bonnie Raitt, says: 'Almost everyone who plays blues learns 'Dust My Broom'. For one thing, it is so appealing because it is so obviously an early progenitor of rock'n'roll. Originally it was a woman's song: 'Get up in the morning and I believe I'll dust my broom.' It meant that she was going to get rid of her old man, 'I will dust my broom on the back of this guy.' That's the only explanation I have of it: the song just sounds good and I like the way the vowels come together.'

Although Little Richard was to stand out from the crowd, the world of blues and rhythm and blues was populated with eccentric, one-off performers, none more so than

Professor 'Fess' Longhair, the New Orleans blues singer and pianist. Fess once got so excited that he kicked a hole in his piano, and Chas White recalls, 'A lot of rock'n'roll is about spontaneity and some of the best New Orleans records came from Professor Longhair coming in and playing rhumba boogies. They got the tapes rolling and that was it. He is as important as Ry Cooder as he brought in South American rhythms and American Indian tribal music.' Richard would see him and think, 'I can do this. I can do just what I want.'

From the age of 14, Little Richard would sing from time to time in a Macon bar, the Tic Toc Room, which was owned by a white couple, Ann and Johnny Howard. It was years ahead of its time: it had a mixed clientele and was also a gay meeting place. Richard said, 'When I was 13. I played there and the people went mad. I played 'Guitar Rag' on the piano.'

Richard would also sell Cokes at the Macon City Auditorium, working for local promoter Clint Brantley. There was a constant stream of stars performing or waiting to leave for the next town.

Bud kicked Richard out of the house for his effeminate behaviour and the Howards allowed him to stay on their premises. Richard said of the Howards, 'They adopted me and bought me a car. I went to school and Ann was like my mother for many years. Johnny passed away and I got famous but she wouldn't take any money from me. They had a lot to do with me loving people today.' Richard never forgot their kindness and sometimes dedicated 'Miss Ann' to her ('When I'm with Miss Ann, I'm livin' in paradise.')

Richard often performed at the Tic Toc Room, invariably performing 'Caledonia'. He also had bookings drumming up support for Dr Nubillo's medicine show. Richard's interest in turbans and capes was down to Dr Nubillo, who also 'carried a black stick and exhibited something he called the Devil's child—the dried-up body of a baby with claw feet like a bird and horns on its head.'

The trumpet break in 'Atlanta Boogie', a 1951 record from Tommy Brown, may not sound very hip, but otherwise this is rock'n'roll all the way. Tommy Brown from Atlanta influenced many Georgian musicians, including Little Richard and James Brown and possibly Johnnie Ray, whose 'Cry' is like his 'Weepin' and Cryin''.

Ike Turner's Kings of Rhythm Band featured Ike's cousin, Jackie Brenston. On 5 March 1951 they recorded 'Rocket 88' for Sam Phillips in Memphis. It was largely instrumental with three short vocals: its energy has made Phillips call it 'the first rock'n'roll record', but then that would have to be something he'd produced. The record was released on Chess and topped the R & B charts, but there was friction as Ike Turner resented the billing, which implied Brenston was the star.

'I always liked that record,' admitted Little Richard, 'and I used the riff in my act. When we were looking for a lead-in for 'Good Golly Miss Molly', I used that and it fitted.' In several later interviews, Richard says he wrote 'Good Golly Miss Molly' in Macon, but, according to the record label, it is not even his song.

Little Richard was never taken to court for breach of copyright, but it is possible that backroom deals were made to credit and compensate original songwriters and publishers.

All these links to earlier records have changed my perspective on Little Richard: he wasn't the great originator that I thought he was in the 1950s. Nevertheless, he brought this wonderful stuff to our attention and added his own magnificent spin. It simply illustrates that nobody lives in a vacuum.

In 1950, 17-year-old Richard was approached by Ethel Wynnes, who ran the Winsetta Patio club, 160km (100 miles) south of Macon in Fitzgerald, Georgia. The singer with B Brown and his Orchestra was sick and following a recommendation, she invited Richard to join them for a few dates. When the band played to white audiences in Georgia, Richard sang some contemporary hits ('Goodnight Irene', 'Mona Lisa'), which were well received.

B Brown told him to bill himself as Little Richard, echoing the stage names of many blues performers. There was Little Willie Littlefield and Little Walter before him and Little Willie John and Little Milton shortly afterwards. Sometimes the 'Little' denotes their youth.

There was also Big Joe Turner, which sounded good although in his case, he was mocking his obesity. Fats Domino with his first record 'The Fat Man' was getting the joke in first. On the female front, there was Big Mama Thornton and Little Esther, who later performed as Esther Phillips. In 1952 Little Esther and Little Willie (Littlefield) recorded a duet, 'Last Laugh Blues', an early Jerry Leiber and Mike Stoller song, for Federal.

In June 1952 the jazz and standards singer Billy Eckstine was given a gold record by the Harlem Record Dealers Association. He was touring as 'the biggest boon to the record business in a decade', but he never made the R & B charts again: things were changing.

Little Richard also toured with Sugarfoot Sam's Minstrel Show from Alabama, on the chitlin circuit, clubs for Black performers which took their name from the food associated with the Southern poor, especially Blacks. With the Minstrel Show he was not just Little Richard but also Princess Lavonne. Because the audiences regarded it as good clean fun, many of the Black clubs in the South featured drag artists, even having an annual ball in New Orleans. The entertainment had developed from the minstrel shows, to offer fun and entertainment rather make than any political point, and Little Richard loved it.

Richard also developed an interest in doo-wop. Henry Nash knew Richard from school, where Richard was interested in the sounds Henry could make with a saxophone. When Henry was forming a doo-wop group, the Dominions, Richard was with them for some months, but he was never really a team player.

He did, however, love doo-wop, commenting on the Spaniels: 'Yeah, those boys could sing. They're on it, especially that bass man and my man, the smooth voice of Pookie Hudson. My goodness, if I was in a group, I'd like to be in the Spaniels." When asked which Spaniels' records he liked best, he named 'Baby, It's You', 'Stormy Weather' and 'Goodnight, Sweetheart, Goodnight'.

Richard also sang with a travelling circus owned by the King Brothers and then he was invited to join the Tidy Jolly Steppers, again performing in drag, for $10 a week. After that, he teamed up with two other drag artists and they worked on the L J Heath Show at Bailey's 81 Theatre in Atlanta, where Richard performed four times a day. Their *Broadway Follies* production toured the South. Another vocalist on the show was Chuck Willis, later known for 'What Am I Living For'. Willis had a hang-up about his balding head and always wore a turban, turning what would have been a liability into an asset.

Richard also found himself working alongside B.B. King and Jimmy Witherspoon – all good experience.

The most significant influence, though, was Billy Wright, the self-proclaimed Prince of the Blues, though he mixed blues with gospel and boogie-woogie. He had his first Top 10 R & B successes with 'Blues for My Baby' and You Satisfy' in 1949 for the Savoy label. He had a similar style to Louis Jordan. 'Billy's Boogie Blues' (1949) contains the line, 'That gal rocks me, rocks me with a steady roll' and has a playout that was copied by Frankie Lymon in 'Baby, Baby'.

I'm partial to his 1950 single 'Stacked Deck': he's going to play cards with his girlfriend but as he goes through the cards, rather like 'Deck of Cards', you realise he is going to win because he is the King with his crown. It's a shame that Richard never recorded a tribute album to his early heroes: it would been good to have heard contemporary versions of songs like these.

Billy with coal black hair and gold teeth was in his early 30s and wore loud clothes. He had had his hair curled, and he applied heavy make-up for the stage. Billy encouraged Richard to be flamboyant, have a pompadour and slap on Pancake 31. Wright was also a female impersonator, so Richard was impressed.

Wright introduced Richard to a white disc jockey, Zenas Sears, who played Black records on Radio WGST in Atlanta. As a result, Little Richard was signed to RCA and was recorded on 16 October 1951 at that radio station using Billy Wright's musicians. So Little Richard was on RCA some four years before Elvis, although this is not as impressive as it sounds. RCA released his two singles with little promotion, so why did they bother?

In 'Every Hour', you can hear strains of the agonised blues that Richard later recorded, such as 'Can't Believe You Wanna Leave' and 'Early One Morning'. 'Why Did You Leave Me' is darker and Richard is writing about California, a place he only knew from a map.

The famed jazz critic Leonard Feather (born in London in 1914) wrote the entertaining 'Get Rich Quick' with his wife Jane, while Jane and Little Richard wrote 'Taxi Blues', an odd song about a singer beating up his girlfriend. Still, that was common in songs of the period: Big Joe Turner in 'Honey Hush' is threatening his partner with a baseball bat.

The first single was released by RCA in December 1951 and reviewed in the trade paper *Billboard*: 'From Macon, Georgia comes Little Richard, an 18-year-old blues shouter with a voice high in pitch but stylistically lowdown. Currently making personal appearances in Kentucky and along the Dixie circuit, he is presented among new RCA Victor discs with 'Taxi Blues' and 'Every Hour'.' So, *Billboard* had the correct information on Richard's age though they never referred back to it. As 'Every Hour' sold quite well, Billy Wright's record company asked him to record it – instead, he wrote a companion song, 'Every Evenin''.

Through Zenas Sears' airplay, Richard's single had some local success. 'Every Hour' was regularly played on *Randy's Record Store,* a programme from Nashville. Bud Penniman had changed his mind: he was impressed with his son and made sure it was on the jukebox at the Tip-In Inn on Woodliff Street, Macon.

Around this time, a piano-pounding R & B shouter from the South would take the stage sporting a six-inch pompadour, rhinestone shades, embossed shirts, heavy lipstick, and heavier jewellery – and his name was not Little Richard.

His name was Esquerita.

Well, actually his dad was Eskew Reeder and he was born Stephen Quincy Reeder (S Q Reeder) in Greenville, South Carolina in 1935. He played piano from a young age and his roots were in gospel. He dropped out of high school when he was 15 and joined the Heavenly Echoes in New York. They took him on the road and he recorded with them. In a world of eccentrics, Esquerita was distinctive. 'Esquerita was the first with the high wavy piled-up hair, lipstick and women's sunglasses,' says Dr John.

Esquerita played the chitlin circuit in the Deep South and he was gay, Black and camp. He was over six foot and looked crazy and was bringing humour to rock'n'roll. A powerful pianist, he used his huge hands to good effect, but his voice was not as strong or flexible as Richard's.

When Richard was playing for Sister Rosa, who sold 'blessed bread' at the Macon bus station, as well his regular chore of washing dishes, Esquerita came into town. Richard called him 'Excreta', though not to his face: indeed, they used to refer to each other as 'Miss Thing'.

When Richard invited him home, Esquerita played 'One Mint Julep' on the treble keys of the family piano and Richard was impressed: he was now determined to be a pianist as well as a vocalist. Richard said, 'He also taught me his obligato holler, the "Whoo!".'

But Richard wouldn't use this yet.

RCA thought that Little Richard had made a promising start but needed better material. The bandleader Joe Thomas and the pianist Howard Biggs had a songwriting partnership in New York and the company asked them to submit songs for the next session. There was a jump blues 'I Brought It All on Myself', a very confident, Louis Jordan-styled 'Ain't Nothin' Happenin'' and a slow blues 'Please Have Mercy on Me', which was derivative of Percy Mayfield's ballad, 'Please Send Me Someone to Love'. In 1956 Joe and Howard had one of their songs recorded by Elvis Presley, 'I'm Gonna Sit Right Down and Cry (Over You)'.

Richard himself wrote 'Thinkin' 'Bout My Mother', an autobiographical song about a boy who works away from home and is thinking fondly of his mum.

This session on 12 January 1952, like the first, took place at WGST. The songs had professional arrangements and are good performances. Richard had increased confidence but wasn't yet the Richard that we know and love.

One of his favourite singers was Ruth Brown and he loved her 1953 record 'Mama, He Treats Your Daughter Mean'. Herb Abramson of Atlantic Records talked about her 'million-dollar squeal' and now we can see how easily Little Richard incorporated that into his own performances. But not just yet.

Richard read of Ruth Brown being robbed of $10,000 in jewellery and furs from her car. At the time, she was eating in the Bailey Hotel in Pittsburgh *en route* to New Jersey for a show. The report told Richard that she was doing well and that there was money to be made if you had the talent and the right breaks. But Little Richard's day-dreaming was forgotten as he had to confront reality.

On Valentine's Day 1952 Bud and his daughter Peggie were drinking at the Tip-In Inn with his buddy, Frank Tanner. Frank was throwing firecrackers into the stove and laughing. Bud told him to leave but outside with his friends, he made an even greater noise. When Bud went to quieten them, he was shot dead. Frank was arrested and was convicted by a jury on 5 June`1952, but the case was later dismissed. Ten years later Frank asked the Penniman family to forgive him 'and we did', said Little Richard.

'The police were quite glad that Bud had gone,' reflected Richard. At the time, Leva was pregnant and her twelfth and final child, Peyton, was born two months later, on what would have been Bud's birthday, 5 April 1952.

RCA released 'Get Rich Quick' and 'Thinkin' 'bout My Mother'' as a single, but Little Richard was in no state to promote it. *Billboard* commented in its inimitable style, 'Ork and chanter cut this raucous, carefree number solidly. Backing is in ragtime style.'

This was followed by 'Ain't Nothing Happenin'' combined with 'Why Did You Leave Me?' from the first session. The fourth RCA single was 'Please Have Mercy on Me' and 'I

Brought It All on Myself'. 'The warbler turns in a good vocal on this blues-weeper as he asks his girl to show him a little mercy. Ork backs him in bluesy style,' said *Billboard* in November 1952.

A New York manager, Horace Edwards, asked Little Richard to join Percy Welch and his Orchestra for a tour of military bases around Macon. Their pianist Luke Gondor gave Richard some advice on playing the piano.

The US R & B chart in *Billboard* is, as you would expect packed with Black records, but not exclusively. In 1952 one of their No.1 records was Johnnie Ray's 'Cry', which shows that crossovers were in both directions. To my astonishment, Pat Boone had four US R & B hits, including 'Love Letters in the Sand'. Clearly, white artists were picking up sales in Black areas. Similarly, *Billboard* reported that Fats Domino and his six-man band had a month's residency at Grady's Supper Club in Nashville for $2,500 a week.

R & B accounted for only 5% of the total record sales in 1952 but it was possible for a big hit to sell 250,000 copies. Million sellers by R & B artists were rare, but that was to change.

A major film in 1953 was the 3D extra-terrestrial drama, *It Came from Outer Space*, based on a Ray Bradbury story. It is mentioned in 'Science Fiction/Double Feature' from *The Rocky Horror Show* (1973) and its title predicted the rise of Little Richard. (Come to think of it, there is certainly a Little Richard element to *The Rocky Horror Show*. 'Sweet Transvestite' would have been perfect for him.)

As Richard's elder brother, Charles was fighting with the marines in Korea, Richard was the principal breadwinner and needed regular employment, no matter how menial. He was back washing dishes at the Greyhound station in Macon for $15 a week. When Richard wanted to criticise his boss, he would go 'Awopbopaloobop Alopbamboom', little knowing that he had created his passport to fame.

The Macon promoter Clint Brantley owned the Two Spot on Fifth Street and booked bigger attractions for Macon City Auditorium. As a former musician, Brantley recognised Little Richard's talent. He told him, "Get yourself a band – there's plenty of work available."

CHAPTER 2
Specialty Acts

I. Art for Art's Sake

In the 1990s it amused me that Virgin Records was described as an independent record company. Indies weren't meant to be giant conglomerates like Virgin, although Virgin had started as one.

The real indies are to be found among the American record companies of the 1940s and '50s. The larger companies were slow to appreciate the potential of Black artists and their music and although there were major stars (Louis Armstrong, Duke Ellington, Count Basie, Fats Waller), most Black performers recorded for smaller labels. This was an opportunity for businessmen in the big cities, where they formed companies, created dedicated radio stations and opened record stores. Some were opportunistic, some were gangsters, but most of them were enthusiasts like Art Rupe.

Art Rupe (Arthur Milton Goldberg) was born in Greensburg, Pennsylvania on 5 September 1917 and was raised in nearby McKeesport, both close to Pittsburgh. He was the son of a second-hand furniture salesman. The family did not have much money but he did well at school, attended a business course at Miami University, and then went to Los Angeles. He had a vivid imagination and had hopes of being a screenwriter in the developing film industry called Hollywood. Life, though, had other plans, not least war service maintaining Liberty ships. Their steel became brittle in the North Atlantic and he learned the importance of getting things right.

Art Rupe found it difficult to break into films but he could make a living by producing and selling records to the Black community. The record industry faced problems after the war, notably a shortage of shellac, which had mostly come from Japan. This made it harder and more expensive to press records, although a vinyl alternative was being developed, and it also meant that the majors like RCA and Decca were reducing their rosters. Good artists were looking for new homes.

Rupe had $600 and he spent $200 in buying some current R & B, blues and gospel releases and playing them over and over to determine what worked and what didn't. He looked at the structure of the songs, the rhythms, the instruments used, the length of instrumental passages, and how the singers performed. With his knowledge of business administration, he considered how records were marketed and he appreciated that success was built around jukeboxes.

So, with two business partners, he started the Juke Box label and they knew from the start that would not be able to finance big band recordings. Their first release was 'Boogie No.1' by the Sepia Tones in 1944. It was fun but the music was too frantic for dancing. Still, it sold several thousand copies and gave Juke Box a good start.

Juke Box had its first big R & B success early in 1946 with 'R.M. Blues' for Roy Milton and his Solid Senders, a jump blues outfit. The track had an accentuated offbeat and is one of the precursors of rock'n'roll. It was one of the first records to sell a million copies in what was regarded as a race market, although Ella Fitzgerald and Billy Eckstine won Gold Discs with crossover sales.

Roy Milton continued with hit records until 1953, including 'The Hucklebuck' (1949) which laid the foundation for twist records. Frank Sinatra famously hated rock'n'roll but he covered 'The Hucklebuck'. Milton was also a drummer and he often had a snare drum by his microphone which gave his records a stronger beat.

Looking for gimmicks, Rupe had the unusual idea of calling Roosevelt Sykes the Blues Man and Marion Abernathy the Blues Woman. The public might like to guess who the Blues Man and the Blues Woman were. The first hit was with the Blues Woman's 'Voo-It, Voo-It!' and its innuendo-packed lines, "I've got a man that gives boogie all night long."

After a second Roy Milton hit, 'Milton's Boogie', Rupe realised his partners were crooked and so he left Juke Box and set up Specialty Records with Milton as his first artist. He created a distinctive yellow, black and white label for brand awareness.

Rupe saw his main audience as being in Los Angeles which, because of the war, now had a large Black population. If the records could also sell in the south and perhaps nationally, so much the better.

Milton's glamorous pianist Camille Howard had her own singles including 'X-temperaneous Boogie' in 1948, and 'Money Blues', a rewrite of 'Why Don't You Do Right?' in 1951.

Art Rupe was friendly with two brothers who were bandleaders – the elder Joe Liggins, with his Honeydrippers, and the younger Jimmy Liggins, with his Drops of Joy. Joe was doing exceptionally well on the Exclusive label, topping the R & B chart for 18 weeks with 'The Honeydripper' in 1943.

The owners of Exclusive, Leon and Otis René, owned a shellac pressing plant, but they didn't have the facilities or the finances to utilise the new vinyl format. As a result of the shellac shortage, they were selling 'The Honeydripper' over the odds at $1.85. It was still a huge success despite cheaper covers from Roosevelt Sykes at 50 cents (RCA's subsidiary Bluebird label) and Jimmie Lunceford (Decca) at 75 cents, an indication that RCA and Decca wanted Exclusive out of the way.

Soon Exclusive ran into financial difficulties and in 1950, Joe Liggins brought his band over to Specialty, where Jimmy was doing okay. Their successes included 'Tear Drop Blues' (Jimmy, 1948), 'Rag Mop' (Joe, a great dance track released in 1950), 'Pink Champagne' (Joe, R & B No.1 for 13 weeks in 1950: not quite rock'n'roll but getting there) and 'Drunk' (Jimmy, 1953). On 'Drunk', the band was billed as Jimmy Liggins and his 3-D Music as Rupe was always looking for gimmicks. Jimmy's was an unlikely success story as he had been shot in the mouth. 'Rag Mop', incidentally, was a Black cover of a white original, which was a pop hit for the Ames Brothers.

By 1948 the price of singles had levelled out to 79 cents, but there was a new threat to record companies from the Petrillo ban. The president of the American Federation of Musicians, James Petrillo, called on union musicians to boycott recording studios until increased levels of pay were agreed.

And that was the reason for 'X-temperaneous Boogie'. Roy Milton had been in the studio close to midnight when the ban took effect. They had a few minutes left and Rupe said, 'What can we do?' Milton's pianist, Camille Howard, improvised a boogie, hence the title and another hit was born.

As the ban didn't involve the singers themselves, ingenious ways were found to circumvent this, both Frank Sinatra and Bing Crosby recording a cappella. Columbia had a studio in Mexico and some American recordings were made there.

Although Art Rupe was Jewish with no strong beliefs, he loved the sound of gospel music and much of that was a cappella. It made sense to sign a gospel group, the six-piece Pilgrim Travelers. They tapped their feet as they sang, causing Rupe to publicise them as 'Something New – Walking Rhythm Spirituals'. They harmonised (and tapped their feet) beautifully on 'Jesus Met the Woman at the Well'.

In 1951 Art Rupe added the Soul Stirrers to the label and their first single, 'Jesus Gave Me Water' sold 65,000. This record was preserved for all time by the Library of Congress in 2022, inducted at the same time as Queen's 'Bohemian Rhapsody'. Part of the reason for its preservation was because the Soul Stirrers was featuring their young singer, Sam Cooke, and perhaps for the first time, there was sex appeal with a spiritual group. Girls would be screaming when the Soul Stirrers performed and Cooke realised in 1957 that he should be stirring his soul elsewhere – but more of this later.

Once the Petrillo strike had been settled with modest increases, Rupe wanted to make his label as profitable as possible. For a start, he wanted a proper office. When Speciality started, he was simply hiring a room with a desk and a phone, but in 1949, they operated from 8508 Sunset Boulevard, a famed location in Hollywood.

As well as the record company, Art Rupe had Venice Music for music publishing, so if he could find good, original songs, so much the better. He had a booking agency, Herald Attractions, more to help the artists than fleece them. Although Little Richard was to complain about royalties, Rupe paid standard rates and gave his artists correct six-monthly statements on record sales and songwriting royalties. There were dubious characters in the record business, but Art Rupe, although a hard businessman, wasn't underhand. He didn't claim songwriting royalties for songs he hadn't written. However, he wasn't generous and he didn't like being challenged.

The union allowed a company to record four songs in a three-hour session and Rupe didn't want to waste time and money by recording only two or three. He encouraged bands to rehearse before recording. There was no multitracking back then, so the band would be playing together and a mistake meant starting again. Art learned how to become a good producer and he did the splicing and mastering of the tapes himself.

Artists never had exclusive rights to a song so that anybody might cover it, and indeed, music publishers were keen to have cover versions, preferably for different markets. Art Rupe saw the sense in owning both record and publishing companies and so he encouraged rival versions to his own artists. In 1956 it didn't bother him that Pat Boone was covering 'Tutti Frutti': quite the reverse because it meant more songwriting income.

It is overlooked that Black performers were often covering white artists. The Orioles were almost a covers band as they sang 'Crying in the Chapel' (Darrell Glenn), 'In the Chapel by the Moonlight' (Shep Fields) and 'You Belong to Me' (Jo Stafford). 'You Belong to Me' sounds very odd today as you wonder what Jo Stafford's partner is doing galivanting around the world and seeing the sights, but it is really a song about conscription and the poor guy is a soldier. Even Louis Armstrong was persuaded to record covers including 'Sincerely' and 'Only You', where his playful trumpet solo is at variance with the song.

The major labels (RCA. Mercury, Decca, Columbia) were slow in finding new Black artists and songwriters, so they largely depended on hearing good new songs and determining how to record them for the white market. We will see how this played out in the rock'n'roll era with Bill Haley, Pat Boone and Elvis Presley. Sometimes the songs ('Sixty Minute Man', 'Shake, Rattle and Roll') had to be watered down for the white, teenage audience. As Jerry Wexler at Atlantic brilliantly put it, 'Rhythm'n'blues is black music for black artists. Rock'n'roll is black music for teenagers.'

Clarence Fountain from the gospel group, the Five Blind Boys of Alabama, commented. 'Some of the white artists are very good but we have stronger voices and can reach more depths and more highs. It is the hand of the Lord that leads us and makes us do the things that we do.'

In 1950 Rupe signed an excellent new singer/songwriter Percy Mayfield, who was marketed as a blues balladeer. He topped the R & B charts for two weeks with his plaintive 'Please Send Me Someone to Love', which in three minutes manages to be a love song, a prayer and a comment on the stability of the world after the war.

In 1952 when Mayfield was returning from an appearance in Las Vegas, his car hit a parked truck and he was covered in debris. Pronounced dead at the scene, he did recover and although his injuries prevented him from performing, he recorded for Chess and Imperial. It's unfortunate that Art Rupe lost contact with him because he could have written brilliantly for Little Richard. Instead, Ray Charles hired Mayfield as a staff writer for his label, Tangerine Records and he wrote 'Hit the Road, Jack' and 'The Danger Zone', another song about global politics.

Rupe knew New Orleans was full of R & B musicians and he went there in 1952. He told radio listeners that he was seeking talent and any potential artist could come to Cosimo Matassa's studio for an audition.

Back in New Orleans, the drummer Earl Palmer was playing jazz clubs for very little money but having fun. Dave Bartholomew asked him if he would play on his records and then Fats Domino's starting with 'The Fat Man' (1949) and 'Every Night about this Time' (1950), the two records that established Fats. The big one for Specialty came with Lloyd Price's 'Lawdy Miss Clawdy' in 1952. Palmer developed a backbeat with a heavy emphasis on the second and fourth beats. He always considered the best example of his style was on Fats Domino's 'I'm Walkin'', a million-selling rock'n'roll classic.

Both Bumps Blackwell and Little Richard were fearful of Art Rupe, who after all was the man with the money. Bumps, in his turn, could be overbearing when dealing with Little Richard in the studio.

Art Rupe may have lost Percy Mayfield as a chart name, but now he had immense success with Lloyd Price. 'Lawdy Miss Clawdy' was a No.1 R & B record for seven weeks. It was such a great New Orleans sound that Fats and Dave formed their own partnership, which was then heard on Fats' hit records. Unfortunately, Price's other songs at the time weren't too strong and the fact that they followed 'Lawdy Miss Clawdy' with a song called 'Oooh-Oooh-Oooh' tells you everything.

In June 1952 Specialty entered the country market with four singles, and they opened a southern branch in Jackson, Mississippi. Johnny Vincent was to find and record the talent but under strict written guidelines from Art Rupe: 'The singer should be way in front of the music. However, at no time should the rhythm be lost. Feeling and soul are more important than good technique. Keep praising their efforts, but remember, you are the director.'

Louis Jordan and his Tympany Five was one of the most successful bands of the post-war years but he joked about his ethnicity to appeal to white audiences. Take 'Saturday Night Fish Fry', which topped the R & B chart for 12 weeks in 1949 and crossed over to pop. It is like a musical version of the vaudeville comics, Amos'n'Andy. In that same year, LaVern Baker was marketing herself as Little Miss Sharecropper.

Ivory Joe Hunter recorded the standard, 'Blue Moon' and *Ted Mack's Amateur Hour* was won by seven-year-old Gladys Knight who sang Nat 'King' Cole's 'Too Young' and pocketed $2,000. You can still hear her on *YouTube.* She was too young for that song and Nat 'King' Cole at 33 was certainly too old.

Art Rupe played the market very well and even before Little Richard, Specialty was the most successful independent R & B label on the west coast. That's surprising because Art Rupe did not believe in paying for airplay, which was known as payola. He figured that if he released good records, the disc jockeys would have to play them or lose credibility.

Mind you, he had tried it. Art Rupe wrote to the Cleveland DJ Alan Freed, on 17 April 1953. 'Saul Bihari had quite a discussion with us relative to the promotional plan he has worked out with you, and he was very generous in his praise of the results you are giving him. It pleases us very much to go along with you on the same basis. I will send you $50 on the first of each month with the understanding that you schedule at least five sides we specify in a list of records we will mail you periodically.'

Within six months, Freed was wanting more, asking Rupe to switch Specialty to a distribution company run by his brother. They fell out over it but in 1955 Freed approached Rupe for a loan to pay legal fees over the ownership of his licensing name, 'Moondog'. He wrote, 'There are probably plenty of people who could come up with it but I do not want to jeopardise what I am building with bad guys in the business entering the picture.' Freed, evidently, did not regard himself as a bad guy.

When Lloyd Price visited Macon, Richard was impressed by his black and gold Cadillac. Price told Richard to send Art Rupe a tape of his original songs, even if only sung a cappella. Richard sang a gospel song, 'He's My Star', and one of lost love, 'Wonderin'', which were recorded as a favour at a local radio station. With his falsetto, Richard sounded like Clyde McPhatter, but that made sense: at the time a McPhatter platter meant money in the bank. Sometimes, Richard would sing a secular version of 'He's My Star', then called 'She's My Star'. He enjoyed this song without doing much with it. Art Rupe thought that Little Richard had potential, although he had no concept of what would develop.

And anyway, before that, there was Don Robey.

II. The Night Before Christmas

Although Art Rupe and Don Robey both owned record labels concentrating on Black performers and musicians, you could hardly get a bigger contrast in conducting business. The urbane and fastidious Rupe differed from the intimidating Robey, yet through their efforts they brought Black R & B music into the mainstream. Robey was a gangster, no doubt about that; an archetypal gangster you might say, unsmiling with cold eyes and never without bodyguards, although he was tough enough to deal with most problems on his own. Even his business partner and booking agent, Evelyn Johnson, acknowledged how threatening he could be. For all, that he did love the Black R & B and gospel music that he was promoting.

Don Robey had been born in 1903 in Houston to an African father and white mother and he referred to himself as a Black Jew. Little Richard said, 'Robey was a Black guy who looked like a white guy.'

In his teens, Don Robey played dice and cards to make money. He was good but he had marked decks so that he could make a little more. He was a safe pair of hands for receiving stolen goods and acting as a fence.

The Second World War brought about the demise of the big bands because of conscription and petrol shortages, which restricted touring schedules. The new era would herald in smaller units like Louis Jordan and his Tympany Five and solo vocalists touring on their own and relying on local musicians for accompaniment. Robey saw his opportunity: he invested in night clubs and established regular venues in Houston for touring Black performers. He opened the Peacock Dinner Club with top entertainment for wealthy diners and gamblers, but he never gave a sucker an even break. The house took rather more than it should and there was a financial arrangement with local prostitutes.

In 1949 Robey formed Peacock Records with his own artist, Clarence 'Gatemouth' Brown, as its first signing. Gate had a double-sided hit with 'Mary Is Fine' and 'My Time Is Expensive'. The original single omitted the songwriting details, but Robey had submitted the song titles under his own name. When he was told that he had to show songwriters on record labels, he often put his own name or his pseudonym, Deadric Malone, Deadric being his middle name. Any legitimate writer would be ill-advised to voice his concerns.

Among the songs that have Don or Deadric as composer are 'Ain't Nothin' You Can Do', 'Further Up the Road' (which became a key song in Eric Clapton's repertoire), 'I Pity the Fool' and 'Turn on Your Lovelight', so clearly Bobby Bland got a real bad deal. Robey claimed credit for Johnny Ace's classic, 'Pledging My Love'.

At first Don Robey was releasing gospel music in Houston on his own label, Peacock, and he had some fine groups – the Dixie Hummingbirds and the Five Blind Boys of Mississippi among them. Gospel had a regular, loyal following but Robey was more interested in secular music that could be promoted throughout the country and even appeal to a white audience. He noticed that Nat 'King' Cole was moving away from his jazz trio and was clocking up huge middle-of-the-road hits with 'The Christmas Song' (1946), 'Nature Boy' (1948), 'Mona Lisa' (1950) and 'Too Young' (1951), all for Capitol Records. It was lucrative, in the first instance, to have white artists covering Black hit songs, but why shouldn't the Black performers themselves cross over to the mainstream?

The colour of mainstream entertainment was white. The TV documentary *Nat 'King' Cole: Afraid of the Dark* (2014) describes the racism that Cole faced and the difficulties of being the only Black TV star in Hollywood. The producers wanted to package him as something he was not: that is, white. Lena Horne has spoken about how she had to pretend she wasn't Black in MGM musicals: for example, 'Don't move your mouth too much when you sing.'

Robey became interested in record distribution and radio playlists, and how records might sell in other parts of the US. As usual, he looked for the flaws in the system and how he could exploit that, but to his credit, he appreciated that Black R & B might appeal in a big way to white record-buyers.

We now have a complicated situation which involves Don Robey, bandleader Johnny Otis, the songwriters Jerry Leiber and Mike Stoller, a Memphis radio station, and the singers Big Mama Thornton, Rufus Thomas and Elvis Presley.

Johnny Otis, born in 1921, was the son of Greek parents, growing up in Vallejo, close to San Francisco. In 1941 he was so stunned by Count Basie's orchestra that he became proficient on drums, vibes and piano. He played in casinos and in 1946, he led a band to accompany the Ink Spots on a worldwide tour. He was soon making his own R & B hits and in 1948 he discovered the Robins (later the Coasters) and Little Esther (later Esther Phillips). He usually toured as the Johnny Otis Rhythm & Blues Caravan. Because of his dark complexion and musical interests, many thought he was Black but he was Greek.

Don Robey had had an affair with a barnstorming blues woman, Big Mama Thornton, a real match of fiery temperaments, and although they had moved on, he loved her voice and her personality. In 1952 the bandleader Johnny Otis asked fledgling songwriters Jerry Leiber and Mike Stoller for a song for Big Mama, to be released on Peacock Records.

Taking stock of her larger-than-life personality, Leiber and Stoller wrote 'Hound Dog', and Jerry was to comment, 'She was the biggest, the baddest, the saltiest chick you could ever see. I had to write a song for her that basically said, "Go fuck yourself!"' Thornton, 25 but looking older, recorded the song with Johnny Otis' band. It was a personality performance full of yelps and howls and it topped the R & B chart for seven weeks – a nice little earner for Peacock Records.

We don't know why Robey didn't claim a songwriting credit himself, but Otis was doing him a favour because he was signed to another label, Savoy. The label said 'Hound Dog' was written by Leiber, Stoller and Otis. Leiber and Stoller took legal advice and it was shown that Otis wasn't the songwriter – and that was that, at least for the moment.

As Robey was also a booking agent, arranging tours of the South for his artists, he developed business interests in Memphis. David Mattis, an owner of WDIA, had sectioned off a room in his radio station for use as a recording studio. There was plenty of blues talent in Memphis and he could produce their records for Duke and promote them on his own station. Robey sweettalked Mattis and it led to a merger ostensibly called Duke/Peacock, although Robey planned to remove Mattis as soon as he could.

The most influential disc jockey on WDIA was Rufus Thomas. He loved Big Mama's 'Hound Dog' and created an answer version, 'Bear Cat', which he recorded for a new label in Memphis, Sun Records, owned by Sam Phillips. It was a rewrite of 'Hound Dog' and Sam Phillips listed himself as the composer. It climbed to No.3 in R & B charts.

Don Robey was livid. He told David Mattis that this was extreme disloyalty. Rufus Thomas should have recorded this song for Duke/Peacock – and what's more, they should have the publishing on it. Thomas was lucky to keep his job (and possibly his life!) and he did stay with the station until 1974.

Then, in 1956, 'Hound Dog' was recorded by Elvis Presley and became a multi-million seller. The label credited Leiber and Stoller. Johnny Otis forged a document which stated that the three of them testified they had written the song together. It was shown to be fake and Leiber and Stoller got their rewards. Despite that, Otis would later be ordained.

Returning to Memphis in the early 1950s, B.B. King had formed a superlative band of local musicians, the Beale Streeters, who could play in the city, accept touring and recording dates and back other performers as appropriate. They included Earl Forest (drums), John Alexander (vocals, piano), Junior Parker (vocals, harmonica) and Rosco Gordon (vocals, piano). B.B. couldn't join them too often because he was making a name for himself: starting in 1951, he was having major R & B hits, 'Three O'clock Blues' and 'You Know I Love You'.

Born in 1929, John Alexander was the son of a preacher and had played piano and organ in church. He served in the navy after the war although he never got further than Virginia. He learned how to handle a gun and developed a fascination with firearms.

In 1952 Robey recognised that Alexander had a plaintive, romantic voice and he recorded him with the Beale Streeters, having major R & B hits with 'My Song', 'Cross My Heart' and 'The Clock', renaming him Johnny Ace in the process. He was a fine-looking lad with high cheekbones who quickly found a female following. He had more versatility than his ballads would suggest and he was twinned with Big Mama Thornton for his own song, 'Yes Baby'.

His revolver was generally empty and he would point it at people including his girlfriend and threaten to shoot them. Sometimes he would put the barrel to his own head and pull the trigger. Even if there was a bullet in the revolver, he reckoned he would be all right, insisting that when you spin the carriage, the weight means that the cartridge should stop at the bottom.

Johnny Ace and Big Mama Thornton had been booked for a big show at the Houston City Auditorium on Christmas Eve 1954, when Johnny Ace was teasing Big Mama Thornton and pointing his gun at her. This made her uneasy. A minute or two later, Ace put the gun to the side of his own head and pulled the trigger. The gun was loaded; blood was everywhere, and Johnny Ace was rushed to hospital where he died on Christmas Day, just 25 years old.

The authorities accepted Big Mama's explanation and Johnny Ace's death was deemed an unfortunate accident from someone who should have known better. However, because of Robey's reputation, there are doubts. It seems unlikely that he would have been responsible: Johnny Ace was making him money in record sales, songwriting and touring commissions. Furthermore, how could he sure Johnny Ace would point the gun at his own head and not somebody else's?

Still, Don Robey could see the financial potential of his death. The death of country singer Hank Williams on New Year's Day 1953 had stimulated a national interest in his music. Robey would do the same with Johnny Ace. He had a romantic single ready to go, 'Pledging My Love'. The song was written by Ferdinand Washington, who had written for B.B. King and Lowell Fulson but he had to share his credit with Don Robey, who insisted on calling him 'Fats'. In 1956 Fats – sorry, Ferdinand –wrote a wonderful song for servicemen overseas, 'I'll Be Home', originally recorded by the Flamingos and a UK No.1 for Pat Boone.

'Pledging My Love' topped the R & B charts for ten weeks, remaining on the listings for five months. It made the Top 20 pop charts as did a white cover version from Teresa Brewer: she was following her hit 'Let Me Go, Lover'.

The tribute singles included 'Johnny Has Gone' (Varetta Dillard), 'Johnny Ace's Last Letter' (Frankie Ervin), 'Why Johnny Why' (Linda Hayes), 'Johnny's Still Singing' (The Five Wings) and 'Salute to Johnny Ace' (The Rovers).

Ever the opportunist, Don Robey found his way into the albums market with *The Johnny Ace Memorial Album.* When Robey signed a young blues singer, Jimmy Lee Land, to Duke, he renamed him Buddy Ace. He released his first record alongside Johnny Ace's final record, 'Still Love You So'.

As soon as 'Pledging My Love' was a hit, Bing Crosby of all people sang it on the radio and there have been numerous versions since – like the Platters' 'Only You', it is the perfect wedding song. You can choose from LaVern Baker, Solomon Burke, Roy Hamilton, Emmylou Harris, Tom Jones, Jerry Lee Lewis, Little Milton, Aaron Neville, Percy Sledge, Johnny Tillotson and a duet from Diana Ross and Marvin Gaye. His 'Never Let Me Go' was revived by the Impressions in 1962 and Luther Vandross in 1993 and it was performed as a duet by Bob Dylan and Joan Baez on the Rolling Thunder tour.

Johnny Ace's songs are heard in many films, including *Mean Streets, Bad Lieutenant* and *Back to the Future*, and Paul Simon paid tribute to him in his song, 'The Late Great Johnny Ace' (1981), which is as much about John Lennon as it is Johnny Ace. According to the song, Paul Simon sent away to Texas in 1954 for a photograph of Johnny Ace and it came back signed, 'The late great Johnny Ace'. Can't be true but it does sound like the sort of thing Don Robey would do.

When Little Richard signed with Don Robey in 1953, Don Robey was thinking that Johnny Ace would be his crossover artist and so he missed out on Little Richard's potential. Maybe he had him too early but it was more likely that their personalities did not gel.

Early in 1953 Little Richard formed a band, the Tempo Toppers, with Barry Lee Gilmore, Jimmy Swann and a guy called Shorty. They also included the husband-and-wife team of Raymond and Mildred Taylor, who worked independently as the Duces of Rhythm.

Barry Lee Gilmore from Memphis could lift a chair in his mouth and dance around with it. When I saw Little Richard in Liverpool in 1963, he too danced around the stage with a chair in his mouth, but no one has ever believed me. I had come to doubt it myself but now I've discovered Barry Lee Gilmore, I can see where Richard got it from, and so I'm confident it did happen.

On 2 January 1953 Little Richard made his first appearance in New Orleans, at the Dew Drop Inn on Lasalle Street. His appearance led to a further residency at the Tijuana Club and he met guitarist Earl King who shared his musical experiences and was to have his own R & B hit with 'Those Lonely, Lonely Nights' in 1955.

A regular visitor to the Dew Drop Inn was the cowboy actor Lash LaRue, who had a stage act with a bullwhip and a guitar. He made numerous westerns but his career came to an end when *Hard on the Trail* (1972) was spiced up with porno footage. He was so remorseful that he gave up acting and became an evangelist.

At the Club Matinee in Houston, Richard met another charismatic figure, Johnny Otis. Richard told him, 'I am the King of the Blues – and the Queen too.' Otis was to comment, 'He looked good and he reminded me of Dinah Washington.'

RCA wasn't renewing his recording contract, but Little Richard impressed Don Robey and was signed to his Peacock label. What could be a better-named label for Little Richard than Peacock?

At the first session on 25 February 1953, Richard was working with the Duces of Rhythm, the Tempo Toppers and the Roy Montrell Orchestra. However, the billing on the first single was 'Duces of Rhythm and Tempo Toppers (Lead: Little Richard)'. Ridiculous: there's no way that potential purchasers would remember that. Three of the songs were written by Raymond Taylor: probably all four, although 'Always' credits Robey.

The first single combined 'Ain't that Good News' and 'Fool at the Wheel' and was positively featured in *Billboard* with a photograph of the group: 'The Duces of Rhythm are a husband-and-wife team, Raymond and Mildred Taylor. Ray plays the piano, trumpet, trombone and organ, while Mildred's an ace drummer. The Tempo Toppers, who handle the vocals, are a terrific group of singers. Little Richard sings lead with the group.'

'Fool at the Wheel' told of a drunk with a new Ford who doesn't even 'slow down for children going to school'. The mood of the song is all wrong and sounds more like a novelty. A bass voice sang the solo line which ended the record. Richard referred to the fool 'slippin' 'n' slidin' all over the road'. That phrase would come in useful.

'Ain't That Good News' was a curious song and performance. Richard related how he was blues crazy while surrounded by gospel harmonies. It was trying to appeal to both markets but was confusing and odd.

The second single was released as the Tempo Toppers featuring Little Richard. The main side, 'Rice, Red Beans & Turnip Greens', praised Southern soul food and was a companion to Hank Williams' country hit 'Jambalaya'. In the song Richard was talking to a waitress and the performance included a break for saxophone and organ. Whoever wrote the B-side, 'Always', needn't have bothered. It's a vocal group performance of an average song and Little Richard feels constrained.

Robey enjoyed pushing people around and Richard with his sexuality and irritating mannerisms was an easy target. When Richard questioned him one day about royalties, Don Robey "jumped on me, knocked me down and kicked me in the stomach. It gave me a hernia that was painful for years.' It was just another day at the office for Don Robey.

Although the two singles hadn't sold well, Robey then recorded him with the Johnny Otis Orchestra, along with sessions for two other performers, Joe 'Papoose' Fritz and Luvenia Lewis. Richard recorded 'Maybe I'm Right', 'Directly from My Heart', 'I Love My Baby' and 'Little Richard's Boogie', but they were not released until Richard became famous. Don Robey didn't think he had what it took for the big time.

However, on 'Little Richard's Boogie', Richard was closing in on his hit-making sound, although it featured Johnny Otis' vibes rather than Richard's piano. Richard was singing about how good a singer, musician and dancer he was. I agree with *Billboard's* assessment over a reissue on 10 March 1956: 'After 'Tutti Frutti' anything released by the artist might seem an anti-climax. But here Little Richard rides the Johnny Otis Band in a fast and furious rhythm opus that could easily be a repeater. It certainly is an outstanding juke box offering.' It wasn't a hit single, but new fans would have enjoyed it.

'Directly from My Heart' is a passionate love ballad, enhanced by Richard's vocal tricks. In 1971 the Mothers of Invention featuring Frank Zappa with Don 'Sugarcane' Harris's electric violin recorded a sensational five-minute version that brought Richard and the blues to a new generation of listeners.

'Maybe I'm Right' was a slow plodder, written by Richard himself and enhanced by his heartfelt vocals. He was experimenting with his voice and its uniqueness was coming through. 'I Love My Baby' is as uninspired as its title, although the line 'She's got another man, trying to me get killed' takes you by surprise. Richard's ending is similar to what he would do with 'Kansas City'.

Joe 'Papoose' Fritz had a song called 'Real Fine Girl'. One verse sounds familiar:

She's a real fine queen, she's built for speed,
She's got everything that a good man needs.

After the session in October 1953, Richard made one-off appearances, working with the Tempo Toppers and with Johnny Otis. Although his Duke/Peacock session was a marked development, he wasn't to make another record for almost two years. By then, his transformation was complete.

Okay, Richard hadn't made hits for Peacock but by now the competition was fierce. *Billboard* calculated that there had been 15m R & B singles sold in 1953 and they were often bought by white teenagers, although there was still segregation. There were 75 companies releasing R & B records and many of the best-selling records came from the smaller companies.

In Nashville Little Richard played the New Era Club and slept at the YMCA as white hotels wouldn't let him in. On that booking, Little Richard befriended the R & B duo Shirley and Lee and got to know their musicians. Those musicians developed into the Upsetters and they worked with Little Richard on the road through his hit-making period.

The drummer was Charles Connor and the saxophonist Wilbert Smith, later known as Lee Diamond. Wilbert wrote Aaron's Neville's classic R & B single, 'Tell It Like It Is' in 1966.

Charles Connor had been born in New Orleans in 1935 and when only 16, he was playing drums for Professor Longhair at the Hi-Hat Club, but Longhair didn't like playing away from New Orleans. Little Richard was the ideal employer as he wanted young guys who would look cool and had some showmanship (but not too much). He wanted a hard-driving sound and he took Connor to Macon's train station and had him play along with arriving trains. 'I want your drumming to sound like a choo-choo train,' Richard explained.

Out in the streets of Macon, Richard was certainly getting his own good booty. His sex life was varied — he once called himself omnisexual — and he enjoyed voyeurism, so he'd drive around town with a prostitute Fanny, she'd pick up guys, and he'd watch her have sex with them. After a gas-station worker reported their activities, Richard landed in jail. A sympathetic magistrate learnt that he was a travelling musician, so he was told to get out of town and not to do it again, an impetus to get the Upsetters on the road.

Connor told *Now Dig This* that he had made love to over 2,000 women while on the road. He said, 'A lot of women wouldn't give their boyfriends oral sex, but they'd give it to musicians who weren't going to talk.'

Little Richard and the Upsetters had a station wagon with their name on. They sang hit songs by Roy Brown, B.B. King and Billy Wright and if the audience was right, they would bring the house down with the innuendo of 'Tutti Frutti'. They loved it in Macon, which was a good place to play because of the military bases.

Phil Walden was a white kid from Macon born in 1940, and who would later manage Otis Reeding and establish Capricorn Records. He saw Little Richard in 1955, opening for Amos Milburn ('Chicken Shack Boogie', 'Bad Bad Whiskey') at the City Auditorium. 'Amos Milburn disappointed me – he was just a fat guy sitting at a piano,' he recalled, 'but Little Richard destroyed me. He did an off-colour version of 'Tutti Frutti' and he waved to all the gay guys, his 'sisters', in the audience.'

In October 1954, WDIA from Memphis, now the nation's leading Black music station, banned all records with suggestive lyrics and double entendres, so clearly Little Richard was not alone. The station felt that Black music was about to break through, and innuendo-driven songs might lead to complaints and block its progress.

Through being in the forces, Lloyd Price's career had lost its impetus. Price was stationed in both Korea and Japan and he would write to Art Rupe, saying 'Please get me out of here.' When he returned to America, he met Little Richard, who felt his own career was going nowhere. Lloyd Price told him to make a demonstration record for Specialty and send it to Art Rupe in Los Angeles.

Meanwhile, Art Rupe had told his producer Bumps Blackwell that they should seek out someone as good as B.B. King or Ray Charles. It had not occurred to Rupe that he should find somebody who was totally unique.

That would be Little Richard.

CHAPTER 3

The Big Easy and the Little Richard

I. There Is a House in New Orleans

Living on Merseyside as I do, I've been hoping for scheduled flights between Liverpool and New Orleans because flying from the Liverpool John Lennon Airport to the Louis Armstrong International New Orleans Airport sounds beguiling.

Although New Orleans' musical history is so great (Buddy Bolden, Louis Armstrong, Jelly Roll Morton, Sidney Beçhet, Fats Domino, Irma Thomas, Dr John, the Neville Brothers and the Marsalis family), Little Richard was only there briefly. He never lived in the Big Easy but he made most of his key recordings there, time that was extremely well spent.

A good case could be made for New Orleans having a more distinctive and identifiable sound than that of Chicago (electric blues), Detroit (Motown) or Nashville (country). The music of New York or Los Angeles is too varied to be quantified.

New Orleans is the home of jazz, but there were no recording studios there in the first decades of the twentieth century. Louis Armstrong invariably recorded in Chicago and New York. The gamechanger was Cosimo Matassa whose recording studio is now legendary.

Cosimo Matassa was born into a Sicilian family in New Orleans on 13 April 1926. His father John ran Matassa's Market, a family store still running today on Dauphine Street, and a jukebox hiring company with a partner (Joe Mancuso). They named it the J&M Amusement Service. They operated from a shop building on 818–840 Rampart Street. Cue, Louis Armstrong's 'South Rampart Street Parade'.

They serviced around 60 jukeboxes in the neighbouring bars and clubs and as you can imagine, jukeboxes had rough treatment.

Joe Mancuso realised that none of the records by local musicians were being made in New Orleans: hence, a marketing opportunity was there. Although only 19, Cosimo bought recording equipment and a disc cutter and advertised for business at the J&M Studio, 838 North Rampart Street, in 1947. The studio was only 16 feet by 18 feet with a small control booth. The charge was $15 an hour plus the cost of tape and discs. You got Cosimo himself as the engineer, largely because he didn't want his equipment being damaged. He had no great technical ability but he knew when something sounded right and he would then press the 'Record' button. He was a pleasant, affable guy who kept up-to-date with studio technology.

In the spring of 1956, Cosimo Matassa moved the studio to larger premises at 521 Governor Nichols Street. And by the early 1960s, the record business being what it is, some regular clients were going bust or moving onto something else. Cosimo collated several local labels into Dover Records so that they could share promotional costs. All went well with Robert Parker's 'Barefootin'' and Aaron Neville's 'Tell It Like It Is' and then Dover went under. Cosimo retained his love for the music and worked at the Jazz City studio but also helped with a grocery store now run by his sons.

In 2012 Cosimo Matassa was inducted into the Rock & Roll Hall of Fame for 'musical excellence'. He died at the age of 88 in his beloved New Orleans. He said of his production work, 'If you didn't know who I was, I did my job', hardly the philosophy of Harvey Philip Spector.

II. A Living Volcano

A familiar story is that Little Richard was washing dishes at the Greyhound bus station in Macon and sent a demonstration tape to Specialty Records in Hollywood. Although that is true, the implication behind it is not. Little Richard for the most part was on the road with the Upsetters and because he had to help support his family, he worked at the bus station when he had no bookings. He was managed by Clint Brantley and had a contract with Peacock Records. In other words, he was a working musician rather than a dishwasher.

On 9 February 1955, 'Little Richard and his Upsetters' (to use his introduction) recorded two of his compositions at WMBL studio in Macon for Art Rupe in Los Angeles and submitted by Clint Brantley to look more professional. At the start, Little Richard says, 'Mr Rupe, you are now going to hear Little Richard and his Upsetters.'

'Baby' is close to the Little Richard we know and love: a mid-tempo beat number where he is playing around with his voice and developing his personality. 'All Night Long' is a blues with B.B. King-styled responses between the lines. The production is wayward, but the talent is there. In the beefy sax break, Richard encourages the musicians to give of their best.

Art Rupe was employing Bumps Blackwell to produce sessions for Specialty: in later interviews, Rupe would maintain that he produced over 90 per cent of Specialty's product but this claim is as outlandish as some of Richard's. He did, however, oversee and authorise every release and he did splice tapes to make a finished product, although this had led to cataloguing problems as to who did what at Speciality and when.

An intriguing mix of French, African and American Indian descent, Robert Alexander 'Bumps' Blackwell was born in Seattle, Washington in 1918. He learnt to play piano and then vibes, an instrument popularised by Lionel Hampton, but during the war he worked for Boeing, making parts for the B-29 bomber. Bumps was fired from the Tacoma Shipyards on the grounds that he was Black. Local politicians got him reinstated, and the workers welcomed him back, which he celebrated by organising a benefit dance. Once the war was over, he formed his own band, grandly called the Bumps Blackwell Orchestra and at different times, they accompanied Billie Holiday, Ray Charles and Billy Eckstine.

In 1953 Bumps was planning to study classical composition at UCLA but he was also asked to produce Sonny Knight for Aladdin. Impressed with his efforts, Art Rupe offered him a fulltime job at Speciality and his first sessions in 1955 were with the zydeco accordionist Clifton Chenier ('Boppin' the Rock', background music today but ahead of the pack then) and the balladeer Jesse Belvin (the anguished doo-wop of 'Where's My Girl'). When he went to the Shrine Auditorium in Los Angeles to record gospel music, he heard the Soul Stirrers with their exciting young vocalist, Sam Cooke. He could appreciate that Cooke was a fine vocalist with an outstanding stage personality and he thought that one day he might persuade him to cross over to secular music.

But first it was Little Richard. Richard kept calling Specialty to see if they had heard his songs, and Rupe's secretary kept stalling. Rupe had Bumps Blackwell locate the demo and they liked it. He had been on Peacock, but Don Robey hadn't recognised his potential. Indeed, Richard was mad with Peacock for having his credit almost as an afterthought on the label. A record distributor from Atlanta, Paul Glass, who happened to be around, agreed with Art and Bumps. That's three yesses then.

Rupe told Richard that he would like to record him but what about Peacock, was there still a contract? There was but Don Robey had wanted nothing more to do with him. Not that Robey admitted that, of course. Robey told Rupe that he had big plans and didn't want to let him go, but he could be persuaded for $600. Rupe must have been impressed to pay out so much, although it would be deducted from Richard's future royalties.

And so, several months after sending the tape to Art Rupe, Richard was invited to Cosimo Matassa's studio in New Orleans. There would be two three-hour sessions in J&M, the afternoon of 13 September and the following morning, an indication that Rupe and Blackwell recognised his potential.

Richard travelled with three local musicians – Henry Nash (also his road manager), Lee Diamond and Charles Connor – but they weren't expected to play: it was to show them what a real studio was like. They were surprised to find it was a room in the back of a furniture store. It had been a tough journey: it was raining hard and the wipers on the Chrysler didn't work.

The session would feature the cream of local talent – Lee Allen (tenor sax), Red Tyler (baritone sax), Justin Adams (guitar), Frank Fields (bass), Earl Palmer (drums) and Huey 'Piano' Smith (piano). Today this would be a group to die for but back then, they were simply musicians who knew what they were doing. Little Richard wasn't expected to play piano: he was booked as a singer. There is some studio chat from the first session where Huey Smith discusses an introduction which confirms he was on piano and not Richard. In a later interview, Smith was dismissive of his elementary playing, but then you'd never add 'Piano' to your name unless you're good.

Bumps and Cosimo Matassa spent 40 minutes balancing instruments and once satisfied, the tracks were recorded as though in concert. On the first day, they recorded three of Richard's songs ('Lonesome and Blue', 'Wonderin'', 'All Night Long') and Jerry Leiber and Mike Stoller's 'Kansas City'.

'Lonesome and Blue' was a mawkish ballad with Richard in his top register, performing well but the song was only average. 'Wonderin'' with its piano triplets needed some vocal back-up to turn it into doo-wop. 'All Night Long' had drive and personality, Little Richard going up and down his vocal scale with screaming, howling and some unintelligible words in the sax break. He was losing any inhibitions he might have had.

In 1952 Jerry Leiber and Mike Stoller wrote 'K.C. Lovin'' for Little Willie Littlefield. The title wasn't part of the lyric and the song is better known as 'Kansas City'. It is about a man who wants to leave his woman and is looking for a new one in Kansas City (as you do). Most of the words are familiar but Little Willie does have one verse that is rarely sung:

Gonna pack my clothes, leave at the crack of dawn,
My old lady will be sleeping and she won't know where I've gone.

Little Richard recorded the song in 1955 – a version that wasn't issued until 1957 – and it seems that he didn't know the song well and it was, more or less, a try-out in the studio. His girl's in Kansas City and he's going to bring her home.

In 1958 Little Richard reworked this final section for 'Hey-Hey-Hey-Hey', which was the B-side of 'Good Golly Miss Molly' and credited himself as the sole songwriter.

When the Beatles recorded 'Kansas City' as a track for *Beatles For Sale* in 1964, the songwriters were listed as Leiber and Stoller. This was a multi-million selling album and it was years later that Little Richard's publishers complained that it infringed the copyright of 'Hey-Hey-Hey-Hey'.

But when Richard recorded 'Kansas City' that afternoon in 1955, it was a strong performance of a song that had yet to be a hit.

A couple of miles away, the Dew Drop Inn and Hotel on LaSalle Street was a famed local venue, noted for its drag acts. Indeed Esquerita made his reputation there. Richard wanted to see it – quite likely, he and his party were booked into the hotel – and Bumps Blackwell took them to it.

Bumps also invited the songwriter Dorothy LaBostrie, who worked as a cook, as Little Richard who was going to sing her song, 'I'm just a Lonely Guy' the following day. She was a single mum who, as luck would have it, had written raunchy songs for Dinah Washington ('Blowtop Blues') and Big Boy Myles ('Mickey Mouse Boarding House': surprisingly, Walt Disney didn't sue).

In 1959, she wrote a wonderful R & B ballad for Irma Thomas, 'Don't Mess with My Man' and an equally fine soul ballad for Johnny Adams, 'I Won't Cry'. Adams was living in the same apartment block as LaBostrie: she heard him singing in the bath and offered him the song. It's a fine performance but it could have been a monster hit for Sam Cooke. 'She was a good lyricist,' said Bumps Blackwell, 'but she used the same melody for all her tunes.'

When they were talking, Richard mentioned 'Tutti Frutti', a song he sang in clubs when the mood was right, and as there was an old upright around, Bumps asked him to play it. Richard said this wasn't about ice cream. He was unsure about performing it with a lady present, whom he didn't know and wanted to impress. Dorothy didn't object and he sang it with his back to her.

'Tutti Frutti' contained what would become the battle cry of rock'n'roll, 'Awopbopaloobop Alopbamboom', but there was no way the original lyrics, which were about gay sex, would have found airplay.

Tutti frutti, good booty
If it don't fit, don't force it.
You can grease it, make it easy.

The original lyric also said: 'Miss Lucy is juicy' and 'Miss Tight is all right'.

You'll recall the story of Sam Phillips at the Sun studio in Memphis hearing Elvis, Scotty and Billy jamming on 'That's All Right, Mama' and declaring that this was the sound he was looking for. Now, one year on, Bumps Blackwell had a similar epiphany. Bumps saw it as a novelty song with enormous potential and he asked Dorothy to clean up the words and bring it to the session tomorrow. It would be the most profitable 20 minutes of her life.

In the morning, Little Richard started with three of his own songs. 'Maybe I'm Right' was a lachrymose ballad, competently performed but with nothing new on offer. 'Directly from My Heart' was one of his best ballads, but it didn't improve on his version with Johnny Otis. Then there's a mid-tempo groover, 'Baby', in which Richard declares that he is 'the sweetest man in town'. The song was based on B.B. King's 'Don't You Want a Man Like Me', a 1954 blues/calypso single on RPM Records, and shouldn't really be attributed to Richard. Dorothy's own song, 'I'm Just a Lonely Guy', was a decent ballad with some potential but not enough originality for the charts. Richard said in 1988, 'That sounds like Ray Charles. They wouldn't let me sing like Little Richard.'

That's four songs in the session and the musicians would be breaking union rules to make it five, but probably a few extra dollars did the trick.

So then it was 'Tutti Frutti'.

Little Richard played the piano and Earl Palmer worked out how to match him. He lacked Huey 'Piano' Smith's finesse, but his forceful approach was ideal for this song. Art Rupe was to say, 'Richard could only play in one key, but he was good.'

Dr John was impressed. 'Richard changed something in the New Orleans groove. Instead of a shuffle, he could play the eighth note thing on the piano. He used it on 'Tutti Frutti' and a lot of other records. A lot of other people started using that shit.'

Going into the sax break, Little Richard went into his greatest scream. He was sometimes called the Georgia Peach, but the Georgia Screech was equally applicable.

Bumps told Art Rupe that Little Richard's 'Tutti Frutti' had as much potential as Chess' new rock'n'roll hit, Chuck Berry's 'Maybellene'.

As there were no echo facilities at J&M, Art Rupe would take the session tapes and add echo in Hollywood. This would be processed as the master tape, so the alternative takes can sound a bit flat.

Rock author John Collis contrasts the different approaches on early rock'n'roll records: 'There is very spare instrumentation on Chess records but a lot of the artists are like that. Eddie Cochran is often not much more than an acoustic guitar and a cardboard box, and yet he turns out great rock'n'roll songs. With a bit of reverb, Chuck Berry and Bo Diddley could fill out any space they wanted. Little Richard is different as there is a solid New Orleans sound there, but it is comparatively spare when compared to the Beach Boys.'

John Jorgenson from the Hellecasters: 'The fans weren't picking out the players on the early rock'n'roll records at first. They didn't care about specifics. They just wanted a beat like Little Richard's or Gene Vincent's. Some of those songs were really stupid but if the melody was right, people dug it.'

Little Richard's first Specialty single, released at the end of October 1955, combined 'Tutti Frutti' with 'I'm Just a Lonely Guy', which was good news for Dorothy La Bostrie. It entered the R & B charts and was No.2 for six weeks. *Billboard* called it 'A cleverly-styled novelty with nonsense words delivered rapid-fire. The singer shows a compelling personality and an attractive vocal style.'

Billboard soon nominated 'Tutti Frutti' as the Buy of the Week: 'Having already take the South by storm, this disc is now making big strides in most Northern markets. Still a top seller in Atlanta, Durham, Charlotte, Nashville and Richmond, the record is snowballing in Los Angeles, Baltimore, Pittsburgh and Detroit. Total impact of the record already ranks it among the nation's Top 15.'

Film director John Waters, born in 1946, said: 'When I first heard him, screaming, "Awopbopaloobop Alopbam boom", he scared my grandmother. I thought, "What the hell is that?" It was a sound unlike anything I had ever heard in my life, even outside of music, so he had me from the very first moment I ever heard him. And then when I saw him, I thought, "Oh, my God." And I still have the moustache that really was a tribute to him.'

If 'Tutti Frutti' had ended after a few seconds, that still might have been enough. It has one of the most explosive starts ever put on record. It is up there with the opening chord of 'A Hard Day's Night', Gene Vincent's 'Well-l-l-l' on 'Be-Bop-A-Lula' and Noddy Holders yelling "It's Christmas". Richard remembered being at home in Macon and hearing 'Tutti Frutti' on WLAC out of Nashville. He said, 'Ma, that's me!'

Phil Walden recalls seeing him in Macon: 'I saw him downtown shortly after 'Tutti Frutti' came out. He was twirling a parasol and I said to my friend, "That's Little Richard." He crossed the street and walked right by me and I said, "Tutti frutti" and he said, "Aw rooti!"

'Tutti Frutti' established Little Richard's style of pounding piano, falsetto wailing and a camp performance, but is 'Tutti Frutti' a great song or stupid nonsense? Keith Richards said it best: 'With 'Tutti Frutti', the world transformed from monochrome to glorious Technicolor.'

The American novelist Truman Capote surmised, 'If the Rolling Stones' lyrics made sense, they wouldn't be any good.' You can adapt that quote for Little Richard.

Andrew Gold: 'We could have a good discussion on whether meaningful lyrics are really more important than vapid, silly lyrics. When Little Richard goes "Awopbopaloobop Alopbamboom", he is saying, "I'm having fun, I'm making sounds" and he is showing people how his feelings go. You can have lyrics that are good English like "I trusted you and you broke my heart", but it won't mean anything if it isn't expressed with emotion. 'Tutti Frutti' is a much better song than a lot of songs that are actually good English and it is also a great, great record.'

Loudon Wainwright: 'I would love to have written 'Tutti Frutti', whatever it means. I've written plenty of dumb songs myself and they're fun to write.'

Jennifer Warnes: 'You know what joy books and literature can bring and Leonard Cohen brings the excitement of the written word into music. Very few rock'n'rollers can do that. Leonard brings poetry and prayer into his songs and that speaks to the soul more directly than (sings) "Awopbopaloobop" (laughs) but that can speak to the soul too (laughs).'

In June 2007 MOJO dubbed 'Tutti Frutti' No.1 in a chart of *100 Records that Changed the World.* The record was described as 'a torrent of filth wailed by a bisexual alien'. MOJO said, 'One can only imagine how it must have sounded when the song exploded across the airwaves'. (I don't have to imagine: I was there.) Second was 'I Want to Hold Your Hand' and third, 'Heartbreak Hotel'. In 2021, *Rolling Stone* rated 'Tutti Frutti' No.43 on its list of the greatest 500 songs of all time.

Art Rupe had funded a classic rock'n'roll record 'Tutti Frutti' but it was signed, sealed and delivered before he had even met Little Richard. He invited him to Los Angeles to discuss the record and see what else he had.

Art Rupe maintained that he never fleeced Little Richard and certainly he was never a thief like Don Robey and some of the others. However, Art Rupe was an opportunist who took advantage of Little Richard's lack of financial acumen, so much so that Richard complained bitterly from the 1960s onwards that he had only had a half-cent per record from Specialty when he was expecting two cents.

Trouble is, Richard didn't leave his contracts to run their course. Sensing a hit and seizing an opportunity, Art Rupe said, 'I know you're short of money. How about me giving you $50 upfront for the publishing rights on 'Tutti Frutti'?' Oh dear, dear, dear: Richard's fault I know, but Rupe would guess that he wouldn't seek legal advice. With all the reissues, the cover versions, film and TV rights, and airplay royalties, 'Tutti Frutti' accumulated millions of dollars. Richard's fault, but Rupe should have shown compassion.

Richard complained about his lack of royalties throughout his life. Still, Richard did have high expenses as he lived in a hotel for the last 20 years of his life and yet left an estate of $40 million. That's a teaser – we'll cover it later.

The songwriter John Marascalco who wrote for Little Richard said, "I didn't realise that a lot of the record companies owned their own publishing companies. They licensed songs to themselves at whatever rate they wanted."

One Specialty artist Sonny Wright described Art Rupe to the writer Bill Millar as 'a cold, self-serving and unresponsive man who automatically assumed he was superior.' One day Rupe invited him over to his house . . . to do the gardening. Fortunately, Wright had the wit to say, 'I signed a contract to cut records for you, not to cut your lawn.'

Most performers felt they were being fleeced by the record companies – Bo Diddley, Chuck Berry, Jerry Lee Lewis, Buddy Knox among them. They accepted it because it was the way it was, and in Buddy Knox's case because he didn't want to be thrown out of an upstairs window. The performers made their money on the road, providing their managers were not too crooked. Little Richard was happy on the road with the Upsetters.

Art Rupe had rudimentary recording facilities close to his Hollywood office because the engineer Ted Brinson had a garage with some recording equipment. Some tapes have emerged: perhaps Richard was getting songs down so that they could be copyrighted or to determine what musical arrangements would be suitable.

'Tutti Frutti' was Little Richard's first real attempt to get onto the charts, certainly the pop charts. 'Tutti Frutti' entered the R & B charts on 26 November 1955 and although it couldn't dislodge the Platters with 'The Great Pretender', it reached No.2. It remained on the charts for 21 weeks, very good for a song with a novelty lyric. 'Tutti Frutti' crossed to the US pop charts, not admittedly in a big way but it was No.17 on the Top 40 for five weeks. We will explain why it stalled in the next section.

Just as 'Tutti Frutti' was entering the charts, Little Richard was taken away from promotional work for a session at Radio Recorders in Hollywood. He was backed by Tom Harwell (guitar), Lloyd Lambert (bass), Renald Richard (trumpet), Clarence Ford and Joe Tillman (saxophones) and Oscar Moore (drums, from the Nat 'King' Cole Trio). Although Richard could have played piano, Bumps preferred to separate vocal and piano parts.

This was not a productive session, but perhaps it wasn't intended to be. 'Miss Ann', 'Slippin' And Slidin' and 'Long Tall Sally' (referred to as 'The Thing') were under consideration for the next single and possibly they were working them through for a session in New Orleans. The first take of 'Long Tall Sally' was too slow, but Richard could have been testing it with the musicians so that they got to know it.

Having said that, there were two fine masters. 'True Fine Mama' was a call-and-response record with Little Richard in full voice. It had an outstanding introduction, later modified for 'Good Golly Miss Molly'. Returning to 'Baby', Little Richard gave a much better performance of an average song. It included the line, 'Baby, don't you wish your man looked like Little Richard?' Maybe he knew the song wasn't too convincing and was embellishing it.

Honey Chile was a popular New Orleans DJ – indeed, Fats Domino wrote a song about her. She knew a 20-year-old woman Enotris Johnson, who was trying to raise some funding for a family operation. She had written a jokey lyric – 'Saw Uncle John with Long Tall Sally, Saw Aunt Mary comin', So they ducked back in the alley' – and Honey Chile thought it could be developed into a song. Bumps said, 'This is a song, huh?' and Honey Chile said, 'You better make a song out of that or I'll never play any of your records again.' Payola in reverse, but no harm done. Richard loved 'duck back in the alley', and the song became 'Long Tall Sally'.'

Enotris also wrote 'Miss Ann', which developed into a strong ballad, very typical of Richard's work but needing more fire. In any event, Richard was to return to it. Note the use of girls' names –a default position for teenage songs. Enotris was to write one other lyric for Little Richard, 'Jenny, Jenny', and these songs provided her with income for the rest of her life. However, she had married a minister, Willie J Johnson, and apart from the cheques, did not want to be involved with rock'n'roll. She died in Bogalusa, Louisiana in 2015, having outlived her husband, her daughter and her granddaughter.

There is an extraordinary essay by W T Lhamon, 'Little Richard as a Folk Performer' in a 1985 edition of the academic *Studies in Popular Culture*. He takes 'Miss Ann' back to a devotional riddle from 1511, but it is unlikely that Richard would have been seen this, let alone rewritten it. There are similar words in Blind Lemon Jefferson's 'Got the Blues' (1926) and possibly Richard took a few phrases from that. Hardly matters if he did. That's the blues tradition and Richard knew how to update and adapt it.

Little Richard had had previously recorded 'Kansas City' and now he combined it with a new song, 'Hey-Hey-Hey-Hey' and took several shots at it. At one point, Bumps says, 'Keep going or do you want a rest?' The 'Bring her home, what's wrong with you?' riff is rather like Ray Charles and the Raelets. To promote 'Tutti Frutti', Little Richard looked extravagant. He had a pompadour, wore make-up and had fashionable if somewhat baggy clothes. As his record company was in Hollywood, he would become the go-to artist for rock'n'roll films. Lavishly made-up, he called himself the Georgia Peach and the bronze Liberace and was as camp as Boy George. Little Richard would say from time to time, 'Liberace has his brother George and I have my brother too.' This was true – both had brothers as valets. Art Rupe told him that it was unwise to highlight similarities with Liberace.

Kid Creole: 'Little Richard's moustache, like mine, is an old Cab Calloway 1940s thing: a lot of guys had pencil-thin moustaches then. Little Richard was a big idol of mine. Most performers will only say things that are appropriate, but Little Richard blurted out the most outrageous statements. He will tell you that Pat Boone only recorded his songs because Black music wasn't accepted in those areas. I love Little Richard's sincerity. I love his early stuff and he is one of our greatest entertainers.'

It's easy to be wise after the event but Clint Brantley had never signed a management contract with Richard. This enabled Bumps Blackwell to arrange his appearances and effectively manage him, giving Richard another close link to Art Rupe.

When Brantley realised he was out of the picture, he checked out James Brown again. Brown had established the Famous Flames and they had adapted 'Baby Please Don't Go' as performed by Billy Wright. He had renamed it 'Turn Your Lights Down Low' and now James called it 'Please Please Please'. Brantley sent a demo to Don Robey who made him an offer but a better one came from Ralph Bass at Federal/King Records. 'Please Please Please' became an R & B hit in April 1956 and would become Brown's famed closing number in which he went manic and would refuse to leave the stage. Within the course of six months, there had been three crazed R & B hits, 'Tutti Frutti' (Little Richard), 'Drown in My Own Tears' (Ray Charles) and 'Please Please Please' (James Brown). 'I Put a Spell on You' (Screamin' Jay Hawkins) was just around the corner. Just where was all this wonderful music going to take us?

In September 2020 Cat Stevens chose 'Tutti Frutti' as one of his *Desert Island Discs*, and he commented, 'The first record I ever bought was by Little Richard. I'd never heard anything like that before.'

III. Boone Companion

There are innumerable social issues connected to the rock'n'roll explosion of the mid-1950s, covering race relations, the so-called 'generation gap', sexuality, fashion, technology and the structure of the popular song.

The Brill Building songwriter Paul Evans recalls, 'I used to listen to the older singers like Perry Como, Doris Day and Nat 'King' Cole with my family, but once I discovered Elvis Presley, Little Richard and Chuck Berry, I was banished to the basement with my own radio. I can still hear my father shouting, "Turn that damn radio down!" This was the first music to belong to just one generation. Rock'n'roll was a parting of the ways and a weapon in our hands. My generation celebrated our music and nobody else's.'

Bo Diddley: 'All the American whites were against black music. A black cat would record a song, a white cat would cover it, and the white kids would buy his record. That's how Pat Boone got famous. Even if a white kid wanted to buy my records, he'd have been scared to take them home because of what his folks might say.'

The Eurovision songwriter Bill Martin says, 'The best introduction to any record anywhere is Little Richard's 'Tutti Frutti' with 'Awopbopaloobop Alopbamboom'. It's nonsense but it grabs you immediately. That's good advice for songwriters; grab the public's attention as soon as you can.'

But you risk becoming a laughing-stock. Pat Boone is put down in rock history books. He was a decent ballad singer ('Remember You're Mine', 'Love Letters in the Sand') but he never should have tackled rock'n'roll ('Tutti Frutti', 'Long Tall Sally'). I have a 16-track compilation album from 1986 called *Jivin' Pat*, which contains those two titles along with 'Good Rockin' Tonight', 'Honey Hush', 'Money Honey' and incredibly, Fats Domino's 'The Fat Man'. ('They call me, they call me the Fat Man because I weigh 200 pounds'). They have their vitality drained from them and it makes me wonder who on earth bought them. Well, me obviously, but these shops see me coming.

All those songs originated from Black artists and Pat Boone was recording them for white teenagers. This was down to history as more or less, the US radio stations and record companies were set up along racial lines. A large record company such as RCA might cater for the whole population with its so-called 'race records' aimed at Black record buyers.

But it was not a one-way street of just white artists covering Black songs. The Black doowop group, the Orioles topped the R&B chart in 1953 with 'Crying in the Chapel', which had been a country hit for the cowboy star, Rex Allen; 'Mona Lisa' was sung in Italian in the film *Captain Carey, USA* and became a standard associated with Nat 'King' Cole', and although Tony Bennett recorded the original of 'Blue Velvet' in 1951, it was also an R&B hit for the Clovers.

In 1954, Bill Haley and his Comets began his run of rock'n'roll hits with 'Shake, Rattle and Roll', and curious white teenagers sought out the original from Big Joe Turner. Turner's song had sexual overtones and Haley, to avoid censorship, cleaned them up. To be fair to Haley, he had a great band and he still made a good record.

Taking us back to 1955, Pat Boone commented, 'My first hit was with 'Two Hearts, Two Kisses (Make One Love)'. A group called the Charms on the DeLuxe label made the original R & B record and I locked myself in a room in Chicago and spent a day and a half singing that song over and over. I'd never heard or sung anything like it and so I had a crash course in R. & B, which was becoming rock'n'roll, and we got a good feel on that record.'

Back then, Pat Boone was more concerned about the grammar in his songs than political overtones. 'I had transferred from North Texas State to Columbia University. This is one of our great universities and Randy Wood at Dot Records was asking me to do Fats Domino's 'Ain't That a Shame'. I said, "I know it's a hit song, but can't we change the title to 'Isn't It a Shame'?" We tried it but it didn't sound like rock'n'roll. I wound up recording it as 'Ain't That a Shame'. I was majoring in English with a No.1 record and I thought, "They are going to expel me for this." They didn't and "ain't" became a good word. It's now in the dictionary.'

That wonderful quote sums up Pat Boone's attitude to rock'n'roll and, if I'd thought quicker, I would have said, 'But what about Fats Waller's 'Ain't Misbehavin'', which was written in 1929?'

Although we now know that the radio DJ Alan Freed received payola, he only played the music he loved and that he knew teenagers would also love, irrespective of their colour. His *Moondog Matinee* show had nationwide popularity and he presented package tours and rock'n'roll shows for New York theatres.

When Little Richard recorded 'Tutti Frutti', Art Rupe felt he had a hit record. He had no objection when his friend Randy Wood at Dot Records wanted to release a cover version by Pat Boone. The lyric was amended by Joe Lubin and we will cover that in the next section.

Pat Boone's record scored a double whammy as the A-side was a cover of the Flamingos' doowop hit, 'I'll Be Home'. Both sides charted for Pat Boone with 'I'll Be Home' at No.4 and 'Tutti Frutti' at No. 12, though Lord knows how these charts were compiled as you couldn't buy one side without the other. Pat Boone's single sold 1.5 million and Little Richard's 650,000 which meant that over 2m American teenagers had 'Tutti Frutti' in their collections. As Richard had written the B-side of a million-seller, Art Rupe as a music publisher was very pleased.

Pat Boone too. In 1955 this handsome, wholesome college graduate with white bucks had Top 10 hits with covers of 'Two Hearts' (Otis Williams and the Charms), 'Ain't That a Shame' (Fats Domino) and 'At My Front Door' (El Dorados). However, because of the criticism of his leaden 'Tutti Frutti' and 'Long Tall Sally ', he never recorded up-tempo R. & B. again.

Little Richard had deliberately sung 'Long Tall Sally' as fast as he could. Chas White: 'The black guys were making the records and the white guys were covering them and having hits. Pat Boone was notorious for this. He did 'I'll Be Home', 'Ain't That a Shame' and 'Tutti Frutti'. Although Richard agrees that it helped to bring him across to white people, he was still very annoyed. When they did 'Long Tall Sally', Bumps Blackwell said, 'Let's get the lyrics going so fast that Pat Boone won't be able to get his mouth together.' A similar thing happened with Black jazz guys in the 40s, a lot of them played very fast chords so no white musicians could keep up with them. It was a one-sided affair, it was exploitation, it was racism and criminal larceny of the original.'

Steady on: there are two strands here. One is whether white artists should be covering Black records and the other is whether they did it competently.

Pat Boone. 'The original records couldn't get played on white radio stations. I couldn't change that but by doing their songs, I brought attention to these artists and the original versions, and they acquired a bigger audience. In most cases, the artists wrote their own songs, so they were delighted I was doing them, no matter what they said later. Little Richard never criticised me in 1956, as I was a catalyst in bringing artists like him to mainstream America.'

Academic and music writer Mike Brocken: 'I would defend Pat Boone a little bit. The idea of regarding everything Black as being authentic and everything White as being inauthentic is a hackneyed way of looking at popular music and it doesn't have a great deal of substance to it. Jerry Wexler from Atlantic Records said, "Nobody wanted to listen to Pat Boone and they wanted to hear Ruth Brown" but that is clearly not the case. Although I personally think Pat Boone is rubbish and his music is terrible, lots of people didn't think that way and he has his place in history. He was a conduit, and the way that American teenagers got into rock'n'roll and African American music would not have been the same without Pat Boone.'

Bobby Vee. 'Pat Boone is not responsible for the way our country was: he was just a guy looking for material. It could be said that he introduced the white population to Black R & B and Black rock'n'roll. They might not have heard it otherwise until much later. The upper mid-west where I grew up was agricultural and I came to rock'n'roll through country music. I was listening to the country station, and they started playing Elvis Presley and Carl Perkins. I didn't hear the Moonglows, the Spaniels and all those other great doo-wop groups until a couple of years later when I started going to New York City and was working at the Brooklyn Paramount.'

Songwriter Otis Blackwell: 'The white radio stations wouldn't play Little Richard's version of 'Tutti Frutti' and they made Pat Boone's version the hit. Would Elvis have done 'Hound Dog' if it had not been for 'Tutti Frutti'?'

What seems to be ignored is that Elvis Presley also recorded Little Richard's songs – 'Tutti Frutti', 'Long Tall Sally', 'Rip It Up' and 'Ready Teddy' (two more than Pat Boone!) – and so surely he is as much at fault as Richard, though he has no trouble with the phrasing on 'Long Tall Sally'.

Mike Brocken: 'You can also argue that girls bought Pat Boone's records over Elvis Presley's because Presley had an element of danger, of sexual promise. Pat Boone was skimmed milk as opposed to the full dairy product.'

Indeed, Little Richard regarded Elvis' covers as the ultimate accolade, even telling *Rolling Stone*, 'I thank God for Elvis Presley. I thank the Lord for sending Elvis to open the doors so I could walk down the road.' When Richard left rock'n'roll in 1958 to become a minister, Elvis sent him a gilded Bible, which he had autographed, hopefully 'Sincerely, Elvis' and not 'Sincerely, God'.

Specialty Records, although owned by a white man, Art Rupe, made records for the Black market and he dismissed both Sam Cooke and his producer Bumps Blackwell when he found them sweetening Sam's soulful voice with a white vocal group. Bumps took Sam round the cornet to Keen Records and they had a US Number 1 on the pop charts with the plaintive ballad, 'You Send Me' in 1957.

Of the 14 No. 1 records on the US charts in 1955, 13 were by white American and the other by a Cuban. By 1961, there were 21 No. 1 records, 7 were by Black American artists and 14 white, including a German. That's only a snapshot but it shows that things were changing.

Also, and we will come to this, Little Richard never, ever objected to the Beatles doing his songs, probably because they were being given a new and unexpected lease of life.

IV. Long Tall Sally – The British Contribution

Speaking as a Brit, I know there are precious few decent rock'n'roll songs from British writers. Ian Samwell's 'Move It!' for Cliff Richard and Johnny Kidd's 'Shakin'All Over' would fight for top place but there's not much below them. However, if you look at the songwriting credits for 'Tutti Frutti', you may find a Brit has been included, Joe Lubin. How does he come to be there?

'Tutti Frutti' started life as a dirty song around drinking dens in the American South. Little Richard picked it up and could claim it as his own as the original songwriter had not registered it – and probably never would. A New Orleans songwriter, Dorothy La Bostrie, wrote some new words and Little Richard's original hit single was credited to Richard Penniman and Dorothy La Bostrie.

When Pat Boone covered it for the white pop market, Randy Wood, the owner of Dot Records, thought it might be a bit risqué for radio playlists and for a performer as wholesome as Boone. And who better than Doris Day's songwriter to tidy it up? My guess is that Randy Wood asked for a revised lyric and Art Rupe commissioned Joe Lubin to do it. This sort of thing happens from time to time and normally the new songwriter wouldn't get a credit: the songwriter might have been slipped $100 for the rewrite.

But Pat Boone's single came out with the credit of Penniman, La Bostrie and Lubin. He can only have been added with the permission of the publisher – that is, Art Rupe. He agreed presumably because a Pat Boone hit meant big bucks, and his single did sell over a million copies.

Joe Lubin's share of the songwriting would have been one-third from the sales of Pat Boone's version and any other version which copies Boone (precious few). However, over the last 50 years when there has been a new version, the credit has often been Penniman, La Bostrie, Lubin.

As I see it, nobody has paid much attention to Joe Lubin and his part in the story. In 2001 I met his cousin Clive Kirsch at BBC Radio London, and although Joe was ill (and indeed died a few months later), he was up to writing some emails. I obtained his story and wrote about him for *In Tune* magazine and then when he died, the *Independent*.

As a music historian I was very interested in Joe Lubin. Before the Swinging Sixties, very few British songwriters had any success in Hollywood, the exceptions being Joe Lubin and the Liverpudlian Jack Brooks who wrote 'That's Amore' for Dean Martin.

Joe Lubin was born during an air raid in Brick Lane in the east of London on 7 June 1917. He told me, 'As long as I can remember, I have been singing anywhere and everywhere, which led to me writing my own songs and then trying to sell them.'

Following an injury, Joe Lubin was discharged from the RAF in 1941. He became an air raid warden in London and entertained civilians in shelters. He recalled, 'We got used to wartime living and it was almost business as usual. One day I took some songs to Denmark Street. There I was in the rain, feeling sorry for myself, not even aware of the falling bombs. I stopped a small man coming out of his office and walking towards his Bentley. It was Noel Gay.' Lubin introduced himself to the noted songwriter and publisher, who returned to his office and gave him an advance of £10. Soon his songs were being recorded and Vera Lynn had success with 'I'm Sending My Blessings' and Anne Shelton with 'Till Stars Forget to Shine', both in 1944.

In 1948 Joe has success with 'The Shoemaker's Serenade', which was recorded by Petula Clark, the Five Smith Brothers and the Radio Revellers. The song did not find an American outlet, but Lubin moved to New York. He said, 'TV was in its infancy, and I wrote bits and pieces and spot songs for the medium. I met Danny Kaye who was going to appear at the London Palladium. I told him that he should include a Cockney song and wrote 'A Paper Full Of Fish'n'Chips' for him. I was at his opening and Danny took the town by storm.' Lubin wrote additional verses for Kaye to perform at a reception in Buckingham Palace, hosted by Princess Margaret.

Back in New York, Lubin married a magazine illustrator. He encouraged her to accept an assignment at Paramount Studios in Hollywood and they settled there. 'I wanted to sell my songs to the movies, although I knew that musicals were out.' With some royalties from England, Joe started Carmel Records. 'My wife and I went to the Black area and in no time at all, we got to know some very good, young musicians. We went into a small recording studio and recorded four songs, two singles. I got an independent pressing plant to press up 500 DJ copies, but the only DJs who played them were on home-based radio stations that only reached 50 people. None of the big, white stations wanted to play them. It was Snow White radio.'

The radio programming led a curious assignment: 'The publishers of 'Tutti Frutti' had heard about a white Jewish songwriter who was producing Black records. They called me in to clean up the song so that Pat Boone, who was a million-selling artist, would record it."

The amendments were minor: Richard's 'She knows how to love me, yes indeed' became 'She's a real gone cookie, yes sirree'.

Much to Little Richard's annoyance, Joe Lubin received a writing credit and thus has his name on one of the cornerstones of rock'n'roll. The changes are so simple and straightforward that you wonder why Richard and/or Rupe (who had wanted to be a songwriter) hadn't made them themselves without involving a third party.

Joe Lubin produced the 1958 rock'n'roll hit by Jan and Arnie, 'Jennie Lee', which was recorded in Jan Berry's garage: 'I knew I had made a hit record but I had no contract with these two underage kids. I asked a lawyer to draw up a contract quickly, giving them a good royalty. Then I phoned some good musicians and recorded the overdubs. Word got around as I got lots of phone calls from record companies who wanted to buy my master.'

Still wanting to write for films, in 1958, Lubin set his sights on Doris Day. Joe recalled, 'I wanted to meet Marty Melcher, Doris Day's husband and manager and the toughest man alive. I gatecrashed his office and talked as fast as I could, not showing any weaknesses. He said he needed a novelty song and there and then, I sang one. He liked it and said that Doris would record it next week. I felt he was playing games with me, so pushing my luck, I said I'd like to submit songs, if any, for the next Doris Day movie. He said they would be starting one soon and they would need three songs, but he didn't give me the script. I went outside and waited in my bashed-up car until I saw him leave. I went into the office again and said, very confidently, that Marty had asked me to find a script for him. There it was, in front of my eyes: *Teacher's Pet* with Doris Day and Clark Gable. I called my wife and told her I'd be home late and started to read it. My home was four miles away from Marty's office and by the time I got home, I'd written a first draft of the title song and also 'The Girl Who Invented Rock'n'Roll', which was to be sung, at the time, by Marilyn Monroe, although that was not to be, and it was sung by Mamie Van Doren. I stayed up all night and finished a third song, 'Teacher's Pet Mambo', for a comedy sequence in which Clark Gable is too clumsy to dance with Doris Day. The next morning, dog-tired and to Marty's surprise, I took them in to him.'

Melcher used Lubin's songs and he wrote several more songs for Day, including the title songs for *Please Don't Eat the Daisies* (1960), *Move Over, Darling* (1964) and *The Glass Bottom Boat* (1966).

Lubin worked on the television series, *Bonanza!* and *The High Chaparral*, but he declined an offer from his friend Dick James to publish the Beatles' songs in the States. Although Lubin continued to write, he did not write any more hit songs. When I spoke to him in 2001, his files had been destroyed in a recent California earthquake. 'I have a printout of all the songs held on the publishing organisations' computers and for the life of me, I can't remember many of them.'

Lubin regretted his bad health but was proud of his children and grandchildren. He added, 'To quote Ira Gershwin, "Who could ask for anything more?"'

Joe Lubin died on 9 October 2001, aged 84.

CHAPTER 4

You Sure Have Started Somethin'

I. Classic Singles

1956 is a year that transformed popular music, arguably a year above all others, and although Elvis Presley was leading the charge, Little Richard wasn't far behind. Crucially, Elvis Presley, Little Richard, Chuck Berry, Carl Perkins and, in the UK, Lonnie Donegan were all making an impression at the same time – with Buddy Holly and the Everly Brothers waiting in the wings.

Little Richard started 1956 touring with the Upsetters and building up his following. There were now family ties as his drummer, Charles Connor, had married his sister, Peggy. Connor thought that 'Tutti Frutti' was a great stage number.: 'Little Richard wanted 'Tutti Frutti' to have more energy than the record, not just the simple backbeat that Earl Palmer played. It was to be more on the bass drum.' That's telling you, Earl.

However, Art Rupe didn't want the Upsetters for the next record: he preferred the New Orleans session musicians. Not that Art Rupe knew a great deal about record production – he just knew that when you recorded Little Richard, you put that voice way out in front.

The J&M Studio in New Orleans were to have a busy year in 1956 and they had now moved to bigger premises at 523 Governor Nicholls Street in the French Quarter, close to Basin Street, famed through Louis Armstrong's 'Basin Street Blues'.

Little Richard arrived on 3 February 1956 to record the next single which would probably be 'Long Tall Sally' backed with 'Slippin' and Slidin''. The musicians were Edgar Blanchard (guitar), Frank Fields (bass), Lee Allen (tenor sax), Alvin Tyler (baritone sax) and Earl Palmer (drums).

'Slippin' and Slidin'' was pumped up with Little Richard playing the engaging opening riff and belting out the lyrics. There was a powerful tenor sax break from Lee Allen, but who could say what the song was about? UK bluesman Dave Kelly says, 'The Little Richard record I love is 'Slippin' And Slidin'' which I am doing with the Blues Band, but obviously his greatest record is 'Tutti Frutti'. Both are absolutely marvellous as well as the definitive 'Long Tall Sally'.'

Roy Young: 'I loved 'Slippin' And Slidin' but I like anything that Little Richard did. It was all mind-blowing. His voice is incredible, really soulful. He could have recorded anything and I would have loved it.'

Chas Hodges from Chas and Dave: 'It is such a good band on those early records and Little Richard drove them along. The chemistry was right – the right musicians with the right singers. They can't fail to make you feel good.'

Maybelle Jackson, who had written for Guitar Slim, gave Richard 'Heeby-Jeebies', but it was too obviously a copy of 'Tutti Frutti'. Maybelle's own mobility was impaired, but she wrote wild, dance songs with hardly any pauses for breath. However, when writing songs like this you have to be careful that you don't stray into nursery rhyme territory and end up as Freddie and the Dreamers.

There were two songs by Warren Scott: the self-doubting ballad 'The Most I Can Offer', which is fine but out of character for Richard. His other song, 'Oh Why', is about bad luck, the kind of wry novelty at which the Coasters excelled.

Billboard reported: 'Shaw Artists is now handling Little Richard's bookings in the East. As soon as the deal was worked out by Jack Archer, Shaw and Lilian Cumber of Herald Attractions, the act was immediately set to headline the show at the Apollo Theatre, New York, the week of February 17.'

Oh, to have been there. This great show featured Little Richard, the Flamingos, Guitar Slim and Linda Hopkins. Richard performed 'Tutti Frutti', 'Shake, Rattle and Roll' (a nod to Joe Turner and its white cover from Bill Haley) and a song *Billboard* called 'Don't You Wish You Had a Man Like Me', which would have been 'Baby'.

It went well and an advertisement a couple of weeks later said, 'Now available for booking, Little 'Tutti Frutti' Richard. Herald Attractions, Los Angeles.' The ad listed five more rock'n'roll acts, including Marvin & Johnny and 10 gospel acts including the Soul Stirrers with Sam Cooke.

The Theatre Booking Association (TBA) had 40 theatres for Black entertainers around the country and there was a stream of touring variety shows. The two main Black theatres were the Apollo in New York and the Howard in Washington. To the musicians, TBA meant 'tough on Black asses' (Ma Rainey's splendid joke) as the wages were poor, the hotels sub-standard and the working conditions harsh. Usually, the theatre tours were booked for a week's variety, but a tour of one-night stands would be particularly uncomfortable, especially with a couple of hundred miles between engagements.

By and large, promoters tried to establish their performers in New York because that was a centre for booking agents and record distribution. As the songs goes, 'If I can make it here, I'll make it anywhere, It's up to you, New York, New York.'

Little Richard's follow-up to 'Tutti Frutti' was released in March 1956 and combined two great sides, 'Long Tall Sally' and 'Slippin' and Slidin''. 'Slippin' and Slidin'' was the original A-side, but it was soon flipped. *Billboard* said, 'Little Richard has a sock follow-up to 'Tutti Frutti' in this two-sided hit, which should grab plenty of plays in both the R & B and pop markets. 'Slippin'' is a swingy rhythm novelty with a rockin' beat, spicy lyrics and a showmanly vocal performance. 'Long Tall Sally' is an equally effective rhythm novelty with humorous lyrics and another great warbling job by the artist.'

The reviewer was classifying Little Richard as a novelty singer and a week later, *Billboard* reported both sides were showing 'spectacular strength'. The teenage show *National Radio Fan Club* voted it the best of the new releases.

However, rock'n'roll was being condemned across America, and there was a call for NBC to ban Richard's record. *Billboard* reported, 'NBC's song censorship rules are often considered to be decidedly on the prim side, and the Specialty disk was screened before airing. After listening to it several times, however, the censor exec finally shook his head and told the show's producer Parker Gibbs, "How can I reject it when I can't even understand it?"'

In March 1956 Little Richard was arrested in El Paso for dancing wildly on stage. This wasn't racial: Elvis was coming in a fortnight and the police said they were going to lock him up too.

On Easter Sunday, April 1, *The Rhythm & Blues Show of 1956* opened in Richmond, Virginia with a bill to die for: Fats Domino, Little Richard, Ruth Brown, Little Willie John, the Clovers, the Cadillacs, the Turbans and Choker Campbell's orchestra. Other performers came and went as it moved around. The promoters were not using the term 'Rock'n'Roll' in the billing as this was a Black show aimed at Black audiences. Initially, rock'n'roll referred to the white music of Bill Haley but it soon spread to the Black artists who, anyway, used it in their lyrics – for example, Chuck Berry's 'Rock and Roll Music'.

Little Richard loved being on the same bill as Fats Domino: he loved his music especially 'Blueberry Hill' and admired his piano style, although it was way different from his own. Fats was slower and more deliberate while Richard was flair and razzamatazz. Little Richard could beat the hell out of a tune, while Fats drew you into his performances with his good-hearted nature.

This magnificent show could be booked for $3,500 a night or 60% of the gate and as they took $52,000 in ticket money on the first four dates, the promoters who opted for $3,500 had the real deal. Those first dates were in Richmond and then Charlotte and Winston-Salem, both in North Carolina and finally, Philadelphia. That's 1,600km (1,000 miles) of travelling so, writing as a Brit, it seems a trek. The tour moved on to Washington DC, Pittsburgh, Buffalo and Newark, but curiously, New York itself was not on the schedule.

Little Willie John was bad-tempered and couldn't cope. He was a small man with a large voice and a hang-up about his size. At the Apollo, Little Richard brained him with a straightening comb. Ruth Brown said, 'You can't be a star 'til you act like one.' Willie said, 'Bitch, you don't tell me nothing'" She pushed him through some swinging doors and he lost two front teeth. On the positive side, he was the first to record 'Fever' in 1956, soon to be a big hit for Peggy Lee with modified lyrics from Sammy Cahn. Willie was involved in many criminal activities and in 1965 he was convicted for manslaughter, and died in prison three years later.

Another package, *The Rhythm & Blues Revue,* was doing the rounds with Big Joe Turner, Nat 'King' Cole, Sarah Vaughan and Count Basie and his Orchestra, but that show was more jazz than rock'n'roll.

Directly aimed at teenage audiences and with Black and white performers was *The Biggest Rock'n'Roll Show Of 56* with Bill Haley and his Comets, the Platters, Frankie Lymon and the Teenagers, Clyde McPhatter and Bo Diddley. They played an arduous 45 dates across the USA. As *Billboard* reported, 'Once the butt of jokes by radio and TV networks, rock'n'roll music is beginning to emerge as a powerful new audience factor in the minds of the network honchos.'

These tours were unquestionably arduous and doubly so for Black artists: being off guard or making the wrong judgment could land you in trouble. Many of the Black artists were not used to being in white areas. It is doubtful that any education was provided for the Teenagers.

'Chuck Berry and Ike Turner have been much maligned by the press, but they were raised in the Southern states,' says Chas White. 'Ike Turner experienced the Klu Klux Klan. His dad had some disease and had to sleep in a tent outside the house and the Klan bashed him about. It's hard to comprehend what it is like living there when you are living in the British Isles. It was brutal stuff and it did affect people psychologically.'

Little Richard, it would seem, was luckier than most and for all his clowning, he could be astute. He did say in one interview, 'The one thing I didn't allow was for the band to fool with white girls. At that time, we would have gotten killed.'

'Long Tall Sally' topped the US R & B charts and stayed there for eight weeks, with Richard replacing Ray Charles' 'Drown in My Own Tears'. The B-side was almost as popular and went to No.2, so for a couple of weeks, Richard had both the No.1 and No.2 R & B records in the US and they were both on the same single. Both sides were on the pop chart too with 'Long Tall Sally reaching No.6 and 'Slippin' and Slidin'', No.33. Pat Boone's 'Long Tall Sally' went to No.8 on the pop charts, one of the few occasions in that period where he missed out on a gold record.

Meanwhile, Elvis had recorded 'Tutti Frutti' as the opening track on the second side of his first album, *Elvis Presley*. It topped the US album charts for 10 weeks and was on the listing for almost a year.

In May 1956, Little Richard performed 'Tutti Frutti' (oversized white suit) and 'Long Tall Sally' (stylish dark suit) as a screen test for the film, *Don't Knock the Rock*. The audition was included on the 2012 Concord reissue of the LP *Here's Little Richard* and I have put the videos onto my PC. Richard is miming extremely well and dancing in the instrumental passages, and if I'm having a bad morning, I play them.

Little Richard was back in the J&M Studio in New Orleans on 9 May with the usual studio musicians except Ray Montrell from Roy Milton's band came in on guitar. Richard had written a new rocker, 'I Got It', with verses about street sellers, food and sexual activity: 'It ain't what you eat, it's the way how you chew it' was one of Richard's favourite phrases – and one he returns to again and again. There was no concession to the teenage market with 'I Got It' and Greil Marcus described it as 'a marvel from the 50s'.

Richard's ending for 'Kansas City' had developed into a standalone song, 'Hey-Hey-Hey-Hey', sometimes identified by its opening line, 'Goin' Back to Birmingham'.

Twenty-five-year-old Italian-American John Marascalco wanted to make his living as a songwriter. He took 'Ready Teddy', modelled on 'Tutti Frutti', to Bumps Blackwell. Also, he had heard 'Long Tall Sally' one Saturday night and written 'Rip It Up' in church the following morning – the song begins, 'Saturday night and I just got paid.' They both sounded like Little Richard singles. Marascalco's ulcer started playing up, maybe more so when he discovered that Bumps had added himself to the songwriting credits.

The verses in 'Ready Teddy', like 'Long Tall Sally', were largely sung a cappella. A few days later Richard tried 'Heeby-Jeebies' in Hollywood and took it slower, but that took its force away and the sax break sounded perfunctory.

Little Richard topped the bill at the Shrine Auditorium, Los Angeles on a show with the Turks, the Robins and Marvin & Johnny. Asked about a forthcoming convention for disc jockeys, Little Richard said he would arrive 'with a stream of Cadillacs, filled with chorus girls.' 'With all these cuties around,' asked *Billboard*, 'what will happen to the jockeys?'

That was a joke, but payola was becoming a major problem for the American record industry. Art Rupe, being a tightwad, naturally said, 'I thought payola dishonest and unfair, and I resented no-talent disc jockeys picking the music in that way.'

Art Rupe wanted to make great records that the DJs would omit at their peril and he regarded Specialty with its distinctive label as being a hallmark of quality. However, soon he would be unable to hold out against the DJs' demands and Sonny Bono became his bagman.

In June 1956, Specialty released their third Little Richard single, which combined two great rockers, 'Rip It Up' and 'Ready Teddy'. Art Rupe wasn't sure about 'Rip It Up' and

Bumps said, 'Put it out and you can buy me a new suit if it's a hit.' Bumps was well dressed for the rest of the year.

Billboard said, 'Little Richard grooves it up on both sides with wild, rip-roaring abandon that's sure to excite the fans. The exceptional band backing keeps up the frantic swinging pace throughout both sides. Both have big potential in the pop field as well.'

This time 'Rip It Up' topped the R & B charts for two weeks and 'Ready Teddy' went to No.8. 'Rip It Up' made No.17 on the Hot 100 and saw off a cover version from Bill Haley and his Comets, which stalled at No.25. In September 1956 Elvis Presley recorded 'Rip It Up' as the opening track for his second album, *Elvis*. The album included 'Long Tall Sally' and 'Ready Teddy' and it topped the US album charts for five weeks. In the UK the very title 'Rip It Up' was seen by Teddy boys as an invitation to vandalise cinema seats.

Little Richard was often playing stadiums on the package tours and was usually topping the bill. On 16 July, he was part of the *Top Record Stars* package at Maple Leaf Gardens, Toronto, performing for 13,000 people.

Canadian DJ Red Robinson said, 'Little Richard called himself the bronze Liberace. He was flamboyant but fun and I loved his music. He was very personable to talk to and always upbeat, but I certainly found him strange.'

At the end of July, Little Richard played the Labour Union Hall, New Orleans and stayed in the city for two days of sessions with Ray Montrell, Frank Fields, Lee Allen, Alvin Tyler and Earl Palmer. Richard was sorry to leave the Upsetters behind and Rupe said that he could have a session with them in Los Angeles.

Billboard reported that in August 1956, 'Little Richard had just finished a week at Buffalo's Zanzibar Club where he topped previous attendance highs despite the fact that the town had been crippled by the steel strike. Reportedly, plenty of patrons came down from Canada.'

Little Richard nailed 'Heeby-Jeebies' at the New Orleans session at the end of July. The tempo was frantic; Richard sang as though his life depended on it and the sax break was perfect. It was really a reworking of 'Tutti Frutti' though not as strong. A young Otis Redding loved the song and sang it on talent shows, but no recording exists.

At this session they had another Marascalco song, 'Good Golly Miss Molly', but taking that one too fast turned it into nonsense. The title was a phrase from a southern DJ Jimmy Pennick.

The take here contains a verse that was dropped. '*Take it easy Miss Molly, have mercy on me, You know I like to ball but I ain't as young as used to be.*' The absolute winner from these sessions was 'Lucille'. If the record had ended after that 18 second piano introduction, it still would have been a million seller. The guitar, the piano, the bass and drums are perfectly in step in a truly insidious, slinky rhythm – and we haven't heard Little Richard sing or scream or heard the saxophone yet. Wonderful. 'Lucille' is another song that he wrote with Al Collins, although the song is named after Lucille Horne, a New Orleans disc jockey that Richard knew and liked. Although people talk about the wildness of Little Richard's records, there is, especially with the best of them like 'Lucille', a mixture of mayhem and control.

Richard's cousin lived by the railway line in Barn Hop Bottom, Macon and the trains would shake the houses as they passed. That gave Richard the rhythm for 'Lucille' and he had been playing that way long before he met Bumps Blackwell.

The flamenco guitarist Juan Martin loves the track: 'I was never a great fan of the

Beatles. Little Richard appeals to me more with that rock-steady rhythm of 'Lucille' and that rough voice like a high-pitched Satchmo.'

In the film *Green Book* (2018), the modern jazz pianist Don Shirley (Maharshara Ali) is being driven on a US tour by Frank Vallelonga (Viggo Mortensen). Frank puts on the radio and we hear the introduction to 'Lucille'.

Don Shirley: 'Who's that?'
Frank: 'Little Richard. Could you play something like that, Doc?'
Don Shirley: 'I don't know. It sounds fairly complicated.'

Roger Chapman, the vocalist with Family: 'When I was 13 or 14, you had Elvis and Fats Domino and Jerry Lee Lewis and I was influenced by them. I was 15 or 16 when I started singing. I was doing Eddie Cochran and Buddy Holly and Little Richard. 'Lucille' is perfect as is anything by Buddy Holly. I used to hate anything English.'

Rock author Bob Stanley, also a member of St Etienne: 'My parents had a stack of singles 'Teen Beat, 'Jailhouse Rock', 'Red River Rock' – but I loved Little Richard best. I was fascinated by the labels as much as I was their sound. 'Long Tall Sally' is basically one note. You can't imagine Percy Faith doing a version of it. When you hear somebody covering Little Richard, you realise how monotonous the whole thing is, like the Everly Brothers version of 'Lucille'. Their version is fantastic, but it does sound like a droning plane. Their harmonies are a one-note melody.'

An anguished ballad written by Leo Price, brother of Lloyd, 'Can't Believe You Wanna Leave', was performed passionately. It is a terrific performance, so unusual, and it would have been worth risking as an A-side.

There was a strong revival of Faye Adams' No.1 R & B hit from 1953, 'Shake a Hand', which now contained one of Little Richard's screams. A female chorus was dubbed onto the recording for release.

Although Richard could have sung Little Willie John's 'All Around the World', this title here was a new song by Bumps Blackwell and Mackinley Millet. Richard's song praises the new music: 'All around the world, rock'n'roll is all they play.' Opportunism, but why not?

Richard was named the Most Outstanding Up and Coming Artist by disc-jockeys in *Cash Box* magazine.

In the summer of 1956, the Los Angeles label Modern took Etta James, Richard Berry and Marvin Phillips to Cosimo Matassa's studio in an attempt to capture Little Richard's sound. Richard Berry, soon to write and record 'Louie Louie', didn't sound like Richard but he did his best and 'Yama Yama Pretty Mama' is repeating a Richard-styled phrase over and over. Marvin Phillips does a 'Good Golly, Miss Molly' with 'Have Mercy Miss Percy'. The best part of the day was setting up Etta James as a female Richard while she is looking for a 'Tough Lover', a man so tough he will step on Jesse James' blue suede shoes: I never knew he wore them. In early September Richard was back in Los Angeles, playing the Savoy Ballroom for three nights and he also played Wrigley's Field in Chicago, a venue built on chewing-gum sales and the home of the Chicago Bears. One of Richard's responsibilities was collecting the proceeds and Richard would travel with a suitcase stuffed with money. At different times during his career, this is casually mentioned by reporters: useful information for would-be robbers.

Then Little Richard recorded with the Upsetters at Master Recorders in Los Angeles.

The original lyric of 'I Got It' was about the street-sellers in Macon, selling their food. (A similar theme is Elvis Presley's 'Crawfish'.) Rupe liked it but thought the song would have more potential if it were about a girl. Again, you may wonder why he hadn't asked Richard himself to change it as the job went to John Marascalco. Although not released they rehearsed 'Hound Dog' and the Duke Ellington instrumental, 'Caravan'.

Little Richard had wanted to record Big Mama Thornton's 'Hound Dog', especially now it was a huge success for Elvis. It's unusual to hear Little Richard shouting: 'Ah, guitar' and it is the only lively moment on a perfunctory recording.

In October 1956 Little Richard was touring Texas in the *Top Ten Revue* with Big Joe Turner, Etta James, the Moonglows and Bill Doggett. He was impressed by Etta's version of the oldie, 'By the Light of the Silvery Moon' and thought he could rock it up.

Times were changing. In May 1955, the Supreme Court had issued a ruling in *Brown v. the Board of Education,* authorising school desegregation. Think of it: Months after the government had ordered that a system of racial suppression be dismantled, here were audiences of white teenagers screaming their approval and desire for a Black, gay man.

Michael Gray: 'That first hit, 'Tutti Frutti', released in October 1955, was wild, delicious gibberish from a human voice like no other, roaring and blathering above a band like a fire-engine run amok in the night. We glimpsed a new universe. The Sinatra-sophisticates were slain with a shout. Enter glorious barbarity, chaos and sex. With a few others – Fats Domino, Bill Haley, Elvis Presley, Chuck Berry, Jerry Lee Lewis and Buddy Holly – Little Richard laid down what rock'n'roll was to be like, and he was the loudest, hottest and most exhibitionist of them all.'

Earl Palmer is credited with establishing the basic rock'n'roll beat on '"Lucille', but to him it couldn't be played any other way. 'The only reason I started playing a rock'n'roll beat came from trying to match Richard's right hand," he said, 'With Richard pounding the piano like that, you couldn't go against it.'

The new single combined 'Heeby-Jeebies' with 'She's Got It', which was going to be featured in the film, *The Girl Can't Help It.* As *Billboard* reported on 13 October: 'Next to Fats Domino, Little Richard is R & B's most consistent hitmaker. He also has a huge pop following that is buying this in large enough quantities to guarantee early representation on both Pop and R & B charts.'

Both sides made the R & B Top 10 but neither side was on *Billboard's* Hot 100. Certainly, it wasn't Little Richard's finest single, but the momentum should have taken it up the charts.

Little Richard returned to the J&M Studio in New Orleans in October 1956 for two days of recording. Although Richard's song 'Jenny Jenny' is a good one and a deserved hit single, the recording sounds odd. Richard appears to stumble in the middle of each verse and then at the end, he stutters on 'my girl'. The stutter on 'Jenny Jenny' is down to a bad edit when two takes were joined for the record. It was not his finest hour and the song would have benefited from a new session.

Not to worry, as we also have the utterly brilliant 'Good Golly, Miss Molly'. As with 'Lucille', the song has one of the greatest intros of all-time, but what does 'Good Golly Miss Molly, you sure like to ball' mean? Oh, dancing, I get it. In 1970 Little Richard told *Rolling Stone* it was an innocent song but 'balling' as slang for sexual intercourse was around in the 1950s. The introduction to 'Good Golly, Miss Molly' is among the most exciting in the whole of rock'n'roll, but there are precedents. You can hear its origins in 'Cadillac Boogie', a Specialty record by Jimmy Liggins and his Drops of Joy, dating from 1947, and even more so in 'Rocket 88' by Jackie Brenston, who was accompanied by Ike Turner's Kings of Rhythm in 1951.

Art Rupe had been asked about Little Richard appearing in in *The Girl Can't Help It.* He was told Fats Domino was performing the title song. Ever the opportunist, Rupe said that Fats Domino wasn't animated enough and that Little Richard was far more exciting. The song was passed to Little Richard, who had some difficulty with the slick lyrics. Bobby Troup, who wrote 'Route 66' had not imagined such an arrangement and was surprised – and pleased – when he heard it.

So, Little Richard was given Bobby Troup's title song for *The Girl Can't Help It*, the girl in question being Jayne Mansfield. The vocal group the Coasters were in New Orleans and, according to *Billboard*, sang the backing vocals.

Rather out of character, Little Richard recorded the vaudeville standards, 'Baby Face' and 'By the Light of the Silvery Moon', the latter also to be revived by Jackie Wilson.

In the original 'Baby Face', Al Jolson sang 'My poor heart is thumping, You sure have started something', but I'm not sure what Richard sings. He is stumbling on the words. The rest of the take was fine so Specialty approved its release.

A new ballad and a great one, 'Send Me Some Lovin'', was written by John Marascalco with Leo Price. Richard put real emotion into his performance, employing a higher key than usual. Alan Freed called it one of Little Richard's greatest tracks and I agree. When Leo's brother, Lloyd Price recorded the song in the 1960s, he gave it a Motown arrangement.

While in the studio, Little Richard recorded a radio commercial for WLAC Nashville promoting Royal Crown hairdressing with the disc jockeys Gene Nobles and Hoss Allen. Getting carried away, Richard said that even Long Tall Sally used Royal Crown hairdressing, though Richard himself would soon be resorting to wigs.

'The Girl Can't Help It' and 'All Around the World' were combined for Little Richard's new single and despite the publicity around the film, 'All Around the World' was the original A-side. *Billboard* reported: '"All Around the World' is a frisky, fast moving rhythm item. The flip – another great rhythm tune with amusing lyrics – is the title tune from the forthcoming Jayne Mansfield movie about the juke box industry.'

After playing the Elks Auditorium in Los Angeles on 23 December, Little Richard played the Christmas and New Year period on a package show with Ivory Joe Hunter and Guy Mitchell which was performed in-between screenings of *The Girl Can't Help It* at the Fox Theatre, Detroit.

Even though the film did great business, the title song did not have the impact of 'Tutti Frutti' or 'Long Tall Sally'. Was the public starting to tire of Little Richard or was Little Richard tiring of the public? One way or another, Little Richard's career was set for a seismic shift.

In his autobiography, *James Brown – The Godfather of Soul* (Sidgwick & Jackson, 1987), James Brown placed this following story in 1956, although Little Richard didn't have a suit of mirrors until the mid-60s. He described playing Laurel Garden in Newark with Richard. 'By this time Richard and I had a rivalry to see who could outdo the other. I did my usual dancing and powerful singing and we were getting over real good. Halfway through the act, Richard was trying to get them to make me come off stage, but I wanted to do something to really cap it off so I got the Flames to boost me into the rafters, I worked my way across the ceiling, holding the mic and singing, When I got there to the middle, I hung there by one hand above just pleading "Please, please, please". Richard was running around yelling, "Get him down!" Meanwhile, the Flames danced out to the middle of the floor and cleared the people underneath me. I let go, like I was overcome with emotion, and dropped like down like going off a high bridge. When the Flames caught me, the place went wild. Richard never had a chance.'

II. The Girl Can't Help It

Despite all their tawdriness and tackiness, I love rock'n'roll films – give me low grade to Lew Grade anytime.

In the early 1950s, there was a spate of JD (juvenile delinquency) films in America, the most notorious being *The Wild One* (1953 with Marlon Brando leading a motorbike gang), *The Blackboard Jungle* (1955, with Sidney Poitier, aged 28 and still going to school) and *Rebel Without a Cause* (1955, with James Dean in that bright red jacket). But they are not rock'n'roll films. The only rock'n'roll in any of them occurs in *The Blackboard Jungle* when Bill Haley's 'Rock Around the Clock' is played on the soundtrack but not performed in person.

With rock'n'roll records becoming a teenage phenomenon, Hollywood wanted to cash in. Sam Katzman, the King of the Quickies, made *Rock Around the Clock* in two weeks in 1956. It featured the endlessly grinning Bill Haley with his Comets, the immaculate Platters with 'Only You' and 'The Great Pretender', and a Las Vegas showband, Freddie Bell and the Bellboys, with a novelty about a horse, 'Giddy Up A Ding Dong' and 'We're Gonna Teach You to Rock'. (See what I mean about novelty songs; 'Ding Dong' is plain stupid, but 'Tutti Frutti' is fine.) Although no one in the film looks cool, it caused riots around the world. Local authorities in the UK banned the film, and clergymen said it was destroying the country's moral fibre. It wasn't the best rock'n'roll film, but it was the first and a good start.

Bill Haley had done well in *Rock Around the Clock*, but he was upstaged by Little Richard's guest appearance in his second film, *Don't Knock the Rock*. Or was he? Here's the review from *The Times*: 'The playing and chanting – singing is the wrong word – of Mr Haley and his Comets seem harmless, if monotonous and, as someone who opens his mouth and makes noises, Mr Alan Dale is at least to be preferred to Mr Elvis Presley. The primitive and ugly antics of Little Richard and his assistants, however, could have been dispensed with.'

Rex Morton reviewed *Don't Knock the Rock* for the *New Musical Express* and referred to Little Richard as 'an animated golliwog' which would be unacceptable language today. Other writers latched onto this phrase and it was used time and again in the *NME*. None of them had actually met Little Richard and so 'the five foot bundle of joy' from an early press release was also constantly and erroneously repeated.

Little Richard's biographer, Chas White: 'Little Richard looked outrageous in *Don't Knock the Rock*. This bizarre figure came out with a lascivious face, plenty of make-up, greasy hair, a high pompadour and really wild eyes. He was playing a baby grand and he put his foot on top of it and started hammering the keys. Our piano at home was a sacred instrument that you walked around and my aunt played hymns on it. Little Richard was belting the heck out of it and screaming his head off and when he finished, he bowed as if he had played a Chopin nocturne. It was unbelievable.'

Little Richard didn't make many records with his group, the Upsetters, but they were with him in *Don't Knock the Rock.* The intention had been to counteract criticism by making a positive film about rock'n'roll, and Alan Freed even called it 'a harmless outlet for today's youth'. Richard was lucky to have a non-speaking part – Bill Haley has to say, 'I always thought the freedom of the press was a tailor who irons your shirt for nothing.' That's a joke?

In pop culture terms, Little Richard in *Don't Knock the Rock* deserves to be up there with James Dean in *Rebel without a Cause* and Marlon Brando in *The Wild One.* Marlon Brando in *The Wild One* didn't know what he was rebelling against – Little Richard did: the world would be a better place if we all lost our inhibitions and danced.

The generation gap was the subject of *Shake, Rattle and Rock!* which featured Groucho Marx's foil Margaret Dumont leading a citizen's group out to ban rock'n'roll. There were guest performances from Fats Domino and Big Joe Turner, and young and old get together to give the story a heart-warming ending that nobody believed or even wanted.

Elvis Presley or rather his manager Colonel Parker had a choice: either let's make him a smouldering James Dean or Marlon Brando or let's put him in a rock'n'roll musical. Colonel Parker found a third way: let's feature him in a second-rate and predictable Civil War western, *The Reno Brothers*, with Elvis as one of the Reno brothers who would be killed in the final gunfight, oh yes!

Marshall Crenshaw: 'I find many rock'n'roll films unwatchable so many years after the fact. You're waiting for the performances to happen as the storylines are awful. There's a lot of bogus sermonising where there'd be handwringing about the dire effects of rock'n'roll. The society that they were talking about was a conformist, racist society. The whole thing turned my stomach and the scripts of those major studio rock films from the 50s were a drag, except for *The Girl Can't Help It.* That's the one that's good.'

Hollywood was lagging behind when it came to presenting the new music but not to worry, help was on its way and *The Girl Can't Help It* was released for Christmas 1956. It was a feature length film, packed with live (or rather mimed) performances. It had a seven-week shooting schedule, De Luxe colour, stereo sound and even CinemaScope. It had a first-rate script, witty and not too contrived, and a fabulous array of guest stars. Jayne Mansfield's hourglass figure, Eddie Cochran's shoulders, Gene Vincent's Blue Caps and Little Richard's outrageous vocals steal the show. Richard performs the title song (unseen), 'She's Got It' (as Mansfield parades in front of the bandstand in a tight, red dress) and 'Ready Teddy'.

Film critics snubbed rock'n'roll films, but this one deserves to be amongst the films of the century. Fellini paid homage to it in *Boccaccio 70.* The filmmakers were proud to be using CinemaScope and used it for an excellent visual joke: the switch from the black and white beginning to colour and CinemaScope is brilliantly handled.

The American author Garson Kanin wrote a short story, *Do Re Mi,* which was made into a film with Judy Holliday, *Born Yesterday* (1950). It told how a washed-up theatrical agent is forced to groom a gangster's moll for stardom and, in so doing, falls in love with her. The story was updated for the rock'n'roll era by the writer and director, Frank Tashlin, known for his comedies with Jerry Lewis and Bob Hope.

Tashlin almost made the film with Sheree North as the gangster's moll and Orson Welles as the gangster. He ended up with Jayne Mansfield as a brash parody of Marilyn Monroe and Edmond O'Brien as a screen gangster in his only comedy role. Jayne Mansfield impressed Tashlin enough for her to star in his next film, *Will Success Spoil Rock Hunter?*

Frank Tashlin said, 'There's nothing in the world that's funnier than big breasts' and he set out to prove it in *The Girl Can't Help It.* The film is a homage to breast fetishism, in the title sequence alone (a Little Richard song), milk boils and ice melts as Jayne walks by. 'She's only a girl,' says Tom Ewell to a newsboy. 'If she's only a girl,' comes the reply, 'I don't know what my sister is.' Mansfield's performance was parodied by Divine in John Waters' film, *Pink Flamingo* in 1972.

Jayne Mansfield wasn't a dumb blonde: she had studied drama at the University of Texas and UCLA and she had acted in Arthur Miller's *Death of a Salesman.* She had an IQ of 163, so she knew what he was doing and her effect on men (and adolescent boys like me).

Tom Ewell plays the down-at-heel agent, Tom Miller, and Jayne Mansfield his client, Jerri Jordan – no doubt about it, Tom and Jerri are meant as cartoon characters. The joke is that she can't sing but the racketeer Fats Murdoch (O'Brien) knows that isn't a handicap. He switches on the TV and sees Eddie Cochran shrugging his shoulders to 'Twenty Flight Rock'. If such an untalented individual (!) can become a star, then so can Jerri Jordan.

When Tom tests her singing voice, it shatters glass. However, she wails the police siren in Fats' song, 'Rock Around the Rockpile', which she records with Ray Anthony and his Orchestra. Eventually, Jerri shows she can sing with the ballad 'Ev'rytime', but she had kept her talent from Fats because she really wants to be a wife and mother. Looking down, she says, 'Nobody thinks I'm equipped for motherhood.' Ewell takes up her offer and the film ends with a docile Fats babysitting their fifth child.

The Girl Can't Help It is racially integrated and Little Richard is allowed to perform lascivious songs about a white woman – 'The Girl Can't Help It' (unseen) and 'She's Got It'. Frank Tashlin was into animation and so Little Richard must have been perfect for him: he was *Looney Tunes* personified.

When Tom and Jerri go to the Brill Building or its equivalent, Gene Vincent and the Blue Caps are performing 'Be Bop A Lula' in one of the studios. Paul Peek had joined the Blue Caps and he upstages everybody. The moment the Blue Caps toss their caps off is pure magic.

The film includes the Treniers with a live and lively 'Rockin' Is Our Business', the Platters with 'You'll Never, Never Know' and Fats Domino lamenting 'Blue Monday'. The Chuckles with Teddy Randazzo as lead singer and accordion perform 'Cinnamon Sinner'. Eddie Fontaine, known for 'Nothin' Shakin'', does 'Cool It Baby' and he told *Now Dig This* that he received $15,000 for three days' work, which either seems unlikely or he had a brilliant agent. Johnny Olenn and his Band perform 'My Idea of Love' and 'I Ain't Gonna Cry No More'.

Tom Ewell, a former alcoholic, hallucinates about his past love and though it's hardly rock'n'roll, Julie London with her many changes in 'Cry Me A River' is among the highlights. The MOR singer, Abbey Lincoln sings 'Spread the Word' and Nino Tempo, later to have hits with his sister April Stevens, performs an instrumental, 'Tempo's Tempo'. Even Edmond O'Brien joins the fun with 'Rock Around the Rockpile'.

The Girl Can't Help It was a mainstream film for the new, young and vibrant counterculture. The avant-garde French filmmaker François Truffaut said, '*The Girl Can't Help It* was more than a good film, more than a funny film, more than an excellent parody: it is a masterpiece of the genre. It is more beautiful and successful each time you see it.'

Another famed director Peter Bogdanovich said, 'I knew the director of the film Frank Tashlin and although Frank hated rock'n'roll, he got Little Richard and all the guys in there.

It was right at the time that rock'n'roll was hitting so it was perfect timing. Frank was a satirist. He often showed things on which he wasn't really keen but you couldn't tell which side of the fence he was watching from. The film is great fun.'

B.B. King commented, '*The Girl Can't Help It* was the first film that I can remember was accepted as much by the white audience as the black.'

Marshall Crenshaw: 'I like *The Girl Can't Help It*. You can tell the director Frank Tashlin started directing animated cartoons. It's like some really wild Warner Brothers cartoon and it had a cartoonish approach to the live action. Little Richard was wonderful. I love the way Little Richard appears in those rock'n'roll films because often, he sings these wild songs and then he bows at the end like he's just played a minuet.'

Rita Tushingham: 'I loved Little Richard. There had never been anyone like him before. I loved 'Tutti Frutti' and he was amazing.'

Film critic Mark Kermode: '*The Girl Can't Help It* is a very funny film. People think of it as a roadshow movie but it is a proper film. It was brash and vibrant and it was more rebellious than people give it credit for. It isn't just a string of numbers although the performance pieces are important. It is more than that.'

On 18 September 1968 the Beatles stopped working on 'Birthday' in Abbey Road to watch *The Girl Can't Help It* on TV at Paul's home in St John's Wood. Then they returned to the studio to finish the track. No wonder Paul is screaming like Little Richard.

Mark Kermode: 'Little Richard has had a long screen career and he commands the screen whenever he appears. He was in *Down and Out in Beverly Hills* and he has an incredible screen presence. Even when he is up against the world's most glamorous women, he is the one that your eyes are drawn to. I was watching Prince's *Purple Rain* the other day and I had forgotten that Prince's entire act is Little Richard. He is pretty much doing Little Richard in *The Girl Can't Help It.*

III. Delayed Shock

There was opposition to rock'n'roll as it developed in the USA, but it wasn't hard to hear it as radio stations with powerful transmitters were catering to this new audience. Radio transmitters knew no colour bar, so it was possible for white kids to hear Black music so long as their parents weren't around.

It was more difficult to hear rock'n'roll, Black or white, in the UK because the national radio station, the BBC, was at first reluctant to broadcast the new music. The BBC only played rock'n'roll intermittently and you might have to listen to the whole of a request programme like *Family Favourites* to hear one rock'n'roll record. In March 1956, I was 11 years old and longed to hear a record that was climbing the charts, 'Heartbreak Hotel' by Elvis Presley. What a great title and what a fantastic name. Later, when I found out it was his real name, I was amazed.

One day I was off school with a bug and I put on *Housewives' Choice*, a request programme to take the drudgery out of housework. It started after the news at 9am and finished at 9.55 a.m. Then followed an uplifting homily from a clergyman to prepare listeners for the day. This day the minister said, 'I have just heard the most abominable music imaginable. A reputable organisation has released this travesty and teenagers are buying it. It is by someone called Elvis Presley and it is called 'Heartbreak Hotel'.' He played half a minute of the record that was going to destroy western civilisation before telling us again how appalling it was. I was hooked. I got off my sick bed and went out and purchased the record. I knew 'Rock Around the Clock', but this was something different. You could dance to Bill Haley but I had no idea what you did to 'Heartbreak Hotel'. It was unique.

But not for long. Little Richard's battle cry, 'Long Tall Sally', was a hit in the US in April 1956 but because the Specialty label didn't have a licensing deal, its UK release was delayed.

But John Lennon heard it.

One of Lennon's schoolfriends, Michael Hill, explains, 'In 1956 we had a school exchange programme to Amsterdam and three of us went over – Pete Shotton, Don Beattie and myself. John Lennon didn't go, but I don't know why. We were paired with Dutch children and I discovered with the help of my Dutch friend this marvellous record by Little Richard which had been released there. I brought it back to Liverpool and on our first day back, I told John Lennon that I had a record by a guy who was better than Elvis. That got his attention. When he heard the record, he was speechless. It was a pivotal moment in his life; everything followed from that. 'Long Tall Sally' became a staple feature of the Beatles' shows right through to the end, albeit sung by McCartney who felt the same way we did about the record.'

Little Richard told *Rolling Stone* in 1973: 'The best version of all my stuff is what Paul McCartney did with 'Long Tall Sally'. They did it with an outstanding piano, everything, it was just fantastic.'

'I was ahead of John when it came to rock'n'roll. John wasn't interested in anything very much at age 14,' says Michael Hill. 'At 14, you're allowed to do part-time work and I took a job delivering newspapers. I saved enough money and bought records, whereas John and Pete never did any work and so never had any money. They thought I had a magical supply of records from the States, but they came from the local record shop in Elm Hall Drive.'

On 16 February 1957 BBC-TV stepped into the unknown with an early evening programme on Saturdays called *Six-Five Special*, produced by a 25-year-old Oxford graduate, Jack Good. The management forced him to feature jazz alongside skiffle and rock'n'roll and include worthy items on such wholesome activities as mountaineering and sailing. They wanted archery in the UK.

Each week there was a film clip and it was exciting when Little Richard was broadcast to the nation for the first time. Some of us had seen *The Girl Can't Help It* at the cinema, but this clip of Little Richard on the first programme from *Don't Knock the Rock* meant millions could see what he was like. I was 12 years old and yet to see a rock'n'roll film and this was astonishing: I talked about it for weeks afterwards, and obviously, I still do.

Filmmaker John Waters: 'When his songs were huge hits, people didn't talk about him being gay or anything. I don't know if he was beyond that because he was so scary. They didn't even know what he was. He was a Martian more than being gay. It was like he was from another planet.'

Jack Good recalled, 'The management was horrified when I had a clip of Little Richard and after that I would just write "Clip from current film" in the running order, so that they couldn't comment beforehand. I had a studio audience and the BBC didn't want them dancing in front of the cameras because the cameras might be broken by these ruffians. Fortunately, the set designer was on my side and he put wheels under the rostrums. Just before the show, I said "Plan B" and the audience was wheeled in front of the cameras. The

Assistant Head of Light Entertainment said, "You can't do that!", and I said, "I just did!" The technicians were marvellous as we were only allowed five hours of camera rehearsals, including tea breaks, for a 55-minute live show.'

In April 1956 Pat Boone's Dot single 'I'll Be Home' was released in the UK on the London label with 'Tutti Frutti' on the B-side. It became a No.1. It was followed by 'Long Tall Sally' which made No.18, so effectively, two Little Richard songs were hits in 1956.

Towards the end of year, Little Richard's records were finally licensed for the UK. In December 1956 Little Richard had a minor hit with 'Rip It Up' and then he broke through when 'Long Tall Sally' and 'Tutti Frutti' were issued on the same single. The next single was a double-sided smash, 'The Girl Can't Help It and 'She's Got It'. Little Richard was now a star. Indeed, in order to make up for lost time, a series of four-track Little Richard EPs were released in the UK. This is different to the US where there was only a small EP market.

Dave Kelly from the Blues Band was also the brother of blues singer Jo Ann Kelly. 'I introduced Jo Ann to the guitar. We did skiffle, Buddy Holly and the Everly Brothers at talent shows in holiday camps and we usually won. Jo came home with this EP by Little Richard. Rock'n'roll was exciting but Little Richard was even more exciting, so how did he do that? He had a bigger band with saxes and we didn't know that it was really rhythm and blues under a different name.'

In the jukebox charts published by *World's Fair*, Little Richard reached No.2 with 'Long Tall Sally' and went to No.3 with 'She's Got It', although 'The Girl Can't Help It' was the main side for record sales. *World's Fair* was to dub Little Richard, 'Sir Jukebox'. Later, 'Baby Face' was a jukebox No.1 and even 'Kansas City' reached No.2, despite only being No.26 on the sales chart. As Little Richard sang in 'All Round the World', 'You can hear those jukeboxes jumpin', All night and all the day': he knew his market.

Tom Jones, talking about the 1950s said, 'It was a grey boring world until rock'n'roll came along. For adults, it was almost as bad as being under attack. *Daily Mail* called rock'n'roll, "the black man's revenge" and it was seen as unbridled sexual expression.'

David Bowie: 'In 1956 I heard 'Tutti Frutti' and my heart nearly burst with excitement. I'd never heard anything even resembling this.'

Tim Rice: "Tutti Frutti' is a great lyric. It's fun and it's very memorable. I would find it very difficult to be that simple these days. You can have too much experience, too much technique and you can sometimes forget that your basic job is communication, which is the most important thing for any songwriter to remember.'

In the late 1950s, Percy Phillips in Kensington and Bernard Whitty in Crosby had recording studios on Merseyside. In June 1957, two teenagers, Paul Murphy (vocal) and Johnny Byrne (acoustic guitar), made a private recording of Little Richard's 'She's Got It' with Percy Phillips, the first rock'n'roll recording on Merseyside. The next year an 18-year-old butcher's boy, Teddy Taylor (later known as Kingsize Taylor) recorded an impassioned 'Good Golly Miss Molly' for Bernard Whitty. Ted was recording at the same time as the Quarrymen with Percy Phillips for 'That'll Be the Day' but he sounds far more convincing than the fledgling Beatles.

Chas White: 'I was brought up in the west of Ireland and when I first heard Little Richard, it was like getting out of the Bastille after 40 years' imprisonment because the environment was all high-powered Irish Catholicism. I went to a friend's house and he was tuned into AFN, the American Forces Network. I heard 'Long Tall Sally' and I couldn't believe the power and the energy and the vitality and the freedom of it. Rock music has been the most exciting thing in my life, and Richard has been the main interpreter of this excitement. He is the king of rock'n'roll, the man with the Crown Jewels in his throat, the most exciting man on the planet. He went further than anybody else, and he did it first. He said that his music makes the blind see, the lame walk and the dead rise up, and he says, "I am the originator of soul, the king of rock'n'roll." Little Richard was never humble.'

Geoff Davies, the owner of the Probe Plus record label: 'I was very much aware of rock'n'roll coming along and I remember hearing 'Heartbreak Hotel' for the first time on the radio. I was thinking, "What the hell is this, this feller is not singing properly." I was used to crooners and people singing "properly" and this was just amazing. That and Little Richard were my introduction to rock'n'roll. Little Richard was the real king of rock'n'roll and I think he thought so too. It was just amazing stuff – he made the hardest, the dirtiest and the best rock'n'roll around.'

CHAPTER 5

Can't Believe You Wanna Leave

At the start of 1957, *The Girl Can't Help It* was being screened across America and was very popular, deftly combining humour with classic rock'n'roll performances. Despite the publicity, Little Richard's single of 'The Girl Can't Help It' could only manage No.49 on the US Hot 100. Perhaps it was because it was too structured a song for the explosive Little Richard; perhaps it was because Art Rupe wasn't paying payola to any extent; perhaps the public had had enough of Little Richard.

Whatever, it had been six months since Little Richard's last big hit and something had to be done.

There was no denying Little Richard's drawing power as a performer. He sold out the Apollo in Harlem and there was talk of touring Europe and appearing in Australia with Johnnie Ray. Richard appeared at an autograph party in Los Angeles, which would have taken him longer than most as he wrote dedications and messages with his signature, sometimes even adding his telephone number.

When Richard appeared at the Howard Theatre in Washington, the promised session with the Upsetters was arranged. He had two frantic new songs, 'Ooh! My Soul' and ''Keep-a Knockin'', which made for wonderful, explosive recordings.

Although the Upsetters had been on the road with Richard, this was their first Specialty session with Little Richard.

Charles Connor recalled, 'We did 'Keep-a Knockin'' in a small radio studio in Washington DC when we were on tour. I said, "Let's do something that's never been done before", and that was the four-bar drum intro. I got the idea from Richard telling me about the rhythm of the trains when he was young. It wasn't rehearsed – we created it in the studio.'

When Little Richard retired from show business in 1958, a 58-second tape of him singing 'Keep-a Knockin' was said to have been extended by repeating a section to make a standard-length record. This was a strange story and wasn't true. Little Richard had recorded a full version of 'Keep-a Knockin'', of course he had, but the verse starting 'I'm drinkin' gin and you can't come in', was deemed unacceptable for teenagers. It might not get airplay and so the single combined the first verse with, well, the first verse. The song works much better in its unedited state. It is a great performance with Richard exploding with energy.

Slim Jim Phantom, drummer with the Stray Cats, says, 'There's great drumming on the Little Richard records. Charlie Connor who is a buddy of mine did a great job on 'Keep-a Knockin''. Earl Palmer was always a big influence on me. They are rock star drummers to me.'

Fourteen years after Richard recorded 'Keep-a Knockin'', John Bonham played it at a jam session, perhaps just for fun, and Led Zeppelin developed it into 'Rock and Roll', a track on their fourth album. It was used in a nationwide US ad for Cadillacs in 2002.

Led Zeppelin were accused of plagiarism with 'Dazed and Confused' and 'Whole Lotta Love', but this one was overlooked. Still, can you be a plagiarist on a song that has been stolen in the first place when the original recording didn't have such a drum pattern? Indeed, Louis Jordan's record was advertised as a foxtrot. You can see what a minefield plagiarism is.

But 'Keep-a Knockin'' was hardly a new song. The first recording of 'Keep-a Knockin'' was by Bert M Mays with his barrelhouse piano in 1928 who called it 'You Can't Come in'. He claimed composing credit and he could be right. He has an introductory verse which says,

You told me honey you were going away
You didn't tell me who were going to stay,
You needn't go further
Cause I have got another
And this is all I have to say.

Bert then launched into 'No use a-knockin' but you can't come in' and goes through such excuses as 'I'm busy cookin' and you can't come in'. He ends with 'I don't want you and you can't come in.'

'Ooh! My Soul' had energy but little else. It sounded like Little Richard had realised 'Ooh! My Soul' could be a song title but didn't bother to write the song. When 'Ooh! My Soul' was released in 1958, Bingo Beaufort at *World's Fair* described it as a 'powerful religious rocker'. Er, no.

In March 1957, Little Richard played some dates in the Philippines and then toured the East Coast with the Four Robins and the Sepia Dolls. It wasn't expensive to see him. When he played the Madison Ballroom in Detroit, tickets were 75 cents.

The new single in March 1957 was a cracker, combining the pounding 'Lucille' with the anguished 'Send Me some Lovin''. 'Lucille' topped the US R & B charts for two weeks and 'Send Me some Lovin'' reached No.3. 'Lucille' made the US pop charts, reaching No.21, though it deserved better. *Billboard* called it 'a wild, wailing tribute to Lucille'. It added, 'The flip is a switch to a slow-paced blues which strongly resembles the melody of the old blues, 'Birmingham Jail'. Both of these have power aplenty.' Spot on: 'Birmingham Jail' is also known as 'Down in the Valley', which has soul versions from Solomon Burke and Otis Redding.

'Lucille' was released in the UK on the same day as Pat Boone's best record, 'Love Letters in the Sand'. Both of them were in the Top 10 together.

His first album, *Here's Little Richard*, was issued in the US in March 1957. It included six hits – 'Tutti Frutti', 'Long Tall Sally', 'Slippin' and Slidin'', 'Rip It Up', 'Ready Teddy' and 'She's Got It' – and six tracks that hadn't been issued before – 'Oh Why', 'True Fine Mama', 'Baby', 'Miss Ann', 'Jenny Jenny' and 'Can't Believe You Wanna Leave'. It works as a coherent whole and is a brilliant album. What better way to start an album than with 'Awopbopaloobop Alopbamboom'? A new note for a CD reissue of this album by Concord stated, 'Richard introduced even eights that would come to drive most R & B and rock music and still do today.'

Art Rupe was careful with his costs, but this time it worked in his favour. To quote Chas White, 'Art Rupe was so mean that he got the students at UCLA to design the sleeves for Little Richard's early albums. He couldn't have got better people as the music was aimed at students. The covers convey the energy and vivacity of the music. The microphone in front of him is like a lance thrown down by some proud warrior. The perspiration is coming out of Little Richard like a singing volcano.' In other words, you can judge an album by looking at its cover.

Having seen them at a Hollywood club, Billy Berg's, Art Rupe signed up 18-year-olds Don Harris and Dewey Terry, who had been born and raised in Pasadena with shared musical interests. Harris learnt classical violin and be among the first to play an electric violin, notably with Frank Zappa but he had experimented in 1959 on 'Fiddlin' the Blues'. Terry mostly played piano and bass, but they could switch around.

In the mid-50s they were working with doo-wop groups – the Squires and the Cadets (or Jacks actually the same lads), but they wanted success as a duo and signed with Specialty in January 1957. They only wanted to record and perform their own songs. They didn't have hits with Specialty but their songs were later picked up by others – 'I'm Leavin' It All Up to You' (Dale and Grace and then Donny and Marie Osmond), 'Justine' and 'Koko Joe' (both the Righteous Brothers), 'Farmer John' (sped up by the Searchers) and 'Big Boy Pete' (Olympics). But did they really think that anyone was going to buy 'Kill Me (cause I want to die)'?

Don and Dewey didn't have their own hits with Specialty but they met Little Richard and were to work with him on his comeback in 1964. A lot of the time Don and Dewey had a self-contained spot in Johnny Otis' revue.

In May 1957 the London headquarters of Decca Records came to an arrangement to market Specialty around the world. The new single was the frantic 'Jenny Jenny' with Little Richard hollering like a man possessed. The B-side was his power packed ballad 'Miss Ann'. Both sides made the Top 10 on the US R & B chart.

Little Richard played some Canadian dates in June 1957 and there was 'a tremendous crush around the bandstand' when he played Vancouver. It was there that Richard first announced that he would be quitting show business, but nobody paid much attention.

In July, Little Richard entered the world of cosmetics and his first perfume was Princess Cheri, ostensibly marketed for females. You could also buy Elvis Presley's Hound Dog lipstick.

Then stories began circulating about Little Richard's possible retirement. *Billboard* said in August, 'Despite Little Richard's apparent evangelistic kick, Irv Siders of the Gale Agency notes that the chanter is in greater demand than ever and his bookings now carry into October.' Note the word 'apparent': was there some doubt about it?

Just in case Little Richard was serious, Art Rupe wanted a new Little Richard in the wings – and he found one in Larry Williams.

Larry was working in New Orleans for Fats Domino, driving him around in a station wagon. He was a young, married lad who expected to be working with Lloyd Price, his second cousin, when he was demobbed. He met Little Richard in New Orleans and befriended Bumps Blackwell, who was to comment, 'Larry Williams didn't know whether he wanted to be a singer or a pimp. He had long careers in both fields.' More tactfully, Art Rupe said Larry was into 'the sporting life'.

When Lloyd Price returned to civilian life in 1956, he expected to be met with open arms by Art Rupe but he had been usurped by Little Richard. So Lloyd and his manager, Harold Logan, now set up KRC (Kent Recording Company). Lloyd knew the melody of 'Just Because' was okay because he had taken it from an aria he had heard in the army,

'Caro Nome' from Verdi's *Rigoletto*. When KRC released it, ABC-Paramount offered him a licensing deal and reissued it.

Lloyd Price commented, 'I never thought Larry would double-cross me because I had taken care of this guy. He asked me to loan him money so he could go to LA to see his mother. Instead of going to see her, he went straight to Art Rupe's office and told him about 'Just Because'.'

Art Rupe knew it was a good song, so he recorded it with Larry Williams for his first single. Both versions made the R & B charts – Lloyd Price, No.3 and Larry Williams, No.11. Either way the song was recorded in Hollywood, which is where Larry Williams did most of his recordings.

'Just Because' was a decent start and Art Rupe thought he could be the second Little Richard? Larry didn't have Richard's vivacious personality, but he was a good-looking cheerful guy who could bang out chords like Richard and convincingly sing nonsense songs. 'Pick a girl's name and you're away,' said Bumps, Larry Williams chose Fanny – short fat Fannie to be precise.

Rather than deny the Little Richard influence, Larry wholeheartedly embraced it by referring to his hits in the lyric – 'Slippin' 'n' Slidin'', 'Long Tall Sally', 'Rip It Up' and 'Tutti Frutti' – and then for good measure, he added 'Heartbreak Hotel', 'Fever', 'Hound Dog', 'Blue Suede Shoes', 'Honky Tonk', 'Jim Dandy', 'Blue Monday' and 'Blueberry Hill'; a splendid roll-call for a two-minute single. It was shopping-list songwriting and it worked. Larry performed 'Short Fat Fannie' with the energy of Little Richard, even if his range was flatter. Indeed, he adopted the same formula – couple of verses, sax break, another verse and then out, although he added some rock'n'roll whistling.

'Short Fat Fannie' was a huge hit – top of the R & B charts, No.5 pop, Larry Williams had rock'n'roll stardom, but it was precarious as his other businesses could easily be splashed over the newspapers. It took only one dissatisfied girl (or client!) to talk to the press, and of course he could be blackmailed.

Who had ever heard of a girl called Moronie? Well, never mind: Larry Williams' next single, 'Bony Moronie', was a great rock'n'roll record with a contender for the daftest couplet of all-time, 'I got a girl called Bony Moronie, She's as skinny as a stick of macaroni.' Plas Johnson played tenor sax, a musician who would create the theme for *The Pink Panther*. Larry Williams' whistling made for a highly commercial conclusion, the idea coming from Professor Longhair's records. It was a US pop and R & B hit and it made the UK charts. It was played on BBC-TV's teenage show, *Six-Five Special* and Pete Murray remarked, 'I hope she's bony in the right places.'

Like Richard, Larry Williams was a good showman. He could turn his back on his piano and play it behind him which was a good party trick. Art Rupe recalled, 'Larry Williams introduced a chimpanzee into his stage act. This backfired one night as the chimp adopted an air of indifference and proceeded to throw his excrement at Larry Williams.' Richard also had a pet monkey but he never took it on stage – it just annoyed his neighbours.

In August 1957, Specialty Records announced that it would be going into the albums market with a mammoth push. That was hyperbole. Art Rupe had taken on the arranger and producer Harold Battiste with 22-year-old Sonny Bono as a general factotum. Sonny was an office boy who wanted to pitch his songs and learn studio technique.

Art Rupe gave Richard a $10,000 loan (surely he should have been giving him royalties) so that he could bring his family to Hollywood. In another interview, Richard said the money came from his stage shows, which was money that didn't go through Rupe.

At their height, Little Richard and the Upsetters were playing for a $2,500 guarantee which their share of the gate could easily double.

Richard came back from one tour with a suitcase packed with cash. One night, James Brown and the Famous Flames found themselves sharing a New Jersey bill with Richard and asked him for money to get back to Georgia. Richard opened the trunk of his car, reached in without looking, and handed over a fistful of bills. Richard said, 'I used to feel good about that, especially being from the South, having all these people whom we thought hated us, showing us all this love."

Whatever, Richard secured a house – a mansion really – for his family at 1710 Virginia Road West in the Black Sugar Hill area of Los Angeles. Richard's mother was sorry to leave her friends but amazed when she saw the chandeliers and statues. Little Richard had a luxury car, a gold Fleetwood Cadillac, and he loved the home, inviting Chuck Berry, James Brown, Jackie Wilson, Etta James and the Coasters to view it.

Across the road lived Joe Louis, the world heavyweight boxer. Like Richard, Joe Louis had grown up in the South (in his case, LaFayette), but the family had moved north to Detroit after being persecuted by the Ku Klux Klan. Joe Louis had lived his professional life by a strict code of conduct – never have a photograph taken with a white woman, never gloat over an opponent you had beaten, always behave honourably – and he was now playing golf and trying to get the PGA to permit Black players, an issue that was resolved in 1961.

The very personable Brother Wilbur Gulley of the Seventh-day Adventists came to Little Richard's new house selling literature. Little Richard was impressed, and Gulley introduced him to Joe Lutcher, brother of the singer Nellie Lutcher. Joe had led the Society Cats and had had hits in the late 1940s with 'Shuffle Woogie', 'Rockin' Boogie' (on Specialty) and 'Mardi Gras'. Changing his ways, he devoted his life to God and similarly, he sensed something was missing in Little Richard's life. Despite the cash in the back of his car, Richard felt ripped off and was taunted by racists – and, perhaps more significantly, the IRS was after him.

Richard thought that the Seventh-day Adventists were right. There had to be some selection process for going into Heaven. He said, 'We'd been taught that when we die, we go to Heaven. Everybody went to Heaven! Even if you were the biggest drunk in the city, you went to Heaven. If someone was a killer, he would go to Heaven. I thought, "My, my, everybody can't be going to Heaven."'

At the end of August, Little Richard was part of *Alan Freed's Holiday Rock'n'Roll Show* at the Brooklyn Paramount with the Diamonds, Mickey & Sylvia and Larry Williams, a big show with 50 performers. There were plans to bring an Alan Freed package to the UK early in 1958 in conjunction with the Grade Organisation: Little Richard, the Moonglows and Jo Ann Campbell would be supported by UK acts. This was changed to Little Richard and the Diamonds and dropped completely when Little Richard quit the business.

In September 1957, Little Richard played the Howard Theatre, Washington for a week with Larry Williams, Clarence 'Frogman' Henry, Screamin' Jay Hawkins and Huey 'Piano' Smith. If I could be transported back in time, that show would suit me fine. It's odd that Little Richard and Larry Williams were on the same bill as Larry Williams was Little Richard-lite.

In 1956 the beat poet Allen Ginsberg knew that he had to see a rock'n'roll show and he said he saw Fats Domino and Little Richard at the Paramount Theatre in Times Square, although they never appeared there together. Whatever, Ginsberg was amazed to witness 5,000 screaming teenagers, standing on their seats and dancing in the aisles. He had never seen anything like it and enjoyed every minute. The police tried to calm them down, but the noise never stopped. The power of music to reach a whole generation was not lost on Ginsberg.

There had been talk of Little Richard appearing in another rock'n'roll film, *The Hit Parade*, but he soon dropped out. The film's title was changed to *Jamboree* (US) and *Disc-Jockey Jamboree* (UK) and was light on the big hitters. Instead, Richard went with a story loosely based around Alan Freed's career, *Mr Rock'n'Roll,* (mis-)directed by Charles Dubin. It was flimsy but the clips are good – LaVern Baker and Stumpy with 'Humpty Dumpty Heart', Lionel Hampton's title song and cameos from Chuck Berry, Clyde McPhatter and Frankie Lymon. On the double-plus side we have Little Richard belting out 'Lucille' in a great clip with horn players and guitarists moving in line.

'Keep-a Knockin'' was the new single and it made No.2 on the R & B chart. It climbed to No.8 on the US pop chart and he only did better with 'Long Tall Sally'. In the UK, it stopped just outside the Top 20.

The road between gospel and rock was a two-way street and Sam Cooke of the Soul Stirrers wanted Little Richard's success. He was 21 years old and exceptionally good looking.

Ruth Brown described being on tour with both Sam Cooke and Little Richard when Sam wasn't sure whether to cross over. He told her, 'It's easy to get out there but a lot harder to get back in.' She recalled them singing 'Jesus Loves Me' backstage with Sam leading and Richard replying.

Bumps Blackwell arranged a session for Sam Cooke in New Orleans and 'Lovable', was a rewrite of a gospel song 'Wonderful' (recorded by the Soul Stirrers) with the object of affection being a girl rather than God. It was released under the name of Dale Cook, but Bumps hadn't quite got what he was hoping for. He arranged another session, this time in Los Angeles and with a white vocal group. Bumps saw the potential in Sam's song 'You Send Me', and the session was taking place while Art Rupe was in Las Vegas because he knew Rupe would object to a white vocal group, however good, insisting that they wouldn't be soulful.

Unfortunately for Bumps, Art Rupe wasn't in Vegas because his personal life was in turmoil. Art's wife Leonora was leaving him; she was having an affair with saxophonist Jesse James Jones, employed by Art. Art turned up to see how the Sam Cooke session was going and was horrified by the white singers. What's more, Sam Cooke had recorded George Gershwin's 'Summertime' and 'Who's going to buy opera?' Another song, 'Things You Do to Me', was written by Sonny Bono. Art said 'You Send Me' could never be released on Speciality. Bumps said he was quitting, but Art said: 'You're fired' and, turning to Sonny Bono, added, '…and you're hired.' Next stop: Sonny and Cher.

Despite his problems, Art Rupe didn't forget how to cut a deal. Bumps had to forfeit future royalties on Little Richard's sessions in exchange for Sam Cooke's session tapes. Bumps placed them with a new label in Los Angeles, Keen, run by Bob Keane and John Siama. 'You Send Me' became a US No.1 single.

Sam Cooke's songwriting was theoretically with Art Rupe, but Sam wisely but deceitfully listed the song under his brother's name, and the money got to Sam that way. Cooke soon moved to RCA and had many more hits, but he was shot in 1964 having just recorded what would become a Civil Rights anthem, 'A Change Is Gonna Come'. Art Rupe reflected on not accepting 'You Send Me': 'I made a terrible mistake. I shouldn't done it, but I did.'

Rupe took an earlier recording of Sam's 'I'll Come Running to You', and sweetened it in the same way as 'You Send Me' for release.

Clarence Fountain from the Five Blind Boys of Alabama has an intriguing take on Sam Cooke, 'I worked with Sam Cooke all the time as the Blind Boys, the Soul Stirrers and the Pilgrim Travelers were with the same agency. We toured together and made a living. Sam Cooke was fine singing gospel, but his mind was geared to other things, he knew that if they could do it, he could do it too. He didn't really want to sing rock'n'roll once he got into it but money was good and he went for it. He had a good voice, but there was nothing for him to learn with rock'n'roll, it was the easiest thing in the world.'

Chas White: 'The first day I was in Hollywood, I was at Bumps Blackwell's house and I was staying with him. A guy drove up to collect me who looked like Chuck Berry, but it was Bobby Day. He had a Cadillac that looked great when I got into it but when I got out, I could see one side was all bashed in. He drove me to Bumps Blackwell's house. The first night I stayed in a room with the gold disc for Sam Cooke's 'You Send Me' above the bed.'

By now Little Richard had a wild and bizarre image, although that was safer than a Black artist being sexy on stage. An act like Barry White's would have been in real trouble in the 1950s. Nevertheless, at the Royal Theatre in Baltimore, a pair of panties landed on Charles Connor's hi-hat.

Sometimes the Upsetters didn't know when Richard would make his entrance or where he would come from. The band might vamp for a couple of minutes while Richard decided what to do and this built up the excitement. Richard needed this regular band who were used to his ways as opposed to Chuck Berry who would play with anyone who was available.

In West Virginia a hotel manager told the band that they could only be there with their wives. The band had a woman with them, and her husband was downstairs trying to find her. The band sneaked out of the hotel via the fire escape.

In Little Richard's autobiography, he says that he liked watching his band members having sex. Maybe he did masturbate several times a day, but it must be difficult to organise your working life around all this activity. He told *The South Bank Show* in 1986, 'Everybody likes to jack off.' In the same programme, he also said, 'I'm Little Richard but everything is big.'

It does seem that Little Richard was more into voyeurism than gay sex. He told Barney Hoskyns in the *NME* in 1985, 'There was a whole lot to be seen in those orgies, some things you ain't seen the like of in your life. Tree trunks, really! I met a guy, his penis was 18 inches, and sometimes he didn't want people to see it. No girl could have sex with him as he was so big. I would call people in to see it, and we'd say, "Where did you get that from?"'

Richard has reflected: 'Most gay people fall in love with themselves.' His brother and valet Marquette said, 'I knew Richard was changing as he would sometimes read the Bible instead of having an orgy.'

Little Richard met Lee Angel in Savannah, Georgia. She looked stunning – five foot two with a Dolly Parton figure and of white, Black and American Indian ancestry. She was graduating and working as a dancer and stripper. Richard said, 'Angel looked like a white girl, but she was black. She would do anything to excite me.' That included watching someone having sex with her: she was dedicated to Richard and would do anything for him.

Richard dedicated 'Send Me Some Lovin'' to her and she organised many a tour party. Etta James recalled, 'Richard had these parties and they'd say to me, "Don't open the door, you're a minor."'

Angel was interviewed for the book *Rock Wives* by Victoria Balfour in which she describes Little Richard with a great phrase: 'He went into the twilight zone and never returned.' Little Richard was not drinking or taking drugs, but his tours combined orgies with reading from the Bible. Angel concluded, 'I was the woman that Little Richard wanted to be.'

A new white star, Buddy Holly, even joined an orgy. Chas White: 'I said when I first heard it, "This is impossible. Buddy Holly is a real nice chap like a bank clerk," but he was involved in a wild, sexual orgy.'

Buddy Holly also took Little Richard to his family home in Lubbock. His father wouldn't allow him in, but Buddy said, 'Then you won't see me again.' They did enter but his family was not happy. This was when racial barriers were being broken and President Eisenhower was sending troops into Little Rock.

Little Richard was to star in a package tour of Australia, mostly in stadiums and for most of October. On 13 September the *NME* reported that he would go straight from this into a four-week UK tour with the Moonglows, Teddy Randazzo and Jo Ann Campbell, supported by British acts, starting on October 20.

The concert promoter Lee Gordon had been born in Michigan in 1923 but after a few run-ins with the Mob, he moved to Australia. He brought over Frank Sinatra and Johnnie Ray and in March 1957, he mounted the first major rock'n'roll tour of Australia with Bill Haley and his Comets, the Platters, LaVern Baker, Big Joe Turner and Freddie Bell and the Bellboys. How could it fail? It also took the Sydney-born singer Johnny O'Keefe to stardom in his homeland.

His second rock'n'roll tour was to star Little Richard, Gene Vincent and his Blue Caps, Eddie Cochran and the female Elvis with the crazy name, Alis Lesley. She had been born Alice Lesley, which was strangely convenient. She sang Elvis Presley's hits and had worked with the Blue Caps in California.

Gene Vincent's star was waning as he had been unable to capitalise on the success of 'Be-Bop-A-Lula' but he was a productive artist, releasing albums as Capitol's leading rock'n'roll performer. He had a lively act, despite wearing a leg brace, but his black leather look was not created until 1960. The Blue Caps looked like a 1970s cabaret act in zebra-patterned suits. Vincent's attitude to stagecraft was different to Little Richard's. Richard's musicians were there to make him sound great: Vincent was all for letting the musicians shine.

Gene had been touring the States and one of the Blue Caps, Tommy Facenda, had been charged with statutory rape in Minnesota. He told the police that he hadn't gone to bed with a statue. The matter was resolved, and the band was on the road again.

Despite their strange courtship, Lee Angel had fallen madly in love with Little Richard and she hoped to marry him when he returned from Australia.

The tour was well planned, but the distances were still overwhelming. They actually played 25 performances over 12 days at 8 different venues, mostly stadiums, and this is long before stadium rock became the norm. The logistics didn't hit the performers until it started. These are the concerts that they played:

Tuesday 1 October 1957 – 6pm, 8.45pm, Crown Theatre, Wollongong, NSW
Wednesday 2 October 1957 – 6pm, 8.45pm, Newcastle Stadium, NSW
Thursday 3 October 1957 – 6pm, 8.45pm, Brisbane Stadium, Queensland
Friday 4 October 1957 – 6pm, 8.45pm Sydney Stadium, NSW
Saturday 5 October 1957 – 2.30pm, 6pm, 8.45pm Sydney Stadium, NSW
Sunday 6 October 1957 – No show
Monday 7 October 1957 – 1pm., Masonic Hall, Broken Hill, NSW
Monday 7 October 1957 – 6pm, 8.45pm Centennial Hall, Wayville, South Australia
Tuesday 8 October 1957 – 6.15pm, 8.45pm West Melbourne Stadium, Victoria
Wednesday 9 October 1957 – 6.15pm, 8.45pm West Melbourne Stadium, Victoria
Thursday 10 October 1957 – 6.15pm, 8.45pm West Melbourne Stadium, Victoria
Friday 11 October 1957 – 6pm, 8.45pm, Sydney Stadium, NSW
Saturday 12 October 1957 – 2.30pm, 6pm, 8.45pm Sydney Stadium, NSW

The organisers planned jiving competitions with £100 in prize money for each show. Little Richard was inventing rock'n'roll striptease and was carrying a substantial wardrobe, including a supply of bright green turbans.

Little Richard never liked flying and hated the long trip to Australia, which was over 16,000km (10,000 miles). He had a book *The Great Controversy* written in 1858 by Ellen G White, the founder of the Seventh-day Adventists. In Heaven, God had created Satan, a being with freedom of choice, who became God's adversary. Right now, the two were locked in conflict over the future of the world and it would soon be resolved. As this book had been written in 1858, just what did 'soon' mean? Richard thought it would be happening on 1 January 1958, the book's centenary.

When Christ returned, the good people (the Seventh-day Adventists, naturally), whether dead or alive, would be taken to Heaven. The rest would die.

The text preyed on Richard's mind and at different times on the journey, he thought that the plane was on fire or that it was being supported in the sky by angels. During some turbulence, he shouted that he would dedicate his life to God if God would only let him live. Little Richard was not your ideal travelling companion.

The immediate problem for the promoter was Gene Vincent and his Blue Caps flying to Honolulu instead of Hawaii, and so they couldn't make the first show. As the Blue Caps were also contracted to back Eddie Cochran and Alis Lesley, there were further problems which Lee Gordon resolved by asking local artists Johnny O'Keefe and the Dee-Jays to step in. Their recent singles were 'You Hit the Wrong Note, Billy Goat' (Bill Haley) and 'Flip Flop and Fly' (Joe Turner). Because Gene Vincent was missing, Johnny O'Keefe was booed but he shouted, 'Okay, you boo me now but you're gonna love me' and he succeeded with a highly energetic performance. It was also his job to announce the performers via a backstage microphone.

Alis Lesley was unknown, but Eddie Cochran had had a US hit with 'Sittin' in the Balcony'. Oddly, though, the posters said he would perform 'Butterfly' (Charlie Gracie), 'Gone' (Ferlin Husky) and 'A White Sport Coat' (Marty Robbins), not really songs to set stadiums alight. Both Alis and Eddie proved to be solid support acts.

Little Richard and the Upsetters stormed the audience and there were screams from both himself and the audience. With his stage antics, he demonstrated that he was fit as any athlete. After the show, he told a reporter that he was very glad to be in Australia and that he wanted to play Russia. He could draw American and Russian teenagers together to help resolve the Cold War.

The first stadium gig was at Newcastle Stadium in New South Wales and the crowd was enthusiastic from the start. Girls ran forward to grab the handkerchiefs Eddie Cochran was throwing into the audience. The protection barrier around the footlights was pulled down. Drums were broken and another set had to be found quickly. Meanwhile, Dickie Harrell from the Blue Caps improvised by jumping on top of the piano and banging a snare drum under his arm. Unfortunately, he damaged the piano. Not that it mattered as Little Richard was next.

Little Richard was wearing a blue costume, not too far away from some classy pyjamas. He tore the top half into pieces and threw it into the audience, following it with a belt, a ring and a watch. A scramble ensured and it ended with the musicians and the audience fighting for the bare-chested Richard, with the attendants grabbing him and taking him into the wings. He returned a minute later, screaming 'Awopbopaloobop Alopbamboom'. *Newcastle Morning Herald* said that attendants had to 'rescue an over-excited teenager's foot from Little Richard's face'. There were over 5,000 fans at each show in Brisbane Stadium. *Brisbane Courier Mail* thought that Johnny O'Keefe's 'Giddy-Up-A Ding Dong' was the highlight, but maybe the newspaper was banging the local drum. The reviewer said, 'They rocked, they rolled and they screamed the house down, the noisiest night the police squad could remember. The crowd screamed too as Little Richard dispensed with most of his clothing and also at Alis Lesley's tight gold lamé pants.'

The stadium at Sydney was even bigger and over 10,000 attended each show. The revolving stage which was something new for the performers. The police had to stop fans from trying to pull Gene Vincent off stage. He would come off stage and say, 'They almost got me tonight.'

The report in *Sydney Morning Herald* was about the 'shirt, tie, belt, socks and three pairs of underpants which Richard stripped off and threw to the screaming teenagers.' Let's hope he had been wearing four pair of underpants. His striptease was the climax to 'a frantic, ear-deafening rock'n'roll concert.

What's more, 'Alis Lesley in tight-fitting yellow slacks stood on the piano, lay on the floor, wrestled with the microphone, embraced the string bass and sang."

To accommodate the dancers, some ringside seats had been removed. However, the law did not permit a rearrangement of seating without a licence and the organisers were told that this could not continue on the second night. There was to be no jiving in the audience.

Johnny O'Keefe recalled, 'Little Richard was very worried about the Sputnik. Around 8.30 at night, in-between the shows, we were all standing outside the stadium and looking into the sky. It was flying across, and Richard said, "That's it: the end of the world is coming. I don't want to die in Australia. I'm going home".'

After his troubled flight to Australia, the Sputnik was another sign. Little Richard was convinced the world was ending and no amount of logic would persuade him otherwise. So, we can blame the Russians for Little Richard's retirement. The Sputnik spacecraft was all very well but Eddie Cochran was more interested in meeting Bernard Flock, an American marine who was on shore leave in Australia. He could supply American cigarettes.

In Sydney, they recorded a radio show, an edition of *The Ampol Show* with Jack Davey for the Macquarie Media network. Fortunately, it has survived and we have live performance from Little Richard and the Upsetters ('Long Tall Sally', 'Lucille'), Gene Vincent and his Blue Caps ('Be-Bop-A-Lula', 'Lotta Lovin'') and Eddie Cochran, also with the Upsetters ('Whole Lotta Shakin' Goin' On').

On *The Ampol Show*, Richard said, 'I'm going to be an evangelist. I saw all these lights in the sky. That is a sign that the Lord is coming soon. I am going to study and I am going to help the people who are doing wrong so that they can be saved too.'

So Richard knew that he himself would be saved!

Although Richard loved performing, he said, 'I can't serve the Lord while doing this'. The host, perhaps not knowing how to deal with this outburst, gave him a rug of New Zealand wool, and amazingly, held the broadcast back until November: you would think the station would immediately put it on the news.

The second day created further problems. 'Teenagers ignored the ban when Little Richard and his band started their act. When he started to sing 'The Girl Can't Help It', red-shirted youths grabbed their girls and began to jive in the aisles. The police forced a crowd of screaming youths back to their seats when they climbed a wire screen while trying to rush the stage. The police hurried Little Richard out of a side entrance after the show.'

There were two arrests as Lewis Pirator (20) and Joe Zerafa (21) tried to keep a pair of Little Richard's shorts and about 20 other people had the same idea. They pleaded guilty to offensive behaviour and resisting arrest and were both fined £3. Personally, I wouldn't fight over anybody's boxers, but there we are.

Gene Vincent was enjoying the tour and he loved being with Eddie Cochran, whom he knew would be a star. He loved Little Richard too and was constantly amused by his stage performances. Richard would go on last and would usually overrun. Richard did not like travelling with Vincent, who pretended he was going to throw Richard out of the car. When Gene rang home, he told his mother that he would bring home a kangaroo. He was joking, but it is so rare to hear of Gene Vincent making jokes.

On Sunday, the touring party was to perform at an 8.30pm open-air show at Broken Hill, New South Wales. The co-promoter Mel Langdon wanted insurance against rain, but he couldn't get the cover. Very reluctantly, he went ahead and the chartered plane brought in the 40-strong touring party. But there was a union problem and the show on the Sunday night looked like being cancelled. A compromise was reached, and the media announced that tickets would be valid instead for a show at one o'clock on Monday afternoon. As the stadium wasn't available, fans were redirected to the Masonic Hall. Only 350 people attended the show, which, musically at least, went well. An embarrassed Lee Gordon told a reporter, 'Don't tell anyone that I've got anything to do with this.'

The next show was at the Centennial Hall in Wayville, a suburb of Adelaide. Little Richard was interviewed by Merv Hall from Radio 5DN in Adelaide and said Little Rock was caused by a hard core of older people with a hatred of 'Negroes'. He spoke of his family's involvement in religion and said that he wanted to become an evangelist with the Seventh-day Adventists.

Little Richard was told by the Adelaide police that he could not striptease. He wore a glistening black and white cloak and said that he could not take off his clothes as the police had forbidden it. He threw his cloak into the audience. Within seconds, everybody was scrambling for it. The police said that unless everyone went back to their seats, the show would end.

The public was now aware that Little Richard wanted to be a minister, albeit the strangest minister in the history of religion. Little Richard told *Melbourne Herald*, 'My dad was killed and so I am the sole supporter of my mother and her 10 other kids. I've been earning $10,000 a week and now I plan to retire. I don't smoke, drink or go to the movies but I stay inside reading the Bible when I'm not working.' When asked whether he had saved enough to look after this large family, he said, 'No, but that doesn't matter when the world is coming to an end.'

Melbourne Herald reported on the show's 'blaring sound, frantic rhythm and frenzied body contortion.' Little Richard, the star of the show, made his entrance in a green, jewelled turban and a canary yellow suit, partially covered by a crimson cloak. After an amusing striptease, he was soon entertaining the early show audience wearing only his green turban and a pair of pyjama trousers. It took the attendants some time to break up a group of fighting teenagers trying to gain possession of the first pair of pyjama trousers that the showman tossed away."

While in Melbourne, Eddie Cochran appeared on Stan Rofe's *Platter Parade* and left his mark on 3KZ by carving his name on a studio turntable. Four months later, Buddy Holly added his name to the turntable.

There were further shows at the Melbourne Stadium on 9 October, but on the next day, Little Richard said he wasn't doing any more concerts because the end of the world was coming. 'It's that Russian satellite,' he said, 'I'm flying home on Sunday to be baptised. I want the kids to realise that the Lord means more to me than anything. It is a matter of life and death for me to get back to the West Coast by Monday. The man who is going to baptise me won't be able to do it after Monday. My Sydney concert on Saturday will be my last ever.'

Why wasn't Richard baptised already, and why can't he be baptised by somebody else? All totally confusing but he was making things up as he went along. And what about the kids he was addressing – were they going to be saved? Shouldn't he have been telling them what to do?

On that last show in Melbourne, Richard came out with in his robes with an ornate Bible and he said, 'Ladies and gentlemen, I am not going to sing for you tonight. I'm to going to tell you about the Lord.' He read to them for 20 minutes and left the stage. If anything was going to start a riot, I would have thought that would be it, but no, the audience accepted what he had to say: he was a good preacher.

On Friday the touring party returned to Sydney and *Sydney Herald* reported that Little Richard had thrown four rings valued at £4,000 into the Hunter River to prove his devotion after being challenged by his saxophonist, Cliff Burks. 'That's shows my faith in God,' said Richard.

For the Sydney concerts, the audience was told, 'We regret that the New South Wales police department says that there will be no dancing in the hall. You can get a refund. Do you want that?' There were shouts of 'No! No! No!' A reviewer said that 'Gene Vincent transformed the revolving stage into a riot of colour. His floor-level climax to the act first charmed the crowd and then completely enthralled it.'

Richard looked in the Sydney telephone book and found a Seventh-day Adventist, Pastor Conley, at a missionary college. He told Richard to break his contracts and not to delay. 'Let hell come,' said Richard. 'Christ conquered hell.'

Little Richard wanted to return to Los Angeles immediately and dedicate what was left of his life to the Seventh-day Adventists. He would be sued for breach of contract, but that didn't matter. Firstly, the world was about to end, and secondly, all contracts could be broken by an Act of God and this clearly was an Act of God. (Nice one, Rich.)

The subsequent shows were cancelled and Little Richard was returning a week early. A plane that had originally been scheduled for his return crashed in the Pacific and a couple of people were killed. To Richard, this was another sign.

Back in America, Richard gave a press conference and announced he would be studying religion and not performing anymore. He said, 'I've been earning $10,000 a week and now I plan to retire.'.

Little Richard was persuaded to play the Apollo in New York as a favour to Alan Freed, but that was it. The UK tour for November arranged by the Shaw Agency was off. I'm surprised that nasty-looking men in grey overcoats didn't pay Richard a visit, but luckily, the people he offended were not associated with the Mob.

Little Richard wanted out of his Specialty contract with Art Rupe, as he said he wasn't working for the Devil anymore. On the other hand, Rupe didn't want to lose Little Richard, no matter how difficult he was: Richard had seven gold discs.

Richard agreed to a final secular session for Specialty. Rupe had lost both Sam Cooke and Little Richard within a year and ironically, both singers wanted to do what the other had been doing. Rupe told Richard he could stay with Specialty and cut spirituals. The label had a religious catalogue, but Rupe knew how volatile Richard was and it was better that things played themselves out. Maybe he could combine music and evangelism like Sister Rosetta Tharpe.

On 18 October 1957, Richard was recording with the Upsetters, this time at Master Recorders in Los Angeles. This would be Little Richard's final session before he retired. Bumps Blackwell and Art Rupe gave the musicians some advice: 'Richard is going to sing his lungs out, so don't blow solos over him. You calm down and Richard, you go all out.'

'I'll Never Let You Go (Boo Hoo Hoo Hoo)' is a textbook Little Richard ballad, and 'Early One Morning' recalls a girl at school who loved someone else. There's a mellow sax break, unusual for Little Richard, but there's no point to the song.

Art Rupe was keen to record the blues 'Good Morning Little Schoolgirl', Richard less so. 'Okay,' said Rupe, 'It's just so we can get it on tape and then we can study it.' We're all heard that before. We don't know what Richard's problem was, though no performer today would dream of singing 'Good Morning Little Schoolgirl'. On the outtakes, we hear Little Richard calling him 'Mr Rupe' and not 'Art'.

Willie Perryman's 'She Knows How to Rock' captured Richard's style well, although the song could be about a prostitute who wants her money first. Then with only five minutes left, Richard said, 'Okay, we'll do 'Shakin'' in G with just the rhythm.' Richard's cover of Jerry Lee Lewis' 'Whole Lotta Shakin' Goin' On', is not so good because he sounds hoarse. Jerry Lee said that Little Richard wore more mascara than Cleopatra and he was 'something else'.

Don Covay was at the session and although he didn't write any songs, he took over with the Upsetters when Richard had finished. Little Richard called him 'Pretty Boy' and this name was used on his single. The titles were 'Bip Bop Bip (Pretty Boy)' and 'Paper Dollar'. He also recorded 'Switchin' in the Kitchen'. He roughed his voice for this dishwashing song, perhaps coming from Richard telling Don about working in the bus station. The lyric refers to having some fun tonight.

Although Lee Angel had hoped to marry Little Richard there was now little chance. In December 1957 she met Jackie Wilson at the Baby Grand club in New York and their affair lasted for a couple of years, although Jackie was married at the time. Later, Lee partnered Screaming Jay Hawkins but she always held a torch for Richard and hoped they would marry.

Angel was disappointed that Richard never wrote a song for her, but why should he? 'Angel' is an overworked word in song-titles – 'Angel' (Elvis Presley), 'Angel Baby' (Rosie and the Originals), 'Angel Baby' (a different one – Dean Martin), 'Angel Face' (James Darren), 'Angel Child' (Al Jolson), 'Pretty Little Angel Eyes' (Curtis Lee) and 'I Married an Angel' (Sammy Kaye). Okay, write me a love song, Richard, but don't call me angel of the morning.

Little Richard had walked away from the rock'n'roll Christmas shows at the New York Paramount, which would have given him $15,000. The shows were always a nightmare for Alan Freed because he had nightmares about it snowing badly – and now he didn't have Little Richard.

CHAPTER 6

Take My Hand, Precious Lord

So the world didn't end in 1958.

Of course, we are dealing with Little Richard World here, which revolves around his personality and nothing is normal. As far as I know, Richard was out on his own, the only Seventh-day Adventist linking the Russian Sputnik with the end of mankind.

Mind you, the Seventh-day Adventists were wary about getting the date wrong. Before the church itself was established, a key figure William Miller determined that the world was going to end in 1844, but he had misinterpreted a passage in the Book of Daniel. The miscalculation came to be known as the Great Disappointment.

Instead, the Adventists referred to a section of the Book of Revelation about time ceasing to exist – that's when the end of the world would come – but no date was given. There's an element of caution about that, but given the history, it's totally understandable.

I suspect too that the Adventists were happy to have Little Richard on board, no matter how eccentric his views. I've been looking around for their celebrity worshippers and it's difficult to find them – the country singer Roy Drusky, an Isley brother and Prince, although he then became a Jehovah's Witness. Little Richard was high profile and most welcome. Many performers were happy to share their faith: Cliff Richard encouraged his fans to go to church; three of the Shadows were Jehovah's Witnesses, and Pat Boone allowed his swimming pool to be used for baptisms. Rev. Richard Coles was a member of Communards.

Little Richard formed his views and then found a spiritual home for them. He described what happened after he saw the Sputnik: 'Which church shall I join? My mind turned back to childhood and a brief introduction by friends to the Seventh-day Adventist church in Macon; to my friend Joe Lutcher, who was an Adventist in Los Angeles; to the pictures of Oakwood College in the *Message* magazine. I had thought vaguely whenever a glimmer of religion stole over my heart, "If I ever choose an affiliation, it will be with the Adventists." I liked their dedication, sincerity, simplicity of life, and biblical teachings, I saw it as admirable, and it was directly opposed to my former existence.' Richard acted fast. He told Joe Lutcher that he wanted to study for the ministry and Joe set the wheels in motion. The new intake of students at the Oakwood Adventist Academy had joined in September 1957 and now six weeks later, Little Richard was with them. He had a medical to determine his fitness and suitability and then he put what he needed in his lavender Cadillac and drove to Huntsville, Alabama. He was going from the age of rock to the Rock of Ages, but the fact that he kept his Cadillac suggests he wasn't giving up everything.

Being at Oakwood gave Little Richard a break from endless touring, the racism he encountered on the road, and the music business itself — which was perhaps his intention all along. 'I stopped and went to school,' he once reflected. 'I was making $15 a week in Macon, and suddenly, I was making $10,000 an hour on the stage. I went back to school to learn how to count because I didn't know how. I needed to know how to handle money.'

Although Richard said over 100 prayers a day, he was not an ideal student. He would miss lectures and be disruptive. His tutors expected that and they could see he was a natural preacher. He could bring people to the church.

When he was caught asking a deacon's son to expose himself, they forgave him, despite the fact that the church was opposed to homosexuality. It's another indication that they wanted Little Richard more than he wanted them.

Richard prevaricated as to whether singing rock'n'roll was good or bad. In 1970 on one of his forays into rock, he told *Rolling Stone*, 'Eventually I decided to come back into the business and teach goodness because music is the universal language. We are one through God's bouquet and we reach it through music, through joy, through happiness.'

In the record world, it was as though Little Richard had never gone away. His power-packed 'Good Golly Miss Molly' was issued by Specialty as a single in January 1958 and *Billboard* said, 'The frantic cat is at his vigorous best on this rocker. Ork backing is good and helps give side potential. It can click in both pop and R & B marts.'

The *NME* commented that 'Good Golly Miss Molly' was 'Wee Dick in his most frantic form' and the B-side 'Hey-Hey-Hey-Hey' was 'more than usually unintelligible.' It reached the UK Top 10, stopping at No.8.

The phrase 'sure like to ball' has a double meaning. The adult Black audience was well used to dirty terms on records – they loved it, but as Little Richard was also appealing to a young teenage market, he had to take care. Richard was relatively lucky as he didn't have the problems of Hank Ballard and the Midnighters ('Work with Me, Annie', 1954) and the white boys, the Kingsmen ('Louie, Louie', 1963).

The Upsetters worked with Dee Clark and recorded with him for Falcon, a subsidiary of Vee-Jay, in March 1958. He wrote a song in the vein of 'Long Tall Sally' called '24 Boyfriends'. He soon developed his own style and had national hits with 'Just Keep It Up', 'Hey Little Girl' and 'Raindrops'. They appeared at the Apollo alongside the Bill Doggett Combo, Little Willie John and the Pastels.

When Danny and the Juniors were thinking of a follow-up for their landmark 'At the Hop', Dave White recalled a Little Richard record, which began, 'All around the world, Rock'n'roll is here to stay' and it wasn't difficult to turn that into 'Rock'n'Roll is Here to Stay', a sentiment that has resonated down the decades. Also in 1958, Esquerita recorded his own song, 'Believe When I Say (Rock'n'Roll Is Here to Stay)', but it's easy to write a song when somebody else has done it first.

Dale Hawkins, the originator of 'Suzie-Q' (a 1957 US hit), recalled, 'Buddy Holly and I were friends. We hung out in New York for about a month together and he was singing 'Maybe Baby' to me. I said, "That's a great song but I would do it this way. I'd give it a Little Richard feel." He said after recording it, "Don't let anybody think that we did it like Little Richard. He would probably tell everybody that he had discovered us too." (Laughs).'

What Holly says is underlined by a cover of 'Maybe Baby' on Esquerita's 1959 album, *Wildcat Shakeout*. Also, Buddy Holly came up with 'Well...All Right' after hearing Little Richard use this phrase both backstage and in performance.

UK rock singer, Buddy Britten: 'When Buddy Holly and the Crickets did their British tour, I saw one show in London and apart from the hits, they were performing Little Richard songs. Buddy leapt about the stage like a lunatic and he had a very long guitar lead and his guitar was heavily amplified.'

Specialty in the US and London-American in the UK were maintaining a stream of

Little Richard 45s while he was at college. By now, London-American in the UK had released seven EPs, all four-track compilations from Little Richard's Specialty catalogue.

In June 1958, the *NME* said that fans would like Little Richard's new single 'Ooh! My Soul'. As for the B-side, 'True Fine Mama', 'Little Richard takes the lyric in throat-tearing fashion.' 'Ooh! My Soul' wasn't the best of his singles, but it reached No.22 in the UK and No.31 in the US. The B-side had some success in the US.

Bobby Vee: 'Sometimes people think the songs are so simple that they are childish but they capture the spirit of 1950s rock'n'roll, which was "Don't think about it, just do it, let's rock".'

It is sometimes questioned why Little Richard's 'Ooh! My Soul' and Ritchie Valens 'Ooh! My Head' are so similar. When Bob Keane had Ritchie Valens in the studio, he started singing Richard's 'Ooh! My Soul'. Bob Keane told him that it was a simple song and if he made a few changes, then it could be a new Ritchie Valens copyright. Ritchie Valens died in the plane crash that also killed Buddy Holly and the Big Bopper in February 1959 and 'Ooh! My Head' helped to fill out his first and only LP.

In August 1958 the *NME* ran a full-page feature by Keith Goodwin headlined *Little Richard's Back in a Big Way.* Only he wasn't because he was at theological college. According to Goodwin, Little Richard had found a way to make the audience laugh with him rather than at him: I'm not sure that's true.

Little Richard's second album, *Little Richard Volume 2*, was issued in July 1958, but just called *Little Richard* in the US.

The liner note said, 'In selecting the songs for this new album, Little Richard tried to top his first album and included some material for his fans' parents who still may not dig the beat. He feels that if they'll only listen to songs they remember like 'Baby Face' and 'By the Light of the Silvery Moon' done up in the Little Richard style, they'll enjoy this new album.'

Untrue. For a start, those were songs from their grandparents' era and that second album was simply the best of the rest. The contents were down to expediency with some tracks two years old, but it was still a splendid album.

At the same time, Larry Williams, who had scored with 'Short Fat Fannie' and 'Bony Moronie' on Specialty in 1957, was Little Richard-lite. He appeared on package shows, being described as the Atomic Rock Buster – atomic bombs got positive publicity in 1958! The Atomic Rock Buster was on *The Big Beat Show* at the New York City Paramount in March 1958 with Jerry Lee Lewis, Chuck Berry and Buddy Holly and then on a two-week run at the Brooklyn Fox in September with Chuck Berry, Bill Haley and his Comets and the Kalin Twins. Spare a thought for the Kalin Twins who went straight to the UK for a tour with new boy Cliff Richard, who totally eclipsed them.

A performer could be performing four times a day in-between the feature film and this could be tough on your voice. Larry sounded as though he should have postponed the recording session for 'Peaches and Cream'. Also, it must have been challenging to run your pimping and narcotics business when you're stuck in a theatre all day.

Although Larry Williams failed to build on his hit records in 1958, he recorded some wonderful tracks usually working with Rene Hall on guitar, Plas Johnson on tenor sax and Earl Palmer on drums. Occasionally, Ernie Freeman or Art Neville would play piano. He started the year with a brilliant double-header, 'Dizzy Miss Lizzy' and 'Slow Down', both his own songs and both a key part of the standard rock'n'roll repertoire. Surprisingly though, the single only made No.69 on the US pop charts and didn't register on the R & B listings.

Art Rupe slipped up when he released this single by putting different takes of 'Dizzy Miss Lizzy' on the 78rpm and 45rpm, and a second error by not turning it to his advantage. He could have proclaimed – 'Buy both versions of this great song!' That would be commonplace in the 1990s and it would have been unique back then. Art Rupe made a third mistake by confining 'Slow Down' to a B-side when it merited an A-side. Larry Williams was wanting his girlfriend to slow down because she was going too fast: there are many interpretations of that and it was a fine record with good changes in tempo.

On the other hand, 'Hootchy-Koo' was too old-fashioned for an A-side with Larry Williams going back to 1940s R & B. He brought Bony Moronie into the lyric – she'd been doing too much hootchy-koo – 'you know' winks Larry. 'The Dummy' is Larry Williams' weakest song: all about a girl who shows no signs of life until she rock'n'rolls. She turns out to be a dummy from a department store. The song is simply unpleasant and sexist.

Larry Williams' third single of 1958, 'Peaches and Cream', was superficial and lacked his wry humour. It contains a passing reference to another rival piano player, Jerry Lee Lewis' 'Great Balls of Fire'. Little Richard could have done something with 'I Was a Fool to Let You Go' if he'd sung it like 'Can't Believe You Wanna Leave', but this arrangement is let down by routine backing vocals from the Blossoms: even Darlene Love has off days.

A single by Bobby Brant and the Poe-Cats 'Rock and Roll Girl' suddenly has a chorus of 'Good Golly Miss Molly' sung by Big Al Downing. Similarly, Don and Dewey's 'Justine' included a verse from 'Good Golly Miss Molly' and the way they repeat her name sounds like Little Richard and Larry Williams calling to each other. In 1965 'Justine' made the US Top 100 via the Righteous Brothers.

Another performer who owes something to Little Richard is James Brown. Born in 1933, he had had a life of petty crime and had been sentenced when he was 16 to eight years' hard labour. Fortunately for him, he was sent to Alto Reform school in Toccoa and as a pitcher for the prison team, he met the musician Bobby Byrd, whose family sponsored him for parole and got him a job and then he sang in a gospel group with Byrd. They moved into R & B and called themselves the Flames. They met Little Richard at Bill's Rendezvous in Toccoa when he came for an appearance. Richard was gathering crowds in the southern clubs and the Flames were the supporting act. Both Richard and his road manager, Fats Gonder, were impressed. Gonder noted his name and told Clint Brantley about them.

When Richard left for the ministry, Brantley didn't want to return the deposits for any bookings he'd made, so he took a chance and asked James Brown to front the Upsetters and call himself Little Richard. James wanted the work and he was to steal the introduction for his own use: 'And now for the hardest working man in show business today, Little Richard!' He quickly realised it would be better to be James Brown.

James Brown had scored with 'Please Please Me' in April 1956 but in an effort to return to the R & B charts, he recorded 'Chonnie-on-chon'. It's a party song featuring an unmistakable James Brown scream but otherwise is an attempt to board the Little Richard bandwagon. James hadn't had a hit since 'Please, Please, Please' in 1956, but 'Try Me' was around the corner.

Little Richard didn't think they sounded similar at all, telling Barney Hoskyns in 1985, 'I sing from my stomach and Otis Redding and James Brown are just singing from their throats.'

Whereas James Brown was getting away from sounding like Little Richard, several performers wanted to emulate him.

Little Ike from Nashville gives a 100 per cent Richard to 'She Can Rock. The song was written by Ted Jarrett who wrote 'You Make It If You Try', but here he was copping phrases from 'Long Tall Sally'.

Lowell Fulson was a dyed-in-the-wool bluesman, but Chess Records persuaded him to try rock'n'roll. The frantic 'Rock This Morning' is a dead ringer for Little Richard. His best-known songs are 'Reconsider Baby' (Elvis Presley) and 'Tramp' (Otis Redding and Carla Thomas).

Thurston Harris, known for 'Little Bitty Pretty One', cut 'Hey Baba Lena'. It was a standard blues format but the vocal and arrangement with sax solo meant they had been listening to Little Richard.

Johnny Vincent recorded Joe Tex for Ace Records in New Orleans with the session musicians who had backed Richard. They cut the frantic 'You Little Baby Faced Thing' and, adding voodoo references, 'Open the Door'. Joe became famous for his secular sermons such as 'Hold What You've Got' and 'The Love You Save' as well as bumping with the fat lady in the disco era. As a sideline, Joe Tex manufactured counterfeit notes, and the band could either be paid in real cash or twice as much in counterfeit. As he didn't get caught, his copies must have been as good as his Little Richard impersonations.

Screamin' Joe Neal from St Louis released 'Rock'n'Roll Deacon' on the Shippings label. He had a gruff monotone, but his band had the energy of Little Richard's musicians and the title was in keeping with Richard's personality. Joe didn't make another record for seven years and then 'She's My Baby' was again monotonous. Give the man a packet of Zubes.

Harold Burrage came from Chicago and was backed by Willie Dixon's band, no less. Their 1957 offering 'She Knocks Me Out' is great fun as it plays around with the 'Lucille' riff and they followed it with an excellent 'Betty Jean' in 1958.

Big Al Downing had made some impact with 'Down on the Farm' earlier in the year and now he copied Richard's style for 'Miss Lucy' with the middle section aping 'Lucille', a strong competent performance but more inhibited than Little Richard. Big Danny Oliver also had 'Lucille' on his mind when he recorded 'Sapphire' in New Orleans. The song is a warning to his girlfriend and contains a wild, wild piano solo.

The gospel artists didn't often make excursions into the pop field, but Marie Knight followed Little Richard's style with the witty 'I Thought I Told You Not To Tell Them'.

Tony Conn was a demobbed serviceman who took part in an amateur night at the Apollo, even though he was white. He jumped about, stood on his head and sang 'Ready Teddy'. He came third and was signed by Ben Weisman, who was to write film songs for Elvis Presley. Weisman wrote the first single, 'Like Wow', a wild number that was halfway between Fabian and Little Richard.

Bobby Darin had his first hit with 'Splish Splash' in 1958, a rock'n'roll party song that referenced 'Lollipop', 'Peggy Sue' and 'Good Golly, Miss Molly'. 'I have a rock'n'roll hit,' he told a reporter, 'That makes me one of a thousand other guys. Now I've got to prove I can sing.'

In 1958, the Italian singer Antonio Ciacci was having success locally but he wanted international recognition. His hero was Little Richard and so he became Little Tony. Moving to the UK, he became a regular on ITV's *Wham!* And had a UK hit with the easy-paced ballad, 'Too Good'.

Paul Jones from Manfred Mann: 'I was living in Portsmouth in 1958 and I went to Guild Hall, and the headliner was meant to be Craig Douglas. He had just had his tonsils out and he had to cancel, as his voice had not returned to normal. His place was taken by a complete unknown called Roy Young, who had suspiciously blond hair and a black satin shirt and played the piano like a cross between Jerry Lee Lewis and Little Richard. I was hugely impressed and I remained a fan when he was in Cliff Bennett and the Rebel Rousers."

Indeed. In 1959 Roy Young established himself in the Saturday teatime show, *Drumbeat,* the BBC's answer to *Oh Boy!*. Roy Young recalls, 'The producer of *Drumbeat,* Stewart Morris, wanted to make a live album and we went into the studio and did a live run off the floor. Most people were used to making records in which a note could be dropped in if you sang flat or sharp, but this was done with an audience. It was very noisy as they were screaming. I wasn't really a singer for the girls: Adam Faith was more like that. I had an audience of guys who liked my Little Richard style. It wasn't soppy or patter, patter, patter. It was boom, boom, boom. Larry Williams made some great records and I thought 'She Said Yeah' was a great track. I'd have liked to have done that properly in the studio.'

Songwriter Roddy Jackson told the rock writer John Broven: 'Sonny Bono and I wrote 'She Said Yeah' together for Larry Williams. He was on his way out as a big star, and he was trying to get another hit with that. It didn't sell, either. The Rolling Stones recorded it as a lead track on an album and I received a cheque for $5,000 at a halfpenny a record and then the BMI performance monies. Paul McCartney recorded it in 1999 for *Run Devil Run*. Venice Music was pretty honest with me.'

Through his single with Paul Peek of the Blue Caps, Gene Vincent got to know of Esquerita and he mentioned him to his producer, Ken Nelson. Nelson thought Capitol should try its own Little Richard. The first Capitol single, 'Oh Baby', featured madcap piano but wasn't much of a song. The mawkish 'Please Come on Home' was better, enlivened by some yelps, although it makes nonsense of the lyric's intention.

Nevertheless, in September 1958, *Billboard* acknowledged Esquerita as 'the find of the year'. They loved his new single, 'Esquerita and the Voola', which was wacky piano exotica enhanced by operatic screeching. 'Rockin' the Joint' is a typical clubland song, sharing verses with Chuck Berry's 'Reelin'; and Rockin' and adding a Bill Haley chant.

Charlie Gillett wrote: 'If a producer or arranger had been deputed to these sessions, he must have been bound and gagged and put in a corner.' But listen to Esquerita's 'Hole in my Heart': what a pity that was never recorded by Richard.

Like the social commentary in Eddie Cochran's current hit 'Summertime Blues', Capitol released 'Laid Off', easily the best of Esquerita's singles, possessing originality and a relevant theme. It was about a man who had been laid off and as close to a protest song as you got in 1959. It had a feeble ending though with Esquerita simply saying, 'That's it'. There was a good ballad on the other side, 'Just Another Lie'. Another single combined the rocking 'Hey Miss Lucy' with the eccentric 'I'm Battie over Hattie'. As with Little Richard, Lucy and Hattie were probably drag queens.

In September 1958, Little Richard's new single combined 'Baby Face' with 'I'll Never Let You Go'. *Billboard* said, 'Little Richard's at his shouting best on his rockin' revival of 'Baby Face'. 'I'll Never Let You Go' is also in the rocker vein, and the artist uses vocal gimmicks in presenting the tune. Both sides appear naturals for pop and R & B loot.' Not released in the UK until December, it got rave reviews in the *NME* and *Disc,* but they both preferred the B-side 'I'll Never Let You Go. 'Little Richard squeals, squeaks and belts the words out of this medium-paced number with a solid thumping beat in the background.'

The UK record buyers loved the novelty of Little Richard reviving Al Jolson and it went to No.2, his highest UK chart placing. Al Jolson used to say, 'This song was dedicated to me.' Oddly, it stalled outside the Top 40 in the US. In 1962 Bobby Darin showed us another way of updating 'Baby Face' including the line, 'Let's twist awhile.' It was a moderate success in both the UK and US.

Brian Epstein said that Little Richard's 'Baby Face' was one of his favourite records, although he warned the Beatles about using the word 'baby' in songs as it sounded childish.

Having had such a huge hit with 'Baby Face', London-American wanted a strong follow-up for Little Richard and went with 'By the Light of the Silvery Moon', backed by 'Early One Morning'. It made the UK Top 20 but it meant nothing in America, possibly because it had recently been in the charts for Jimmy Bowen. It had been recorded by Jackie Wilson (as the B-side to 'Reet Petite') and Etta James and it had an old-fashioned lyric 'With my honey, I'll spoon'.

Specialty's skill for finding hits in Little Richard's session tapes fell away in 1959 and although seven singles were released, only one scraped into the Hot 100 – and that was 'Kansas City' at No.95. The lower end of the charts was largely based on airplay and so radio stations had no place for 'She Knows How to Rock', 'By the Light of the Silvery Moon', 'Shake a Hand', 'Maybe I'm Right', 'I Got It' and 'Directly from My Heart'. In some cases, tracks had been sweetened by Sonny Bono adding violins or backing vocals.

The UK presenter Keith Fordyce, though, was hoping for big things from 'She Knows How to Rock': 'He rips though the songs like a tornado, one fiery bundle of atomic energy. The accompaniment is an instrumental whirlwind and the whole thing leaves you limp and breathless. A billion bouquets to Little Richard for keeping the rock in rock'n'roll and not making it a vehicle for unpleasant neurotic wails.'

Art Rupe wanted his pound of flesh from Richard's recordings and he asked Sonny Bono to touch up leftovers from the sessions. Bono added backing vocals from the Stewart Sisters on 'Directly from My Heart' and 'Maybe I'm Right'. This led to Richard's third US Specialty album, *The Fabulous Little Richard,* but the dynamics of the original recordings had been lost. To his credit, Art Rupe realised this and told Bono to stop.

A classically trained pianist from the Juilliard Music School in New York, Neil Sedaka put his training to one side and hammered out 'I Go Ape', written with Howie Greenfield. It was effervescent, echo-drenched and fun, and it was effectively Little Richard and Jerry Lee Lewis if they were comedy acts.

In March 1959 Huey 'Piano' Smith asked Frankie Ford to perform his song 'Sea Cruise' and created one of the most commercial records to come from New Orleans. It only made No.14 on the US pop charts, but it was highly infectious and has become legendary for its great line, 'I've got the boogie-woogie like a knife in the back.' Ford was a pianist, so he performed the song for the rest of his life and loved the acclaim.

Frankie Ford's licence place was OOO-EEE, his catchphrase from 'Sea Cruise' and he told me in 1992, when wearing a scarf decorated with piano keys, 'Little Richard and Liberace are at two different ends of the entertainment spectrum, and I put them together. I didn't do it intentionally. It just happened that way, but I've always liked to dress up for work. I don't want to look like I've just come off the bus. Sophie Tucker once told me, "These people have paid to see you, so dress up!"' Frankie added, 'I've got to have a word with Harry Connick. All New Orleans piano players are supposed to be gay.'

Wilbert Harrison cut a bluesy version of Jerry Leiber and Mike Stoller's 'Kansas City'. It was released as a single on Fury in April 1959 and within a week, five previously recorded versions were released, including one by Little Richard. Wilbert Harrison reached No.1 in the US and pulverised the opposition, which is ironic as he would not have had such a huge pop hit without Richard showing the way. However, it was Little Richard's version that made the UK Top 30, though only to No.26. Wilbert's other acclaimed performance, 'Let's Stick Together', was recorded as a one-man band, although the Bryan Ferry version is better known.

In 1959 a young police officer in Los Angeles was about to leave the force when he heard a prisoner singing in his cell. He had been arrested for driving a car under the influence of drugs and alcohol. He asked him to record for his label, Nite Owl, and that's how Ron Holden came to make 'Love You So'. The B-side was a tribute to Little Richard and Larry Williams, 'My Babe', which included the line, 'She's got a short fat fanny'. Did I hear that right? Yes, I did. He's just said it again.

All in all, there are probably only around 50 studio recordings where Little Richard is Little Richard as everybody knows him. If you want more recordings in that vein, then, like Art Rupe, you should go to Larry Williams. However, there are many artists who have tried to emulate Richard, usually with little chart success but their records are worth seeking out and of course, nearly everything is on Spotify or YouTube these days. Here are a few examples that have entertained me.

The Wailers from Tacoma, Washington scored with the instrumental 'Tall Cool One' in 1959. They recorded 'Dirty Robber' in Little Richard's style which included the line, 'Little girl even took my guitar.'

A fine rocker in the Little Richard tradition is 'Rockin' This Joint Tonight' by Kid Thomas who had a Little Richard tribute act in Chicago in the late '50s, early '60s. He looked like him too. In 1965 he had another single, 'Wail Baby Wail', issued under his real name of Tommy Lewis. In 1969 he knocked down a 10-year-old cyclist while driving his van. The boy's father thinking that the jury might return a 'not guilty' verdict, waited across the road from the courtroom. When Tommy Lewis got out of the car, the boy's father shot him and continued shooting until he collapsed and died.

Speciality had a three-year contract with Little Richard and by now he was free to record for whomever he chose. He signed with George Goldner of Gone and End records, known for recording doo-wop in New York. Goldner had a curious offer: with the help of Billy Ward (who recorded 'Stardust') he would record Little Richard singing gospel and lease the tapes to several companies simultaneously, the reasoning being that throughout the US, there were several labels releasing gospel recordings. The 20 recordings can be put into three groups, all recorded in September 1959. There are performances of just Little Richard and his piano, some with Herman Stevens on organ and some with organ and a vocal group.

The albums that came from these tracks were the two volumes of *Pray Along with Little Richard,* which gave way to other albums on different labels through licensing agreements. There were two singles: the gospel favourite 'Milky White Way' was an impassioned performance from someone looking forward to heaven and similarly, 'Troubles of the World' was about wanting to leave the world and live with God. So, in 'Troubles of the World' he wants to leave his family and in 'Milky White Way', he plans to join them in Heaven.

The two-part 'I'm Quitting Show Business' is an extraordinary record with just Little Richard and an organist. He is saying that nobody in show business is going to see the kingdom of God – he sings, 'I'm quitting show business, I want to go straight.' The second part of the single is mostly a sermon in which he tells us that we have to say no to the lowest before we can say yes to the highest. A key line is 'If I die while I'm in my sin, I know that Jesus won't let me in.'

A significant feature about these performances is that they don't relate to the Adventist church. They don't say that the world is coming to an end and many of them are familiar gospel songs like 'Take My Hand Precious Lord' and 'Just a Closer Walk with Thee'.

Bob Dylan was a fan: 'Little Richard was a great gospel singer, but he was looked at as an interloper in the gospel world. They didn't accept him there. And the rock 'n' roll world wanted to keep him singing 'Good Golly Miss Molly', so his gospel music wasn't accepted in either world. I can't imagine him being too bothered about it. He was a person of high character.'

In 1994 I saw P J Proby sing 'American Trilogy' whilst standing to attention and I asked him about it. He said, 'My best friend is God and 'Glory Allelujah' is an anthem and is about the Bible Belt where I was born. I was in Little Richard's church. I was the only white boy there and we both had the same manager, Bumps Blackwell. I joined the choir, and I got all my basic training from Baptist religious music.'

By the end of the Fifties, Art Rupe had lost Richard, Larry Williams was about to be arrested for drug dealing, and Lloyd Price was having million-sellers like 'Stagger Lee', but for another label. Because of its violent lyrics, Price had to cut a special non-violent 'Stagger Lee' for US radio playlists.

And now comes the big reveal – Little Richard's marriage. When he was attending an Adventist convention, he met Ernestine Harvin, the daughter of a naval officer and a prominent Adventist. Richard's brother, Charles, felt that the church was using Ernestine to get Richard even more involved, but that is a cynical way of looking at things. Ernestine was a shy, well-educated secretary and she liked Richard who was wearing a suit and behaving normally. Appearances can be deceptive.

They were married in July 1959 at the church on Virginia Road, Huntsville. According to Harvin, she and Richard initially enjoyed a happy marriage with normal sexual relations. She denied claims that Richard was gay. They certainly enjoyed each other's company and they never critcised each other in the press.

Little Richard was already thinking of performing again and on 6 September 1959, Little Richard began his first gospel tour in Dayton, Ohio and it was well received. By and large, he was performing familiar songs like 'Peace in the Valley' and 'Take My Hand, Precious Lord'.

CHAPTER 7

He Got What He Wanted

I. Mercury Rising

Although Little Richard had made some gospel recordings at the end of 1959, there was no attempt to put them in the mainstream. Most fans did not know of these records, and that is true even today. You may come across these tracks with additional instruments in a forlorn attempt to make them sound more commercial, but it doesn't work. Richard's tracks for George Goldner were so obviously made on the cheap. They were poorly packaged too – *Little Richard Sings Spirituals* has one of the worst Little Richard photos ever.

The best thing for Richard's ego, both for the promotion of his faith and for his fans, would have been hit records, and there are many examples of songs of faith making the charts – 'I Believe' (Frankie Laine), 'Faith Can Move Mountains' (Johnnie Ray), *Elvis' Christmas Album,* 'A Wonderful Time Up There' (Pat Boone) and, in 1963, 'Dominique' from the Singing Nun. But who could help Little Richard make that transition?

In 1960 Little Richard recorded two songs with the Gospel Spiritualetts, 'I Found a God' and 'Fly Away Jesus' and although they were released as a 45 on the Sensational Sounds label, not many copies were pressed.

Then again, Little Richard met the Upsetters in New York, who were backing Little Willie John, and they suggested a secular session with the producer H B Barnum. Richard agreed, provided his name wasn't on the records, although anybody would recognise Little Richard. The singles on Little Star were released under the name of The World Famous Upsetters (which they certainly weren't). The first combined solid workouts of Fats Domino's 'I'm in Love Again' and 'Every Night about this Time' but Richard could have had more fun with the daft lyric of 'I'm in Love Again'. The second single featured Fats Domino's lachrymose 'Valley of Tears' with Richard bashing out triplets. It was coupled with a piano-pounding instrumental, 'Freedom Ride'. The Little Star tracks could have been passed off as Specialty recordings.

Little Richard's name was being kept alive by a brilliant revival of 'Lucille' by the Everly Brothers, which was on the B-side of their second Warner Bros single, 'So Sad', but also a hit in its own right. They took 'Lucille' slower and more dramatically than Richard and the author Michael Gray has described their harmonies on the title line as a 'slow motion vocal fall'. It is more like a different song than a cover. More mundanely, Cliff Richard and Adam Faith duetted 'Ready Teddy' on the Royal Variety Performance.

Inspired by 'Lucille', Ronnie Molleen recorded his song. 'Fat Mama' in 1960. The pianist was Roy Estrada, later a member of the Mothers of Invention.

There is a Roy Young single with an odd title, 'Four and Twenty Thousand Kisses'. 'It was an Italian song that we got from Jeff Kruger,' said Roy Young, 'It was recorded by Adriano Celentano and it sounded like Little Richard but the arrangement was written in the wrong key for me and I couldn't get the Little Richard feel from it. It was too low. No one asked me what key I wanted. It didn't feel right.'

Maybe the producer wanted to take the Little Richard feel out of it. The UK *Hit Parade* magazine thought Little Richard's days were over. 'Rock'n'roll has changed radically. It has become less raucous, more controlled, more subtle in conception. Richard's attacking, pounding manner doesn't suit current teenage tastes and even if more of his electrifying discs were available, it's doubtful they would sell as well as they used to.'

Even sadder was the sharp decline of Larry Williams. His drugs and call girls were a more reliable bet than hit-and-miss singles. Art Rupe had lost confidence in him, fearing that Larry's activities might result in a scandal. There was just one single from Larry Williams in 1960, 'Ting-a-Ling', a lazy rewrite of Johnny Otis' 'Hum Ding a Ling', now incorporating Larry's song titles. The other side, 'Little Schoolgirl', was about a schoolboy romance, presumably to appeal to younger audiences.

Then Larry Williams was arrested for a dangerous mix of pimping, drugs and gun ownership. He was found guilty and put in the slammer for two years. In complete contrast and as part of his ministerial training, Richard worked with Joe Lutcher in downtown LA helping derelicts who found themselves on Skid Row. They would be clothed, fed and sometimes washed as well as being told about Jesus.

Little Richard wanted to make more gospel recordings but with better production values and better marketing plans. Bumps Blackwell was now producing for Mercury Records and his orchestrator was a fast-rising dynamo, Quincy Jones. The package seemed right and the songs were selected. By and large, they would have arrangements by Quincy for classical musicians playing alongside the Howard Roberts Chorale. The result was the LP *King of the Gospel Singers*, recorded in June 1961 and released in November. The title was a powerful claim from a new boy on the block, but then this was Little Richard: no make-up short hair, smart suit and singing like Roy Hamilton.

The sleeve note was by Mahalia Jackson, the most renowned of all gospel singers. She wrote, 'I have been told that he was quite a rock'n'roll star. I wouldn't know about that. I do know that there is soul in his singing today.'

Quincy Jones wrote about how the sessions had moved both him and his musicians, particularly his unscripted sermon during 'It's Real' which revealed his sincerity. Quincy said, 'It was a joy working with Little Richard. Though he was very religious, I noticed that he never lost his feeling for rock and soul.'

I'm with Quincy. 'Do You Care' revealed how beautiful Little Richard's voice could be and his own 'He's My Star' (back again) is given a tender arrangement with an organ accompaniment. He doesn't sound like Little Richard on 'Ride On, King Jesus' but displays an impressive operatic voice, but the track fades on his speech: wasn't that worth preserving?

'Joy Joy Joy', testified to the twin joys of being alive and worshipping. You can sense his feelings on a song about contemporary problems, 'In Times like These' where he changes 'very sure' to 'very, very, very sure'.

Another of Richard's songs, 'He's Not just a Soldier', is overblown with marching troops and the Howard Roberts Chorale, but the song is saying, 'Come and fight in the war against evil.' 'It Takes Everything to Serve the Lord' is another call to arms. The arrangement of 'The Captain Calls for You' sounds like a Broadway musical, while 'Do Lord, Remember Me' is a folk song. There are two spirituals from Thomas A Dorsey, 'Peace in the Valley' and 'My Desire'. *World's Fair* commented that 'Peace in the Valley', was 'beautifully done.

I never appreciated that Little Richard could sing like this and I wish I was as confident about its potential.' Richard commented, 'It was the music I had always wanted to record.'

In October 1961 *Billboard* reviewed Little Richard's single of 'He's Not Just a Soldier' and 'Joy, Joy, Joy': 'Little Richard should be back strongly in the pop market with these two powerful sides. He sings them with his old-time enthusiasm as he tells on the first side about a soldier who is somebody's son. Flip is a potent jubilee gospel disking.'

Maybe Little Richard was not a forgotten star but a mainstream entertainer. *The Times* crossword puzzle for 5 October 1961 contained this clue for 4 Down: Little Richard is so gifted (6, 4). If you've got it, you're a clever dick.

The next single, 'He Got What He Wanted' is a raver in which Richard comments on Adam, Samson and Judas as being people who got that they wanted but lost what they had. His voice sounded beautiful and vulnerable on the B-side 'Why Don't You Change Your Ways', written by Joe Lutcher, which was not on the album.

In the UK a *Juke Box Jury* panel with Petula Clark, Hattie Jacques, Pete Murray and Eric Sykes voted 'He Got What He Wanted' a hit. Sam Cooke told *Hit Parade* it was his favourite Little Richard record. It nudged into the Top 40. Little Richard was appealing to a specialised market and offers for gospel concerts came in. There were plans for a second album with Little Richard at Mercury and although several tracks were recorded, it was never released.

The Little Richard imitators were not having hit records either. You'd never guess Otis Redding was only 20 when he cut his first solo single, 'Shout Bamalama' in 1961 as he sounds like a veteran R & B shouter. It's a nonsense song in a Little Richard bag, not far off 'Haunted House', and there's more of the same on the B-side, 'Fat Gal'. He stuck with the Richard style for 'Hey Hey Baby', his first record for Stax/Volt in 1962.

Little Victor and his Orchestra, no less, are totally forgotten but their 1961 single, 'Papa Lou and Gran', was about a fight between grandparents played out over a frantic 'Good Golly Miss Molly' riff.

In March 1962 Cliff Richard and the Shadows were recorded at the ABC Kingston in Surrey. If you take their hits out of it, the Beatles could have comfortably performed the set. Hank Marvin from the Shadows: 'We loved Ray Charles, Chuck Berry, Little Richard and Fats Domino, but those songs were coming out of our repertoire. We were leaving them behind because they were old hat. The Beatles brought them back. We still did 'Willie and the Hand Jive', which was Johnny Otis, but in general we were getting into the less aggressive style which was making it in America. The Beatles were doing the songs we were doing when we started but they brought their own style into it.'

Little Richard had no idea on how his life was about to be transformed and similarly, the Beatles, the Rolling Stones and the Animals and the other key British groups had no idea that were going to transform the lives of some of their heroes.

Richard, if truth be told, had problems. He was about to lose his home because he could not repay a $3,000 loan. Richard said, 'The guy who told me I owed $3,000 said he would pray for me. I said, "God wants you to answer the prayer." (Laughter).' Richard did consider asking his neighbour Joe Louis to lend him the money, but that would have been too humiliating.

To Richard's credit, he acquired a Bachelor of Arts degree, majoring in theology with minors in psychology and business administration. He could return to performing if he wished, but who knew what his motivations were as they changed so often? For many years, he said that because of his faith, he could never perform from sundown Friday until sundown Saturday, but then something would come up and he would have an equally valid reason for doing it. There is no point in looking for consistency in Little Richard's life and I'm convinced he used religion for his own ends.

Chas White: 'Richard used religion to shock people and Jerry Lee is very much the same. If Jerry is in an intense mood, he will look at you with eyes like laser beams and say, "Are you sanctified, boy?" You freeze, and I didn't know how to handle him at first. One night I was with Jerry Lee and his wife. He turned to her and said, "Are you sanctified, honey?" She said, "I sure am, baby. I am sanctified and glorified as well." She was using humour as her safety valve.'

When the second album for Mercury was abandoned, Little Richard had a gospel session for Atlantic in June 1962, and the tracks which included 'Joshua Fit the Battle of Jericho', 'You'll Never Walk Alone' and 'If You Can't Take It, You Can't Make It' (sounds interesting!) were never released.

Meanwhile, Little Richard was being honoured 8,000km (5,000 miles) from Los Angeles in Liverpool, more particularly at the Cavern Club. Geoff Davies, a regular Cavernite, recalled, 'I thought the Beatles were great and Paul McCartney had an amazing Little Richard-type voice. His version of 'Kansas City' was just right. I knew most of their songs as they came from Chuck Berry, Fats Domino and Little Richard but they gave them such life. In some cases, they sounded better than the originals. I went to see them as often as I could.'

Brian Wake, another Cavernite, recalls, 'Often, when The Beatles had completed their opening set at the Cavern, the four of them would spill out from the tiny bandroom and mingle with the audience. At 15 years old, it was a feat of great courage to push my way through a circle of girls until I was standing right next to Paul. "Excuse me Paul," I croaked, "When you go back for the second half, would you sing, 'Ooh! My Soul'?" "Ooh! My Soul," he replied, 'I'll have to ask George." George turned and faced both of us. "This young man here would like us to do 'Ooh! My Soul' when we go back on." "Ooh! My Soul,", said George, "I don't know, I'll have to ask John. Hey, John, can we do 'Ooh! My Soul' for this lad?" John said, "It's not up to me. It's up to Pete. Pete, are we doing 'Ooh! My Soul' in the next set?" Pete said, "It's not up to me; you'll have to ask Paul." They all laughed, and I was grinning like a fool in this embarrassing circle of Beatles and girls. Minutes later, John and Co were back on stage, guitars and drums poised. Paul moved towards the microphone, shaped his mouth into a perfectly formed letter 'O' and belted out 'Ooh! My Soul'.'

Billy Hatton from the Fourmost: 'Paul McCartney didn't have a black voice, but he had a black feeling to his voice. He could scream with the best of them. I was doing it myself, but you couldn't do too much Little Richard stuff or you'd end up with raw liver for a throat. You can hear me screaming on 'The Girl Can't Help It', which we recorded with Sounds Incorporated.'

Joe Ankrah from the Liverpool Black group, the Chants: 'Derry Wilkie was the first black person that I saw on stage in Liverpool and I thought it was fantastic to see a guy who looked a bit like me jumping all over the place and singing. He loved Little Richard and Ray Charles.' Indeed, Derry was known as Liverpool's Little Richard.

Billy Kinsley of the Merseybeats: 'The Beatles drank soup on stage and wore leather jackets and old jeans. They came on singing 'Memphis Tennessee' and changed my life forever. They were playing rock'n'roll, raw and alive, just as it should be played. Paul jumped into the audience screaming 'Long Tall Sally' while Lennon laid on the floor and played guitar solos.'

The UK promoter Don Arden had presented successful tours with Jerry Lee Lewis and Brenda Lee and in 1962, he put Little Richard, Gene Vincent and Sam Cooke on the same bill as a UK hitmaker, and former Shadow, Jet Harris. After his experiences in Australia, Little Richard hadn't wanted to fly and he came to Europe on SS *Rotterdam*. The compère was Glaswegian comic Bob Bain, who was also a talented musician. He was known as the Gag Slinger as he was fast with one-liners and ad libs and he had written Gene Vincent's 1961 hit 'I'm Going Home'.

Richard was planning to play gospel and he came to the UK with a 16-year-old organist, Billy Preston. Preston recalled, 'We met in church and he was getting ready to go to England to do a gospel tour. Or so we thought! We got over there and it turned out to be a rock'n'roll tour. That was the first time that I had ever played rock'n'roll because until then I had been strictly gospel.'

Maureen Cleave interviewed Richard for the *Evening Standard* before the tour started and she wrote, 'He sat in his hotel room in a black embroidered shirt, his 16-year-old organist asleep near him. He is taller (5ft. 10in.) and plumper, has acquired a wife called Ernestine, and enlarged his moustache, which looked slightly uneven. He said, "I am no longer the king of rock n' roll," he said. "I am the world's greatest soul singer. A soul singer sings from the bottom of his heart, he loves souls, he seeks souls. In America, they call me the male Mahalia Jackson."'

She also revealed that he supported his entire family in apartments in Los Angeles, and that he and his wife lived in a pink and white mansion. He also commented on the world order, 'Sometimes I fast for as long as 15 days. I pray for Europe. I pray that God will put a little bit of Jesus into the heart of that guy Khrushchev.'

The tour opened on 8 October 1962 at the Gaumont on Doncaster. Sam Cooke missed the first house because of fog. Richard came out in religious robes and sang 'Peace in the Valley' and 'I Believe' with Billy Preston on organ. Don Arden told him that he'd better perform rock'n'roll for the second house.

When Little Richard was studying for the ministry, he found many preachers disapproved of show business and dismissed his work completely. Now he had graduated from Oakwood, he was wary about performing rock'n'roll in America and the damage it could do to his current intentions. However, he probably reckoned that nobody in the US would hear of what he was doing in the UK, so what the hell, let's rock.

Richard didn't need much persuasion. Sam Cooke was there for the second house and wowed the audience. Richard was always competitive, and he had to be better. Richard spoke to the band and then went on in darkness. Suddenly he was there in an all-white suit and pounding out 'Long Tall Sally'. The house erupted:

Richard had a further trick when the tour got to Mansfield – and bear in mind that no one in the UK had seen James Brown perform. Chas White recalls, 'The first package show I ever went to was in Mansfield. Sam Cooke was magnificent and then there was the man I really wanted to see, Little Richard. They kept us waiting. Sounds Incorporated was playing this pounding beat which was the introduction to 'Lucille'. One chap in the front was going "Where is he?" We thought he might sing gospel, but we wanted 'Rip It Up', 'Lucille', 'Long Tall Sally' and 'Good Golly Miss Molly'. The beat got harder and the spotlight was on the piano. Richard came running from the back of the theatre and he leapt from the orchestra pit onto the stage, grabbed the microphone and went straight into his songs. He did three or four immense, intense versions of his songs and the sweat was pouring off him. He was a nuclear power station on legs. He climbed on the piano and then fell off and there was a big thump. He didn't move and we all thought, "He's dead, he definitely dead" and Bob Bain shouted, "Is there a doctor in the house?" Two guys brought out a stretcher and put him on it and started marching him down the centre of the hall and then Richard suddenly went, "Awopbopaloobop Alopbamboom" and the whole audience rose up. They had to bring down the safety curtain.'

Chas saw him after the show had finished. 'We met him backstage after this blizzard and he was like St Francis of Assisi. He was going "God bless you, my child." He had just made Pavarotti sound like a squeaky mouse. I knew I had to find out more about him as he was so exciting.'

Sam Cooke was not upset at being upstaged. Not at all: he was receiving a masterclass in stagecraft. He had been uneasy because his rival Jackie Wilson had been able to engage audiences so readily. Sam was learning about how to get an audience's attention and keep it. Although he recorded the smooth and sophisticated *Sam Cooke at the Copa* in 1964, his down and dirty, earthy performance at the Harlem Square Club in North Miami is the one: the album where he merged his gospel training with contemporary soul – and it's brilliant. It shows what he had picked up from seeing Little Richard.

At Brighton, Little Richard stripped to his underpants and left the stage in a bathrobe. With his love of show business, perhaps Little Richard should have considered a Blackpool season and a pantomime.

Norman Jopling wrote about him for *Record Mirror* and he recalls the circumstances vividly: 'When I was 18, they said I could do some interviews – and the first one was with Little Richard. I went to this seedy hotel in Bayswater. Little Richard was in a twin room and sitting on a bed and in the other bed was Billy Preston. He was asleep and he stayed asleep throughout the whole interview. Little Richard was talking about a forthcoming Technicolor Cinemascope story of his life. He was going to play himself and Sidney Poitier would be in a lesser role. As he told me this, he was caressing my cheek and the penny dropped. He said, "You have got such lovely soft cheeks, but you know who has the softest cheeks of all. It's Elvis." I would never find out this in any other job. Richard was married at the time, and he was telling everybody that he was a married man.'

You may have been surprised by what you have just read; Little Richard was still married and yet apparently having a relationship with his 16-year-old organist, Billy Preston.

Richard's marriage to Ernestine was still viable and even though she later said that Richard was not gay, she must have realised what was going on. She preferred to ignore the humiliation and who can blame her?

A very gifted musician, Billy Preston had grown up in gospel music. He maintained that there was another kind of freedom in gospel music, but one very much hidden from the strait-laced authorities. The music was a refuge for gay men and lesbians. 'In the neighbourhood, they made you ashamed of being gay, but in the church, you were almost proud to be part of the gay elite of musicians,' Billy Preston told the writer David Ritz. Billy joined Richard's band in 1962, when he was 16, to play gospel. Preston called the gospel circuit 'a sex circus' and one without a closet. 'Everyone knew that my mentor James Cleveland, who became the King of Gospel, was gay,' he continued. 'James had his own church and a national following. So many other of the major figures – like Professor James Earle Hines out of Los Angeles and Professor Alex Bradford out of Chicago – were gay.'

Richard told Norman Jopling, 'I sing gospel songs but with a beat. God has told me to do this', but once he had got 'I Believe' out of the way, he was rockin'n'rollin'.

Little Richard to *Hit Parade*: 'I never said that beat music was sinful. What I objected to mainly was the lyrics.' Fair enough, Richard, but hadn't you written most of those lyrics yourself?

Jet Harris: 'Little Richard said to me, "You should make love to your guitar." Call it "honey" and all that. That might have worked with an American, but I'd have felt daft going "Hello honey" to my guitar.'

As an additional booking away from the UK package show, the Liverpool promoter Sam Leach had booked Little Richard for £350 to appear at the Tower Ballroom, New Brighton on 12 October, but Brian Epstein gazumped him with £500 and took over the booking.

On 12 October 1962, the Beatles played a lunchtime session at the Cavern and then headed to the Tower Ballroom to support Little Richard, a one-off event on his UK tour. He was photographed with the Beatles and the Chants. Joe Ankrah from the Chants recalled, 'It got to a point that we were so good that people were saying "What are you going to do?" We really didn't know and it was very nice to be at the Tower with Little Richard and everything took off from there. I had never heard of the Beatles and I got chatting to Paul McCartney and he invited us to the Cavern for their next lunchtime session. We went there and they knew where we were coming from. We were just a vocal group: we had no instruments. They played some music for us and Brian Epstein heard it and liked it and signed us. We were with him for about a year.'

Tony Crane from the Merseybeats: 'The weirdest show we ever did was with Little Richard at the Tower Ballroom. We opened with 'Lucille' and we did the Everly Brothers' arrangement. Little Richard came running out when he heard that, he wore a big dressing-gown and he had shaving cream on his face and was calling us names. We were frightened of him. We realised what we had done and apologised to him.'

Rock author Michael Gray: 'Little Richard was a complete madman on stage but in a thrilling way. He stood on the piano and his shirt was soaked in sweat. He threw a ring into the crowd and later threw them his stinky shirt as well.'

The Stage ran a feature on Little Richard: 'A fierce looking Richard Penniman yawned. It was three o'clock in the afternoon but he was tired – very tired. He had got to bed only six hours before. That's the worst of having to tour the country on a hectic series of one-night stands. You get little sleep. The night before he had to travel back to his London base from working in New Brighton. An open Bible lay on the bed alongside Little Richard – he claims to get a lot of help and inspiration from the Good Book. He preaches and plugs the gospel with all the ardent fervour he once dispensed rock songs. When Little Richard was booked for Great Britain he thought it was as a gospel singer, but he was in for a surprise.'

A couple of weeks later at the end of the tour, Little Richard appeared at the Liverpool Empire on a show presented by Brian Epstein to promote the release of the Beatles' first Parlophone single, Love Me Do'. Richard told the Beatles, 'Please don't be offended, but I think you sound like a Coloured group.' On the contrary, the Beatles were flattered by the comparison.

Trevor Morais, drummer with Faron's Flamingos: 'I met Little Richard when I was playing the Empire and he was staying at the Adelphi. A whole gang of us went to see him:

there was me, a couple of lads from the Chants and the Beatles. He had a big turban on for the conk job that makes your hair all flat. He had a lot of guys around him and he sent out for some beers, and he had a huge wad of pound notes. He was peeling them off, go and get me this, get me that. I met him years later in a hotel in LA, the Bon Marche Hotel, and he remembered so much about Liverpool. He reckoned he was a big influence on the Beatles, which he was. "Ooo" – that comes from Little Richard, doesn't it?'

After his UK tour, Little Richard travelled to Hamburg for dates at the Star-Club, which had been opened earlier in the year by the Beatles in St Pauli. It was on Grosse Freiheit, which meant Great Freedom, and this was an area where anything goes – sex and drugs and rock and roll.

The Star-Club was a former cinema, now owned by Manfred Weissleder, who also managed sex clubs and made porno films. He was not a man to cross. He had seen the German teenagers' enthusiasm for beat music at the Indra, Kaiserkeller and Top 10 clubs. He not only wanted a share of the market: he wanted to be the key player. First, he wanted the Beatles on an exclusive contract: they had made the German teenagers aware of the excitement of rock'n'roll music.

Klaus Voormann was part of the audience: 'Astrid Kirchherr and I listened to all those rock'n'roll records like Fats Domino, Little Richard, Chuck Berry and Larry Williams. We heard quite a lot on Radio Luxembourg, but it was hard to get hold of the records themselves. It was particularly nice when we met those Beatle boys. Paul sent us records – I remember the Isley Brothers and the Ikettes. He was sending us 45s of records that he really liked, not necessarily the hits.'

But Manfred Weissleder wanted to go one better than just the UK groups. The British rock'n'roll pianist Roy Young was given a residency with additional responsibilities. 'Manfred Weissleder bought me a new car and my job included travelling to England and signing people up. I had to bring American artists to Germany and the best way was through the promoter Don Arden. I told him that I wanted Little Richard, Chuck Berry, Brenda Lee and Ray Charles, and he thought that I was having a go at him. I said, "No, this is genuine. The owner wants to make the Star-Club famous." Within a couple of days, Don Arden was in Hamburg signing a contract with Manfred. I told him Don Arden was a gangster and would try and rip him off but of course Manfred was one as well.'

Accompanied by Sounds Incorporated, Little Richard played the Star-Club in Hamburg from 29 October to 4 November 1962.

The highlight of Little Richard's act had been his striptease when he threw his sweat-drenched shirt into the crowd. *Star-Club News* had a headline, *Striptease à la Madame Richard*. There was praise for his magnificent physique. The Beatles were at the Star-Club and George Harrison would watch him and caught one of his cufflinks.

More than that, Paul McCartney asked Richard to teach him his singing style. Richard was impressed with the Beatles. He called Art Rupe and told him he should sign them for Specialty, but Rupe said, 'I am only interested in you, Richard. Come back and make records like you did before.' At different times, Richard has claimed that he recommended the Beatles to Specialty and to Vee-Jay but nearly every American performer who came to the UK tells a similar story. In any event the Beatles were signed to EMI whose sister company in the US was Capitol. Capitol at first leased Beatles product to Vee-Jay but this was not Richard's doing.

Nevertheless, his enthusiasm for the Beatles was genuine as one of Richard's UK friends, Graham Knight told *Record Mirror*: 'Little Richard had a photo with the Beatles ready to put up in his gold room at home, and one with Sounds Incorporated too. He said, "Next time I invite Elvis over, I'll show them to him and tell him that they are the best group in Britain".'

Sam Hardie from Kingsize Taylor and the Dominoes: 'Davy Jones was in Hamburg at the same time as Little Richard. Little Richard was backed by Sounds Incorporated who were never right for him because they played everything too fast. He saw Little Richard getting undressed and throwing his clothes into the audience. When Davy went on stage with them, he took out his soiled underwear and he threw it into the audience like Richard.'

Gerry Marsden: 'Little Richard was always crazy and always overrunning. I loved him like mad, but it was like being on a show with Ken Dodd. No one can tell them what to do and they can both go on forever.'

Roy Young: 'One night Richard was right behind me when I was playing standing up at the piano with Tony Sheridan on guitar. I was doing 'Rip It Up'. When I finished, he applauded and was jumping up and down, saying that I sounded just like him. I don't think anything has ever topped that moment.'

Chris Curtis of the Searchers had his long hair and light brown leather jacket in Hamburg. Little Richard likened him to Tarzan and said, 'Do you live in a tree?'

Sam Hardie again: 'I had various black magic books and I was trying to get the spells to work. One of them was how to fly. Richard would give us lectures about the Bible and somebody told him I could fly using black magic and he said, "Sam, you ain't a-gonna fly 'cause you ain't a bird." He was serious about it.'

Did any of the black magic spells work? 'None. I tried love spells and they always backfired on me.'

Publicist Chris Hutchins, who worked for Don Arden and went to Hamburg with the Beatles, recalled, 'One night Little Richard and Billy Preston invited Ringo and me back to the hotel for dinner. It was 2 a.m. and it was just dried-up sandwiches. They tried to talk us into doing whatever they did with each other. Ringo talked about a girl he had taken to a cinema in Liverpool and I talked about the girl I was going to marry, hoping that they would get the message. In the end, Little Richard went to the loo and we made a dash for it.'

Horst Fascher was not so inhibited. The floor manager of the Star-Club wrote in his memoir, *Rock & Roll Music* (2006), 'I didn't fancy men, but Little Richard gave me a blow job that many a woman could learn from.'

Little Richard and Billy Preston had an argument, which led to Richard giving his flight ticket to a German boy he had fallen in love with. Manfred Weissleder bought a ticket to get Billy back home.

Roy Young: 'A couple of years later I was chatting to the Beatles at EMI and we were having a laugh. I saw someone coming towards me waving his walking-stick and it was Don Arden. He had broken his leg. He said, "Come over to Hamburg with me as I am being sued by Manfred." I said, "No way, I don't want to get involved in that." Manfred won in the end, but I'm sure Don made money on the side. Little Richard was being paid £1,500 for the two weeks. I had the money in hundreds and I was giving him cash and Richard is a very honest person. He said, "Roy, you have given me too much. It is only £750." Don was going to pocket that difference."

II. The Everly Brothers Tour

As an impresario, Don Arden's bottom line was always to make money. He had done that with Little Richard in 1962 coercing him to return to rock'n'roll, but a year later, Richard was back in America and concentrating on his ministry, so Arden thought of a tour with the Everly Brothers. They had come over for Arthur Howes in 1962 but Don had had a breakdown and Phil bravely continued on his own. Arden was satisfied that Don was back to full health and an itinerary mostly around Gaumont and Odeon cinemas was resolved for autumn 1963.

As Buddy Holly had made the charts posthumously with his cover of Bo Diddley's 'Bo Diddley' and Bo's praises were being sung by the Beatles, Searchers and Rolling Stones, so it was ideal time for Bo's UK début.

Having secured his headliners, Don Arden added the supporting acts. The Rolling Stones' first single, 'Come On', released in June 1963, was a good calling card. As they had hardly played outside London, they were keen to tour the UK. The tour featuring the Everly Brothers, Bo Diddley, pop singer Julie Grant, Mickie Most and the Rolling Stones was announced in the *NME* on July 19.

Mickie Most had been in South Africa and had several hit records there, mostly produced by himself. He was looking for local talent to produce and indeed, he discovered the Animals in Newcastle.

The tour was to open in London on 29 September and run throughout October. On September 13, the Everly Brothers and their wives flew into London Airport. At a press conference at the Hilton, Don and Phil praised local acts, Matt Monro and the Dallas Boys, but Bo Diddley right on the ball remarked, 'I notice that you have a group here called the Beatles. Now that's a good name – the kids can remember it like we've got the Spindles. And of course Bo Diddley, you don't forget that name.' I can't track a band called the Spindles so that could be a joke, but well done, Bo, for some brilliant self-promotion.

The tickets for the Everly Brothers tour, though reasonably priced between 5 and 15 shillings, were not going well. Some fans suspected it could be another fiasco for the Everly Brothers and stayed away. What's more, there were beat group nights all over the country competing for attention. The tour might lose money – lots of it.

Then Don Arden had a brainwave.

Little Richard.

His 1962 comeback tour with Sam Cooke had gone very well but now he was concentrating on his ministry. He said, 'I want people to forget me as a rock'n'roller. I'm going to be an evangelist like Billy Graham.'

'You've got to remember that Little Richard was paranoid,' says Chas White. 'He had experienced racism in the States and he had seen Chuck Berry go to prison. Whether or not Chuck Berry was guilty doesn't really matter here: Little Richard thought that the authorities might come for him next, but if he were a minister he would be protected.'

Richard was preaching and playing piano and organ in a Seventh-day Adventist church just off New York's Times Square. His normal method of preaching was to say, 'This happened to me' and then talk about himself.

Don Arden knew that the right approach was to flatter Little Richard: he called him and said, 'Richard, I'm in the shit and you're the only one who can help me.' Arden recalled, 'Richard wanted the cash he would have got for topping the bill but that was all right and bless his heart, within a couple of days, he was here.' To some degree, Richard was being hypocritical. Communications were not like today's: he could rock'n'roll in the UK and as nobody in America would be any the wiser: he could return to the church without anybody knowing.

'I'm not surprised that Don Arden got Little Richard,' says John Steel of the Animals, 'He was a tough guy but he also had a lot of charm and could be very convincing. He could talk anybody into anything.'

Okay, Richard couldn't top the bill as the Everlys might head for the exit, but he could perform so ferociously that those sweet country boys would have difficulty in following him. The tour would start without him but he would soon be there.

It is surprising that the Musicians' Union allowed Little Richard, the Everly Brothers with their band and Bo Diddley with the Duchess and Jerome to be touring together. Normally the MU would argue that this was putting British musicians out of work, but, as John Steel said, Don Arden could be very persuasive.

This was at a time of high competition for package tours. Peter Walsh had Roy Orbison and Bob Luman touring with the Searchers and Brian Poole, and Arthur Howes had two tours - Tommy Roe with Billy J Kramer and Del Shannon with Gerry and the Pacemakers.

The autumn tour featuring the Everly Brothers, Bo Diddley, the Rolling Stones, Julie Grant, Mickie Most, the Flintstones and compère Bob Bain opened at the New Victoria Theatre in London on 29 September. An unbilled act was the Rattles from the Star-Club in Hamburg, really as a favour to Star-Club owner Manfred Weissleder, and Arden didn't have to pay them.

On that opening night, the Everlys performed 'Rip It Up' and 'Keep A-Knockin'', but Richard had yet to jon the tour.

Phil Everly, who wore evening dress on stage, was to say of the Rolling Stones, 'They were not dressing for the stage and they looked peculiar but they did a good job and stood out. They were an easy bunch of guys to be around.'

The opening show was perfect for the new kids on the block, although Bill Wyman was 27, as this was the Stones' home territory. Writing to *Melody Maker*, B A Woodridge said, 'Many R & B fans left the theatre after the Rolling Stones and Bo Diddley had appeared and those who stayed chanted for the reappearance of Bo Diddley and the Stones – much to the annoyance of the Everlys' fans.'

Bo Diddley brought over three homemade guitars, sometimes playing one with a rectangular body that appeared to be carpeted. He was a heavily-built man wearing a gold lamé suit alongside the Duchess in her cat suit with gold threads and Jerome Green manically waving four, sometimes six, maracas. Bo told everyone that the Duchess was his sister as he felt this was the best way to protect her.

Because of his experiences in Australia, Little Richard hated flying and he had sailed to the UK for his 1962 tour. As Don Arden wanted him urgently, he had to fly, admittedly with reluctance. Even then, he wouldn't make the opening show.

According to *Record Mirror*, 'Little Richard was talking in the third person and in the language of billboards by saying, 'Little Richard Is Something To See, Something To Hear. It Will Be The Electrifying Little Richard In His Amazing Role Like An Atomic Bomb.' Not that anyone in 2023 would ever liken their sound to an atom bomb. Richard commented on new beat trends with this unlikely comment, 'I used to have my hair four and a half inches high and my wife hated it.'

In a way, Richard had a new rival, Cassius Clay. He was the biggest sporting celebrity of the early 60s, a superb-looking fighter in a sport that was not conducive to keeping your looks. Just like Little Richard, he would claim to be the best-looking man around and he would recite his now-famous raps. Unquestionably, he was taking his lead from Little Richard and it was no surprise when he said Richard was his favourite singer. Ooh! my soul.

June Harris, the reviewer for *Disc,* said, 'Little Richard's dynamic début on the Everly Brothers package tour at Watford on Saturday proved that he is still the greatest, wildest performer in the world. Every Little Richard hit from 'Lucille' to 'Good Golly Miss Molly' was hurled at the audience which stamped, raved and yelled with the artist. The old wild action was there and Little Richard's complete performance was charged with shouts of 'All right!' between songs. By the end of his act, he was stripped of all his clothing except for his blue mohair pants. After he closed the first half, the yells for an encore lasted almost five minutes. This man is tremendous.'

The next night of the tour, October 6, was at the Capitol in Cardiff. Little Richard was told not to overrun because it was a Sunday and they had to follow the rules of the Lord's Day Observance Society. There were two houses with a curfew of 10pm.

Little Richard took no notice: he would observe the Lord's Day as he thought fit. Bill Wyman told *Record Mirror*, 'Richard brought the house down when he jumped off stage, went up the centre aisle followed by members of the audience, out of the front doors, then back in through a side-exit and onto the stage. He partly undressed and threw pieces of clothing into the crowd. He performed way past his scheduled time and his manager had to yell to him, "Richard, stop preaching!" to get him off.'

The Everlys' manager, Jack Rael, complained to Don Arden that Little Richard had been allowed too much time, but Arden sided with Richard. Arden had already asked Richard to stay on for the Shirelles tour which would also feature Duane Eddy or Chuck Berry. He'd been thinking of arranging an Everly Brothers special with the ITV producer, Johnnie Hamp, for Granada, but now Little Richard was a better bet.

As well as the Everlys, Richard also knew how to irritate Bo Diddley and they would frequently argue as to who's on first. If Bo got on before Richard, he would add a couple of numbers to his set. The tour was coming together for the audience and falling apart backstage.

Bill Wyman's thoughts are verified by Derek Wayland who reviewed the show for *Cardiff and Suburban News*. Under the heading, *Little Richard Hypnotises Audience*, he wrote: 'Little Richard's guest appearance in the Everly Brothers Show was the most exciting performance ever given in a pop package visiting this city. I thought the days of rock'n'roll were over – until I saw America's fabulous Little Richard. For almost 30 minutes, I relived the rock'n'roll era as this dynamic entertainer sang the songs I enjoyed hearing several years ago. There was 'Long Tall Sally', 'Tutti Frutti' and many others. Fans mobbed Little Richard after he threw his shirt to a lucky member of the packed audience. If he decides to make a comeback, everything is in his favour. He is the star that other stars make a point of seeing.'

Here's a contrasting review from Tez Courtney for Cardiff University's *Broadsheet.* 'The Everlys topped the bill but unjustifiably in my view. They did their hits but essentially they were popsters for the girlie section of the packed audience. Little Richard and Bo Diddley, on the other hand, were explosive. Bo was a revelation – doing the splits, for example. Richard was at his deranged peak with a thunderous three-sax blasting from the Flintstones.

It was the second greatest rock'n'roll show I've ever seen, just below Little Richard's 1962 tour. A bubblegum beat group called the Rolling Stones was down the bill. They were remarkably short little chaps and Jagger's mincing was met with derision by the Teds, who included Breathless Dan and his friends.'

Graham Knight recalls, 'I remember Richard leaping off the stage and running up the centre aisle. The fans were dancing in the aisle and blocking him in. There were no wireless mics then and so he was just hollering at the top of his voice.' Eventually, Peter Grant and Graham Knight got him back on stage.

Watching the show was an up-and-coming Welsh club singer, Tom Jones, then dressed as a Teddy Boy. After the show, Tom knelt in front of Richard as though he had an audition with the Pope. 'Well, baby,' said Little Richard, 'you sure are some Georgia peach.'

Bob Bain and Little Richard worked out an entrance. Bob would ask the audience whom they'd come to see and Richard off-stage would sing the titles of 10 of his hits one after the other. This would drive the audiences hysterical.

'I'd heard so much about the audience reactions to Little Richard that I thought there must be some exaggeration,' said Mick Jagger, 'but it was all true. He drove the whole house into a frenzy.' One night Richard asked to borrow a shirt from Jagger, who then watched the audience tear it to shreds. When Richard asked to borrow another shirt the following night, Jagger said no.

Part of Little Richard's small entourage was his Bible college friend, Walter E Arties IV. He started praying for Richard in Cardiff as he thought he had been possessed by the Devil.

Don Arden: 'Richard always carried a Bible with him so that he could preach to people on the street. My son David picked it up and looked inside it and found that down all the margins, Richard had written the names of his lovers, along with descriptions of what they did when he shagged them. That was his message to God.' Leonard Cohen is often said to have mixed the sacred and the sexual –but Little Richard was first.

Keith Richards was skeptical of Little Richard's religiosity for other reasons. He thought that Little Richard was a preacher for tax concessions. 'Very little to do with God, a lot to do with money,' he concluded in his autobiography, *Life*. I put this to Chas White: 'I think that's unfair. Richard was paranoid, there's no doubt about that. He did fear racism and he thought that religion might be some sort of protection for him.'

Mick Jagger told *Record Mirror*: 'At Cardiff on Sunday night, we played to two packed houses and Richard drove the whole audience into a complete frenzy. It reminded me of the rock'n'roll riots with the whole theatre jumping as the audience, mainly boys, jumped up on the stage and jived in the aisles.' Some fans came backstage and offered the Stones some grass. The Stones freaked out and told them to leave the theatre. How times would change.

After the show most of the performers were in St David's Hotel, Cardiff with Don Arden and Colin Berlin, and everyone was paying individually for drinks and sandwiches. Arden asked Richard if he was happy with his spot on the show and Richard said that he was happy as he could get back to the hotel early. Arden wanted to move him up the bill to put pressure on the Everlys to improve – or leave.

Mickie Most said, 'I used to go on second and do my eight minutes and then I would go into the audience and watch these great artists. Little Richard was completely different from his records and his act changed every night. He didn't really have an act as such: he would just go out and go berserk for half an hour.'

Mick Jagger agreed, 'I couldn't believe the power of Little Richard on stage. He was amazing. Chuck Berry is my favourite, along with Bo Diddley, but nobody could beat Little Richard's stage act. Little Richard is the originator and my first idol.'

The Rattles got by on very little. Herbert Hildebrand says, 'The tour was fantastic but the promoters said that they had no money for us and so we got £5 a day for the whole band, no hotel, nothing. We were four kids carrying our own equipment and we would open the second half with two songs, and every time the coach stopped in front of a hotel, we had to get out and look in a strange city for somewhere to stay, and it was very hard. Sometimes the bus would stop at a restaurant and we couldn't go in as we had no money. Little Richard asked us to have a coffee with him and he gave us money. It was hard but it paid off and it was good learning for us.'

Dicky Tarrach, also from the Rattles, adds, 'Most of us travelled together in this very big bus. Every day Richard would say, "I am so beautiful today." He had his own natural hair then, no wig, but he was very strange. He had to keep saying, "I was the best yesterday, I am the king of rock'n'roll." If he read a good review he would say, "Yes, yes, yes!" He closed the first half and we were on at the start of the second half and our contract was for two songs, but if Little Richard went on too long, we could only do one. There were a couple of nights where he didn't do a long set and we got three songs.'

Little Richard was determined to be the main act on the bill. Keith Richards writing in his autobiography, *Life*, says: 'Little Richard's stage presentation was outrageous and brilliant. He could have the band thumping out 'Lucille' for ten minutes, which is a long time to keep that riff going, and then he'd come out from the back of the theatre. Richard had checked the theatre, talked to the lighting people – 'Where can I come from?' 'Is there a door there?' – and figured how he could make the most effective intro possible: whether it's bang, straight in or whether to let the riff roll for five minutes and turn up from the loft. He's not just playing any old club where presentation means nothing.'

The tour had a good night at the Gaumont, Wolverhampton and then moved to the Gaumont, Derby where Chas White caught the show: 'Little Richard was the Supreme Commander. He was brilliant, even though Bo Diddley shone like a diamond. The Everlys were doing their songs far too fast. I thought the Rolling Stones were awful but put that down to prejudice and I might think differently today. The Flintstones did a decent job backing Little Richard and I never heard Richard complain about them. What particularly infuriated me was Mickie Most who did 'Johnny B Goode' and 'Sea Cruise' so badly that I was enraged. People were throwing those hard, old pennies at him: he was so terrible.'

Richard had thrown away his cufflinks with his shirt and he asked Don Arden to lend him a pair for the second house. Arden slipped off his gold links and passed them to Richard. They went into the crowd with his shirt and Arden was furious.

The music writer John Stafford saw the show with his girlfriend at the Gaumont Doncaster on October 12 and after the first house at 6.15pm, they went to the dressing room shared by Bo Diddley and Little Richard. Bo signed his autograph book and Little Richard said, 'Hey, what about me? Have I upset you?' John explained that he already had Richard's autograph. He showed it to him with his old address (1710 Virginia Road) and Richard signed it with his new address, now 3931 Manchester Place.

Richard asked if they were going to the second show but they weren't because they might miss the last train. Richard ignored this, said that the second show was always better and he assumed that they weren't going because they didn't have the money. He gave them

£5 for tickets, but John didn't take it as they wouldn't be able to get back home.

It was an eventful interval as Ken Jenour of *Disc* also met Richard between houses. 'After the most frenzied, fantastic act I've ever seen, Little Richard came off stage at Derby's Gaumont Theatre last Friday and calmly told me, 'I am planning to cut an LP called *Little Richard Sings Soft Music*. I know I'm real wild on stage and I just can't help it, but I can sing real soft and sweet.' Then to a tirade of screams and stamping feet, he stormed back on stage. And the whole frantic procedure started over again.'

On Sunday 13 October 1963, the Everly Brothers tour played the Odeon Cinema in London Road, Liverpool, and I went to the first house, fortunately making some notes at the time and keeping them.

There was a long pounding introduction from the Flintstones and we all wondered where Little Richard was. He came screaming down the aisle singing 'Lucille' and followed it with 'Long Tall Sally', 'Tutti Frutti', 'Whole Lotta Shakin' Goin' on', and 'Rip It Up', but he could have been singing anything. His showmanship was remarkable and he clenched the top of a chair with his teeth, held it aloft and did a wild rockin' dance around the front of the stage. He stripped to his underpants and put on a dressing-gown as he closed with 'Hound Dog'. He was on stage for over half an hour.

Also at the show was my friend Andrew Doble: 'The Everly Brothers were disappointing because they could so easily have been much better, but Little Richard more than fulfilled my expectations. His suit was soon covered in sweat and he took it off and came back in a fluffy white bathrobe. It was all part of the show and I thought he was an absolutely great showman. Like Little Richard, Bo Diddley was exciting and had pizzazz but all the time I was wondering if the Duchess was his sister or his girlfriend. I saw the Rolling Stones and I thought they would never make it. They seemed limp compared to the others and I was deeply unimpressed. However, Mickie Most was the bottom of the bill by a very, very long way.'

Another view of the same show from the Liverpool crime writer, Ron Ellis: 'The Everly Brothers were very efficient as though a sergeant major had told them to get on with it and they had brushed their hair forward to give themselves a Beatle look. Little Richard was very good and still doing rock'n'roll and it had never occurred to me that he might be gay. Bo Diddley was great: he didn't move very much but his body swung as he played and he had a weird-looking guitar. Mickie Most was okay as he had a good personality and moved about. I remember him more than the Flintstones and Julie Grant, who just stood still."

Ron went backstage to write a feature for *Record Mirror*. He found Bo Diddley ad-libbing 'Doin' the Monkey at School' with Jerome on maracas and local musicians, the Chants and Derry Wilkie adding vocals. Little Richard was praising Jackie Wilson who was working with his old band, the Upsetters. Richard loved Jerry Lee Lewis and he knew who Billy Fury was. He told Ron that Solomon Burke was going to be big.

Backstage, the Rolling Stones were in turmoil. When Brian Jones wanted to stay in a better hotel, the other Stones learnt that Brian was receiving an extra £5 a week for being the leader of the group. From that night in Liverpool, it was all over for Brian as the leader of the Rolling Stones.

After Manchester, the tour moved to the Odeon Glasgow. Jerry Dawson of *Melody Maker* saw Little Richard there: 'Little Richard is on stage, his face bathed in perspiration. He sings. He jumps and dances. The roar from the teenage audience becomes louder. He removes his jacket, shirt and tie. When he comes off stage, he has a toweling robe around his naked torso and he says, "Well, I made them happy, didn't I?"' He told Dawson that he had been studying theology and that he was planning a dramatic presentation of his own life along gospel lines.

The new issue of *Disc* included an interview with Little Richard who said, 'England is one of the first places I visit in passing on the word of God.' Did he view this as a challenge?

It was off to the Odeon Nottingham on October 23 and the next night it was the Odeon Birmingham. With a party of friends from Rugby, Stuart Colman saw the show in Birmingham. He says, 'Mickie Most was not to be taken seriously and few people took any notice of him. The Rolling Stones wore matching dog-tooth jackets and performed on a small riser which was wheeled on and off with their equipment and all of them clinging to it. Bo Diddley with the Duchess and Jerome were superb. He had Gibson amps complete with angled supports that pointed the speakers up into the circle. Little Richard was totally mad and stole the show. He put everything he'd got into his act which was pure rock'n'roll and this made it very difficult for the Everly Brothers. They began with their hits in ultra-fast form which didn't sit well at all. It wasn't until they sang 'Ain't That Lovin' You Baby' that they began to win the crowd over.'

At the Gaumont, Taunton on 25 October, the police had to control Little Richard who had stripped off while singing 'Whole Lotta Shakin' Goin' on' to ensure that he didn't go the Full Monty, but that whole escapade could have been set up by Richard.

By now the Stones knew they were in control. Keith Richards wrote, 'We were getting bigger and bigger. We were opening the second half of the show and the kids were rocking. That was pissing the Everly Brothers off because they were top of the bill. Our impudence had built up to a point where we knew what was going to happen. There was a new wind blowing.'

The month was rounded off at the Lewisham Odeon, the Rattles' last night as they had a November residency at the Star-Club. Dicky Tarrach said, 'We loved touring with Little Richard and we would tell our audiences about it and then play 'Lucille'.'

There was a bright note when the tour came to the Gaumont, Ipswich. Little Richard and the Everly Brothers talked to schoolchildren and signed autographs. Little Richard said, 'A lot of folks told me it was nice to see me back in show business and 1had to put them right. I said, "I'm in my business, not show business".'

The final show was at the famed Hammersmith Odeon on November 3. The Stones received their best reception of the tour, but paper cups were thrown at the Everlys. However, the Stones weren't to everyone's satisfaction. Writing to the *New Musical Express*, J Worley commented, 'Having seen the Stones at the Odeon, Hammersmith, I can only say that their so-called R & B sounds as anaemic as they look and it is deplorable that they should dare to perform with artists of the calibre of Bo Diddley and Little Richard.'

Little Richard was on terrific form, despite a throat infection, an underpowered microphone and instructions not to go into the audience. He told an attendant who was restraining a fan, 'Hey, leave him alone' and the audience loved this. During his five-song set ('Lucille', 'Long Tall Sally', 'Whole Lotta Shakin' Goin' On', 'Hound Dog', 'Keep-A Knockin'') Richard did 14 leaps into air and concluded with a jump from the piano.

Don Arden admitted that the tour did not make a profit. 'I finished up losing two or three grand but at least the tour had the appearance of success which is almost as important as the real thing.'

Little Richard went straight from Don Arden's tour to another one with the Shirelles and Duane Eddy and still being backed by the Flintstones. Little Richard only appeared on a few dates as he apparently injured his ankle and had to return home for medical treatment. I say 'apparently' because he sailed home, a bizarre decision for someone in pain.

Back in Los Angeles, Little Richard returned to preaching. Don Everly went into a supermarket and found him preaching there. His Granada TV concert with the Shirelles was screened in May 1964. One of the highlights was Little Richard, the Shirelles and Sounds Incorporated performing 'Joy Joy Joy' together. The show was billed as. 'Little Richard's farewell performance'. Well, we've heard that before. Still, Granada said that in good faith. Don Arden had offered him a new tour but he was saying rock'n'roll was evil and Don Arden was the Devil. (Well, he wasn't far wrong there.)

Little Richard declared, 'England is going to be one of the first places I will visit in passing on the word of God.' Only it wasn't. Spurred on by his UK success, Richard started recording again and even told the American audiences how well he had been doing in the UK on his version of 'Whole Lotta Shakin' Goin' On'.

The 1963 tour had been very good for Bo Diddley – he had done what he had set out to do. He had a Top 40 single with 'Pretty Thing' and within a year he had four UK Top 20 albums – amazing! The albums were *Bo Diddley, Bo Diddley Is A Gunslinger, Bo Diddley Rides Again* and *Bo Diddley's Beach Party.*

A highly entertaining film could be made about this October 1963 tour by the Everly Brothers, Little Richard and Bo Diddley. The tensions between all the performers make for entertainment and you have great music too.

And a curious PS: Little Richard's nemesis Pat Boone was touring the UK in 1963 and one of his extracurricular activities was to participate in a charity cricket match for the NME who would be playing the Sussex county team. Astonishingly and impressively, he caught the England captain, Ted Dexter.

Publicity stills, mid-50s

Publicity stills, mid-50s

een test for *Don't Knock the Rock*, 1956

Wrigley's Field, Chicago, 1956

Little Richard, 1956

Club Revilot, Nashville, 1954

Little Richard & Impressions, 2004

New Era Club, Nashville, 1952

New Era Club, Nashville, 1955

Little Richard at the Star-Club in Hamburg with Sounds incorporated

Little Richard performs Lucille in *Mr Rock'n'Roll*, 1957

Little Richard in full voice, c.1956

Gerry Marsden with Little Richard at the Star-Club, Hamburg, 1962.

Little Richard with the Beatles, 1962

THE NIGHT OF NIGHTS

STARRING THE NAME THAT'S REALLY
Big
BIG
BIG

America's No. 1 Rock 'n' Roll Showman
The Dynamic, Sensational Singer-pianist

LITTLE RICHARD!

Hit recorder of "Long Tall Sally," "Tutti Frutti," "Rip It Up," &c.

LITTLE RICHARD!

Remember how great he was in the movie "The Girl Can't Help It"?

LITTLE RICHARD!

Bet you never thought you'd ever have the chance to see him in person

LITTLE RICHARD!

Well you can—and real soon. Just two weeks To-night, Friday, October 12

LITTLE RICHARD!

First ever appearance on Merseyside at the Tower Ballroom, New Brighton

LITTLE RICHARD!

7.30 p.m. to 1 a.m.—Lic. Bars till 12.15
Late transport all parts Liverpool & Wirral

LITTLE RICHARD!

Many great names have appeared at the Tower but here is the Greatest

LITTLE RICHARD!

So HURRY! HURRY! Decide now to buy your tickets this week-end for

LITTLE RICHARD!

On Sale (10/6) at Nems, Rushworths, Lewis's, Hessys, Cranes, Strothers, Tower, &c.

LITTLE RICHARD!

BUT WAIT! . That's not all! In addition to the Sensational Group who will be backing Little Richard look at this Great Galaxy of Ten of the North's Top Rock Groups. They're ALL on the same Mammoth Bill!

THE BEATLES

Yes, the group Parlophone are tipping for the Top with their first disc: "Love Me Do" and "P.S. I Love You."

THE BEATLES

plus
THE BIG THREE
plus
PETE MACLAINE & THE DAKOTAS
plus
LEE CURTIS WITH THE ALL STARS
plus
BILLY KRAMER & THE COASTERS
plus
RORY STORM & THE HURRICANES
plus
THE UNDERTAKERS
plus
THE FOUR JAYS
plus
THE MERSEYBEATS
plus
GUS TRAVIS & THE MIDNIGHTERS

FANTASTIC!

ALL THESE FOR YOU ON FRIDAY, OCTOBER 12th AT THE TOWER BALLROOM, NEW BRIGHTON.
The slickest, most exciting non-stop Show Dance every staged on Merseyside.
NOW DO YOU SEE WHY TICKETS ARE IN SUCH GREAT DEMAND!
Don't Delay any longer — Get yours NOW! You won't regret doing so, for this truly will be

THE NIGHT OF NIGHTS

A BOB WOOLER PRODUCTION

The Liverpool Echo, 1962

Page 2—MELODY MAKER October 13 1962

LITTLE RICHARD COMEBACK WOWS 'EM!

FANS of Little Richard, who had travelled from as far as Dundee for his Monday opening at the Gaumont, Doncaster, were not disappointed.

Bursting back from his four years of self-imposed exile, he pulled out all his old numbers.

With a voice like a rusty megaphone he appears to have discovered the secret of perpetual motion and wrestles with the mike as though it were an enemy (see page 7 for Little Richard's own explanation of his exile).

There was disappointment at first house when Sam Cooke failed to turn up, having been delayed en route.

Surprise

At second house he too won over the fans with "Twisting the night away" and several slow beat ballads.

There was a surprise appearance by Gene Vincent who flew in from Israel minus a work permit. Unable to appear on stage, he sang from the orchestra pit.

On Tuesday, at the Granada, Mansfield, Little Richard was hampered by an attack of tonsillitis. This time, Vincent sang from among the audience.

Jet Harris was warmly received with his new sound.—B. A. and A. C.

CAUGHT in the ACT

★ Organ vogue

JAZZ organ is currently enjoying a vogue in America and on record releases in Britain.

To judge by audience reaction, London's Ronnie Scott Club is obviously on to a good thing in presenting Manchester's Allan Haven on Tuesdays and Wednesdays.

Backed by the rather uncertain drumming of George Walker, Allan certainly swings although his improvisation is hardly adventurous.

On Tuesday, the duo were joined by Harold McNair who played admirably on both alto and flute.—K. D.

★ Paris jazz

THE Horace Silver Quintet and Gerry Mulligan Quartet this week took over the Olympia, Paris. Silver's music brought the ovations because of its warmth and sincerity.

Blue Mitchell's trumpet gained the biggest cheer, but Jimmy Cook's tenor disappointed.

Mulligan's success was expected. Trumpeter Art Farmer's dry, rather intellectual trumpet came over well.—H. K.

★ Vintage Tony

IN his new show (King's Theatre, Southsea) Tony Hancock sings, dances, indulges in ham acting, gives impressions, and supplie[illegible]

Ball success story on Luxembourg

KENNY BALL's success story will be told in Radio Luxembourg's "This is their life" on November 7 . . . Impresario Leslie Grade flies to New York this Sunday for a three-day trip "in connection with films." . . . Joe Loss Orchestra for BBC-TV "Miss World" [illegible]

News in [illegible]

[illegible] braith Band to join Clinton Ford's new accompanying group . . . Clyde Valley Stom[illegible]

Melody Maker cutting p.2, 1962

October 13, 1962 MELODY MAKER Page 7

LITTLE RICHARD aint a rocker any more . . .

God put out the fire

AN open Bible lay, like a talisman, on the bed between sprawled-out Richard Penniman and me.

It was a powerful witness, testifying that Little Richard, rock singer, belonged to the past.

The Richard British audiences will be seeing draws inspiration from the Good Book, selling hot gospel with all the fervour that made him a million seller five years ago.

Simply and sincerely, he told the story in the room of his London hotel.

"I was flying to a concert in the Philippines and the engine of the plane caught fire," he explained.

"I prayed for it to be put out and God did it. That was how my life changed.

"Just after, on a tour in Australia, I told my friends I was giving up my kind of life. They thought I was going out of my head.

"So I took all the rings off my fingers and threw 'em in the sea to show I meant it. Some lucky fish might have swallowed 'em.

"Would have been a lucky man that caught that fish. Imagine sorta cutting up the fish and seein' all those rings. My . . ."

Invested

Richard joined the Church of the Seventh Day Adventists, his wife and family with him. He has no children, lives in a "fine place" in Sugar Hill, California, and owns three apartment blocks near his home.

"I invested my money," he said.

He insists that he is not in show business—"this is my own business. Everything is new. I don't feel I'm makin' a comeback to concerts and things. I'm singing what I like to sing, and other people like it, too.

Electrifying

"Yeah, I still get the same reaction from the audiences. I still blow 'em up. Get as wild as ever."

He leaned forward confidentially.

"They thought I was going out of my head."

"I'm billed as the electrifying Little Richard, see? And I do electrify those kids. I got an electrifying act. And they love it, yes they do. They've come up and told me how they enjoyed it.

"No, I don't need a band on stage. The last time I worked with one was five years ago, like I said. I play the piano, of course, and this boy is good enough for me."

Oh, boy!

He gestured to a sleeping figure, face-down on the next bed.

"That's Billy—Billy Preston. He's sixteen and plays the organ. He sounds like a whole band himself. He's great. Great. You ought to hear him play. Oh, boy! I don't need no band when Billy's around."

Thinner

The Little Richard of today is hardly recognisable as the fierce-looking, mop-haired rocker of "Tutti frutti," "Long tall Sally" and "Rip it up" fame.

He's not so little—"'bout five eleven," he told me. "But I used to be smaller. Well, I was thinner in those days."

The warrior look appears occasionally when he talks feelingly about his music.

The hair style?—"I took it off five years ago," he said briefly.

What did he do at concerts when people requested some of his old numbers?

Won't mind

He grinned. "I sing. He got what he wanted (his latest record) or one of my other numbers. They don't mind, you'll see."

The bedside phone had been steadily punctuating our conversation. It rang again and Richard answered it.

He finished talking, put the phone down and turned back to face me.

To church

"Sam Cooke's comin' in on Monday to go straight up to the show at . . . Doncaster, is it?

"Yeah, well I wish he could stay here for a while. I want him to go through all this talking to newsmen. I just feel like a good rest now, if you'll excuse me.

"I know where I'm going tomorrow. I'm going to our church here in London and I'm going to stay there all day.

"I know nobody'll follow me there . . . that's one place I won't get disturbed. . . .

Chris Roberts

Ifield? He's GREAT! says Don Everly

THERE have been exaggerated reports recently about Phil and me having violent quarrels—and that the Everly Brothers as a team, would be splitting up.

You know, like all families we have our differences. We've argued all our lives. However, at heart, we are real close.

There has never been any question but that we would be staying together.

Right now I'm really very, very happy. Both my marriage and my life generally are just swinging.

My brother, Phil, will soon be marrying Jackie Ertel, from New York City. She's the stepdaughter of Archie Bleyer, head of Cadence Records.

As you may know, our mother is in the Chordettes vocal group that records for Cadence. That's how Phil met Jackie.

Phil and I find that teenage audiences are much the same all over the world—and girls' reactions to our singing seems to be similar wherever we go.

TASTES ARE STANDARD

You see, in all countries now, they see the same TV shows, they hear much the same radio and buy exactly the same records. The kids' tastes are pretty standardised.

Generally speaking, people listen to our sound. However, we are now recording our songs in various languages—German, Japanese, French and even Cajun—which is a language, I believe, from Louisiana.

We plan, too, to make some records in Russian.

We've also found that now there are artistes all over the world, in the teenage pop market, that are just as good as the Americans.

Records come out of England that I can't tell, on first hearing, aren't made here in the States.

We heard a guitar player in New Zealand who sounded as though he were born in Nashville!

Phil and I are looking forward to our British visit more this time than last because of all the friends we have made with you.

AND WE DO WANT TO MEET FRANK IFIELD. WE THINK HE'S JUST WONDERFUL.

look-n-listen

(Times BST-CET)

Medody Maker cutting p.7, 1962

Baby Face, 1957

Don't Knock The Rock

Little Richard and Pat Boone

Ready Teddy, 1956

Little Richard at the pulpit

Little Richard studying the Bible

Back in his comfort zone Joe Lubin discusses one of his songs with Doris Day

Robert A. "Bumps" Blackwell, personal manager, and Little Richard discussing newest hit record—"DO YOU FEEL IT?"

Little Richard with his producer/manager Bumps Blackwell, 1966

Little Richard with Jet Harris, formerly of the Shadows

Little Richard 70s style

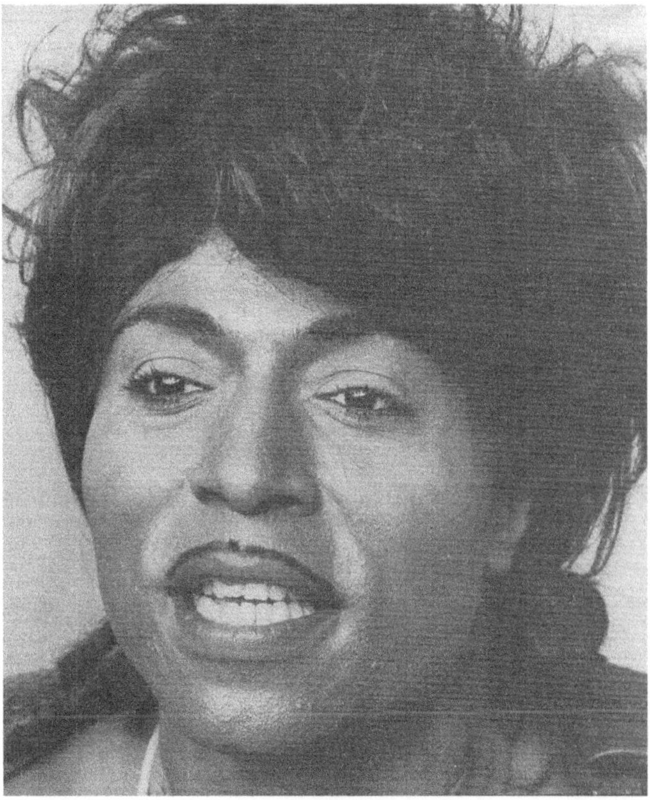

Little Richard in Toronto, 1989 (with Jim Newcombe)

Moss' Empires Ltd.

Telephone: GERRARD 2274
Telegrams: Inland
DEPICT, LESQUARE, LONDON.
Telegrams: Overseas
DEPICT, LONDON, W.C.2.

Cranbourn Mansions,
Cranbourn Street,
London, W.C.2.

Our Ref: JDB/LHH/JJ

4th October, 1962.

Raymond McFall, Esq.,
The Cavern Club,
10, Matthew Street,
Liverpool, 2.

Dear Sir,

With reference to the hiring of Liverpool Empire on Sunday, 14th October, may we remind you that there is a balance of £165. 0. 0. payable on the letting fee. This balance, in accordance with the contract, is due seven days prior to the date of the letting.

Yours faithfully,
For MOSS' EMPIRES LTD.

Chief Accountant.

(Note: The above refers to a one-nighter at the Empire Theatre, Liverpool, put on by Brian Epstein, in conjunction with Ray McFall, the owner of the Cavern Club. Top of the bill was Little Richard. The show was primarily arranged by the promoters to showcase The Beatles on stage at Liverpool's No.1 theatre, and to plug the group's first UK record release, "Love Me Do".)

Bob Wooler

PRINCE LITTLER, C.B.E. CHAIRMAN LESLIE A. MACDONNELL, O.B.E. MANAGING DIRECTOR
T. FLEMING BIRCH, F.C.A. STEWART CRUIKSHANK S. H. NEWSOME DAVID SIMPSON

Empire Theatre, Liverpool, balance payable letter, 1962

CHAPTER 8

Soul Searching

I. The Jimi Hendrix Experience

The official investigation into payola by Congress had highlighted the problems of payola and Alan Freed's career was over. Sure, he had been paid for plays but, in his defence, he only took payola on records that he personally liked or thought right for his audience. Even so, that is no justification for his actions.

Art Rupe had not been accused and had participated only occasionally. Nevertheless, Speciality all but closed down in 1960; Rupe had had enough. He kept his office in Hollywood to promote his existing catalogue and to purchase stocks and real estate.

During its heyday, Speciality had issued only 16 albums: four by Little Richard, one by Lloyd Price, one by Larry Williams and gospel LPs by Alex Bradford, the Soul Stirrers and the Original Gospel Harmonettes. One compilation featured Little Richard, Larry Williams and Lloyd Price. *Gospel Stars in Concert* featured Sam Cooke and the Soul Stirrers and showed their fervour.

Art Rupe was annoyed with himself for not appreciating Sam Cooke's potential as a secular artist and letting Bumps Blackwell walk away with a No.1 record.

Although they were cordial, Little Richard and Art Rupe had effectively parted company in 1957. Art Rupe hadn't been able to retain him on Speciality and he said, 'We did everything to get him to come back including withholding his royalties.' Whoa, you can't do that – well, he just did.

Rupe justified his position with a flimsy defence. 'We said that when you comply with your contract, we will comply with ours. We had to sue him and he countersued and he went his merry way. We put out records that I wouldn't have put out ordinarily including splicing tapes where the timing was atrocious. 'Keep A-Knockin'' and 'Ooh! My Soul' were spliced as best they could be, but the beat was lost where we made the splices.'

Richard had taken legal action in 1959 and settled for $11,000 in exchange for waiving his claim to royalties, but the resentment was always there. He needed a full audited set of accounts from Specialty, but I don't see Art Rupe as one of the real bad guys. I'm sure Sam Cooke had plenty of questions for his manager, Allen Klein and he never would receive credible answers.

Rupe said, "My artists made plenty of money. I didn't share in their personal appearances. I gave him a very fair contract, particularly as an unknown. I gave them a very low rate and I would increase it with time and performance—like you do in any industry," Of course he didn't share in the earnings for personal appearances; he wasn't Richard's agent or manager.

Little Richard's gospel records hadn't crossed over to the teenage market. Art Rupe wanted to bring him back as the Little Richard the public knew and loved. After all, the

British Beat groups were singing his praises as well as his songs. Despite his ongoing problems with Rupe, Richard agreed. Rupe paid $1,000 for Richard's release from Atlantic.

What followed was a session in Los Angeles in April 1964 with the production team of Don and Dewey – that is, Don 'Sugarcane' Harris (bass) and Dewey Terry (guitar). As this was the beat group era, Rupe thought Richard stood a better chance with guitars rather than saxophones, but Earl Palmer was still on drums.

Richard wrote 'Bama Lama Bama Loo', possibly another collection of nonsense syllables but perhaps not. Richard said that when he was young, there was a one-eyed man in Macon who sang and played the washboard for tips and everybody called him Bamalama. Years later Otis Redding recorded 'Shout Bamalama' (1962) and Little Richard 'Bama Lama Bama Loo' (1964).

It is possible that 'Bama' is short for Alabama, but whatever, there wasn't much to the song – and certainly nothing that Richard hadn't done before. Nevertheless, it was engaging and a strong return to Speciality. Richard's voice had matured and he sounded like Tom Jones singing Little Richard – indeed, Tom did record 'Bama Lama Bama Loo'.

Richard's new manager J W Alexander wrote 'Annie's Back' with John Anderson, a soul artist who worked as Kasandra. It was about someone returning home in a new Cadillac: nothing more to the storyline than that. Also recorded was the half-rock, half-calypso of 'Poor Boy Paul', but it sounded like collapso because Richard had too many words to sing. That track was not issued until 1971. Richard also took 'Miss Ann' to the Caribbean.

World's Fair commented that 'Bama Lama Bama Loo' 'was very much along the lines of 'Tutti Frutti' but then that is just what is wanted right now.'

Promoting 'Bama Lama Bama Loo', Little Richard said, 'I have decided to return to the record scene because I found so much of my music being turned into hits by other acts.'

Billboard said, 'Annie's Back – and so's Little Richard. The side really moves along with his wailing. Traditional rock'n'roll.' It reached No.82 in the Hot 100.

Richard had now decided, yes, he would tour the UK again for Don Arden. This would be a lower-scaled affair of club and ballroom dates. Richard brought along his brother Marquette – who hadn't known about the first two tours – as his valet. This time Richard told his family and the church that he'd returned to secular music, probably because he was now thinking of doing US dates.

Richard returned to the UK with guitarist Glen Willings as well as Don and Dewey. The rest of his musicians came from the Flintstones. Richard was favouring a guitar-based sound and was including 'Bama Lama Bama Loo' and 'Annie's Back'. After a couple of shows, Don and Dewey were given their own spot. Perpetually in motion, wearing pink suits and yelling 'Justine', they looked like swimming salmon from a distance, but their sound was authentic.

They all appeared on ITV's *Ready Steady Go!* and Richard had refused to mime. Quite right too: how could anyone, let alone Richard, convincingly lip sync to emotional frenzy?

On 15 May, Little Richard and his band appeared at the Plaza, Birkenhead supported by the Pete Best Four. Pete Best recalls, 'That was a cinema that had some live shows. Little Richard had an argument with one of his band and nearly didn't go on stage. We'd done our spot and the promoter said it looked like Little Richard wasn't going on. Luckily it got solved and the public wasn't aware of this raging argument at the back of the Plaza.'

Little Richard was his usual wild self, standing on the piano and waving his jacket around. 'He was incredible,' says Pete Best, 'I started watching him in the wings, but it was such a dynamic show that I went upstairs to see him from the gods. I was shouting and screaming and jumping up and down like the rest of the audience. He was an all-time great, but then all of us in the Beatles thought he was incredible. When he was in Hamburg, he taught Paul how to do those yells.'

After the UK dates, the entourage performed on the Continent. At L'Olympia, Richard worked 'Ain't That a Shame', 'I Got a Woman' and 'Tutti Frutti' into a long medley. The concert turned into a riot with chairs smashed and windows broken.

Back in the USA, Little Richard was working with a new band, the Guardsmen. As part of the show, Little Richard would sit on a throne, taking that idea from Solomon Burke, who was calling himself the King of Rock'n'Soul.

On 11 July 1964 Little Richard was with Jack Good's studio band on his US series for ABC-TV, *Shindig!* Good was attempting to bring the continuous excitement of his UK series *Oh Boy!* to American audiences with non-stop beat music, and Richard starred in the second programme. As this was being broadcast nationally, Jack Good was warned against having close-ups of Black performers – an absurd rule, and Good broke it. He had Richard singing 'Bama Lama Bama Loo' and 'Whole Lotta Shakin' Goin' on' and in both cases Richard sang the first verse and chorus in close-up. However, the frenzied end to 'Shakin'' with the jacketless Richard on his knees would have been more dramatic in close-up and without the ensemble doing the Frug alongside him. It looked contrived and lacked menace of the original rock'n'roll performances: it resembled an ad for long-lasting Duracell batteries.

Richard sang 'Joy, Joy, Joy', with the Blossoms who included Darlene Love. Indeed, the delight in watching *Shindig* is in identifying the performers on the sidelines – Delaney Bramlett, Larry Knechtel, James Burton. This was a class product ruined by Jack Good equating energy with excitement.

Richard was an inspiration for *Shindig!* and his songs were performed by others, notably the Everly Brothers with 'The Girl Can't Help It'.

Little Richard was keen to have a new recording contract and he admired the R&B catalogue of Vee-Jay Records, a highly successful, independent Black label from Chicago, started by record-shop owners Vi Carter and James Bracken in 1953. Vi's brother Calvin Carter arranged and produced the sessions. Their first success was with the Spaniels' 'Baby It's You' (not the Shirelles' song) in 1953, which made the R & B Top 10.

In 1955 the El Dorados topped the R & B chart with 'At My Front Door', which also made the US Top 20. A follow-up about the back door seemed a good idea, hence 'Bim Bam Boom', where the 'girl' at the back door is six foot two and has escaped from the zoo, hardly the wittiest of ideas and possibly nicked from Georges Brassens' 'Le Gorille' (1952). The El Dorados had another hit in 1956 with the catchy 'I'll Be Forever Lovin' You'. The following year they were featured on the first Vee-Jay LP called *Crazy Little Mama,* as a nod to their 'front door' hit.

Simultaneously, Vee-Jay developed a formidable blues catalogue, starting with Jimmy Reed's 'You Don't Have to Go' in 1954. Reed made several great (but somewhat similar) records including 'Ain't that Lovin' You, Baby', 'Baby, What You Want Me to Do', 'Big Boss Man', 'Bright Lights. Big City' and 'Take Out Some Insurance (on me, baby)' (fantastic title). Reed was often drunk and sometimes Calvin Carter would ask a policeman to lock Jimmy up the night before the session so that he would be reasonably sober in the morning.

Vee-Jay appreciated the potential of 'Duke of Earl' and asked Gene Chandler to record it. The 'Dook, dook, dook, dook of earl' riff was extremely infectious and Chandler was a fine soul singer, even if he didn't stretch himself here. Chandler would wear evening dress, cape, monocle and top hat and sing, 'Nothing can stop me now 'cause I'm the Duke of Earl.' It was a US No.2 and it became a UK beat group favourite via the Chants (who performed it but didn't record it) and Wayne Fontana and the Mindbenders (who did). Among the answer records was 'Duchess of Earl' by the Pearlettes, also on Vee-Jay.

Unlike Specialty, Vee-Jay saw the commercial sense in having white artists on the label. They had worked with the producer Bob Crewe and in 1962 he recommended the Four Seasons, who opened their account with three million-sellers, 'Sherry', 'Big Girls Don't Cry' and 'Walk Like a Man'.

In 1963 Vee-Jay picked up the licence for the Beatles' Parlophone records because Capitol, although affiliated with EMI, wasn't interested. With their new label Tollie, Vee-Jay released singles of 'Love Me Do', 'Please Please Me', 'Twist and Shout' and 'Do You Want to Know a Secret'.

When Capitol realised their mistake, Vee-Jay rode on the back of their publicity and the Vee-Jay album, *Introducing the Beatles*, because a million-seller. Unfortunately for them, this album was widely counterfeited which deprived them of revenue. This was crippling for the label's fortunes, as they had taken on additional staff and opened a West Coast office.

Vee-Jay signed Little Richard in 1964. They weren't sure what to do with him and over 18 months they recorded 26 titles – remakes of his old hits, rock'n'roll favourites and new material. Not only did Vee-Jay let Little Richard down: they also missed the potential of his young guitarist, Jimi Hendrix. Instead, they were wasting their time promoting the shock-horror single 'I Want My Baby Back' by Jimmy Cross.

At the time, Little Richard was being praised by British Beat groups and the Beatles were performing 'Long Tall Sally in every concert. There surely was the tie-in for any publicity campaign. Indeed, 'I'm Down', the B-side of 'Help!', was Paul McCartney's deliberate attempt to write and record like Little Richard.

Vee-Jay's original idea was to record songs of the rock'n'roll era that weren't associated with Richard. He had covered Jerry Lee Lewis' 'Whole Lotta Shakin' Goin' on' while at Specialty, but now he wanted to add his own spin and he opened it with typical Little Richard braggadocio: 'Well all right, everybody. I just got back from my tour over in England. Everybody's talkin' about the rockin' craze over in England. It's a craze – everybody loves it. I just finished my tour in Germany; I just left Italy; I went over to Ireland and Sweden; I stopped over in Belgium and I went over down in France. I went over to Australia, everybody's shakin'; they're rockin' in rhythm; they're havin' a good time and I just made it back to tell you it's time for you to shake. I want you to get it. C'mon over baby, whole lotta shakin' goin' on.' It's a secular sermon and although it's nonsense, it's great fun.

World's Fair said, 'Oh man, is this one wild! If 'Shakin'' doesn't bring Little Richard back to the charts then this business is a mystery. A most powerful changeover.'

It's a mystery then. The track was opportunistic and the production was a mess. Dewey Terry's lead guitar didn't match the barnstorming introduction. It was a mess because everybody was going flat out with little coordination. This was typical of these sessions: instrumental solos all over the place and a pounding rhythm that could accompany a train going downhill.

Richard should have been thinking, 'If I'm going to do 'Hound Dog', 'Money Honey', 'Lawdy Miss Clawdy' and 'Blueberry Hill', what can I bring to the party?' Instead, he was banging his keys so hard that he was close to breaking the piano. Adding all those yelps to 'Hound Dog' was childish. Both 'Short Fat Fannie' (Larry Williams) and 'Groovy Little Suzy' (a new John Marascalco song) had been written in Little Richard's style, so why perform them so poorly? His 'Short Fat Fannie' doesn't even pause for breath, quite a feat, but it's really Little Richard going through the motions.

'Money Honey' is way too fast with Little Richard trying to compensate with his 'Whoos!'. His piano playing is all over the place with the guitarist trying to keep up. 'Lawdy Miss Clawdy' fades as it is getting interesting and has a strong piano part.

Terry Gilkyson wrote 'Memories Are Made of This' about his own family life, but Little Richard ignores or overlooks the charm of the original lyric. Admittedly, Dean Martin had to fake it on his million-selling version as he was going through a divorce and said privately, 'Memories are made of shit'.

On the other hand, *World's Fair* praised 'Blueberry Hill' for its jukebox potential: 'Little Richard has a style all his own and he can make a number swing like crazy. You must simply programme this up-tempo oldie, it's great!'

The best track is the blues 'Goin' Home Tomorrow' with a violin solo from Don Harris. 'Cherry Red', also a blues performance, should have had a stripped-down arrangement: or more to the point, an arrangement. The saxophonist, Alvin 'Red' Tyler had written a good dance song 'Cross Over', but it was not hit material.

Because Little Richard gone down so well on UK club dates in May, Don Arden had announced a new tour for October. Then on the day of the first show, Little Richard cabled Arden to say that he was ill and the tour was off. (Your guess is as good as mine.) When 1,500 fans turned up for the first show at the Queen's Hall, Leeds, they were told that Little Richard wasn't appearing, but you can dance to the Pretty Things instead. The Pretty Things had rubbish thrown at them, forcing them to leave the stage, and the audience received refunds.

Little Richard's career was diving downwards, so what did Vee-Jay do next? Answer: They cut new versions of his Specialty hits. Bad, bad idea, and one that Richard succumbed to time and again. There's far too much happening in 'Lucille' – you've got Little Richard: what more do you need?

The album was released as *Little Richard – His Greatest Hits* as though it were his original recordings. Three titles were carelessly written on the cover ('Oh My Soul' for 'Ooh! My Soul'). The originals were still in print and this was a blatant attempt to make money from the same songs.

To his credit, Richard brought a slowed-down freshness to 'The Girl Can't Help It', and 'Good Golly Miss Molly' has a surprisingly rough vocal, but otherwise it is *Greatest Hits Lite*. Among these remakes, Richard also performs 'It Ain't What You Do', which is full of innuendo.

The turning point in Little Richard's time with Vee-Jay came in January 1965 when he switched to contemporary soul. The tracks were recorded in Los Angeles with Earl Palmer on drums and some meaty saxophones. Sam Cooke's 'Dance Whatcha Wanna' was written for and first recorded by Johnnie Taylor, a good pedigree for an unexceptional song. Like J W Alexander's 'Talkin' 'bout Soul', it was repetitive but good for the dance floor, and it showed some commitment towards making Little Richard relevant to the mid '60s. There was an emotional revival of 'Without Love', the nearest he came to gospel with Vee-Jay.

In 1965, if only he'd known it, Little Richard's luck was in. He was back with the

Upsetters with a revised line-up, which included a hot young guitarist, Jimi Hendrix, who joined in January. On 25 January, Hendrix sent a postcard to his father, saying that he had a job playing for Little Richard and also, that he had been mistaken for Little Richard.

Johnny Allen Hendrix was born in Seattle on 27 November 1942 while his father was stationed in Fiji. His name was chosen by his mother Lucille, who had named him after a boyfriend. When Hendrix's father Al returned, he was horrified and re-registered his name as James Marshall Hendrix. He called himself Jimmy and the spelling was changed to Jimi by his manager, Chas Chandler from the Animals, in September 1966.

Jimi's first musical instrumental was a harmonica. He saw Elvis Presley at the Sicks Stadium in Seattle on 1 September 1957 and a little while later, he saw Little Richard, who was in the neighbourhood visiting friends. (This could have been to do with Bumps Blackwell, who came from Seattle.)

Jimi got a cheap acoustic guitar in 1958 and an electric one in 1959, soon playing with the Rockin' Kings. After a suspended sentence for stealing two cars in 1961, he enlisted for three years in the army. During his service, he played in the King Kasuals. He made several parachute jumps but on his twenty-sixth, he broke his right ankle and was given an early discharge. He found work playing with Hank Ballard and the Midnighters, the Isley Brothers and Sam Cooke. And next a musical parachute jump, playing with Little Richard.

With Little Richard, Hendrix was playing a Sunburst Fender Jazzmaster with a floating tremolo arm and they played impressive venues like the Fillmore in San Francisco and the Whisky A Go Go in Atlanta.

'Jimi was really good,' says Dr John, 'Sometimes Jimi would open with a solo on Freddie's King's 'Hideaway' which he played real tough before Richard came on.'

The American rock writer Peter Guralnick says, 'I don't know anyone who could work a song better in live performance than Little Richard. I'll never forget his headlining a soul show at the Donnelly Theatre in Boston in 1965, bringing the crowd to a riveting climax as he left the microphone and crossed over to the lip of the stage, with an unknown Jimi Hendrix playing guitar behind him. For close to 10 minutes, Richard continued to sing, expound, and expand upon the classic 1950s inspirational number 'Shake a Hand'.'

On 17 April 1965 Hendrix played with Little Richard on Soupy Sales' *Easter Show* at the Paramount on Broadway along with King Curtis, Shirley Ellis, the Exciters and from the UK, the Hollies and Sandie Shaw. There were five shows a day and a film between each performance.

Bobby Elliott of the Hollies explains how it worked: 'The show started at 9 am. with a film and it went through the day as rock show, film, rock show, film. The big band was led by King Curtis and we would run on stage for two songs. The compère was Hal Jackson, and he would say, "OK, folks, fasten your seatbelts because here from little ole England come the Hollies." I had to climb up this ladder at the back of the stage and jump on the drum-kit that belonged to King Curtis' drummer. We would do 'Rockin' Robin' and 'Just One Look', as every act including Little Richard was only allowed two songs and as the week went on and the band got to know us, other musicians would play with us.'

Timing was crucial, which was anathema to Little Richard. Bobby Elliott: 'The audience would see the movie and then the big band would rise up out of the floor. I remember going out for a coffee and coming back and finding Little Richard was being thrown out for overrunning. He had been told to do two songs and he went on for 20 minutes and ruined the schedules. A New York cop was escorting him off the premises and waving a revolver at him. Little Richard was saying, 'I don't understand it. The little white girls love me.' The cop said, 'Do you want your head blown off?' I had only just come over on the plane from Manchester and this was my first time in New York.'

It is difficult to determine exactly what Jimi Hendrix recorded with Little Richard, but one song is certain, 'I Don't Know What You Got (But It's Got Me)', which was written by Don Covay. Covay had written Chubby Checker's smash, 'Pony Time', and his soul songs included 'Mercy Mercy' and 'Seesaw'. He often worked with Atlantic artists and if Richard had not been around, this song would surely have gone to Solomon Burke. Richard emulated Burke's intense preacher-style vocals and it is the best record that Solomon Burke never made. Similarly, Jimi Hendrix matches what Steve Cropper was playing on Stax Records. The full session details are unknown (or unknown to me, at any rate) but the organist, according to *Record Mirror*, was Billy Preston. This makes sense but it assumes that Preston had forgiven Richard for leaving him stranded in Hamburg.

The song is as intense as it is witty as Richard's friends tell him about his wife's affair. It was released as a two-part single and given a UK release by Philips, but other takes have appeared on compilations. The Philips single is definitive. It was produced by Calvin Carter and the other songs on the session were a competent Motown-styled dancer, 'You Better Stop' and 'Something Moves in My Heart' and Richard's own 'Everytime I Think About You'.

If only Vee-Jay had been able to make an album with Little Richard in the same vein. As it was the label was undergoing financial troubles which led to a forced sale in 1966 – and Little Richard would be on the move again. When *Record Mirror* ran a feature on George Harrison at home, its writer, Tony Hall, noticed a single on his jukebox – 'I Don't Know What You've Got' by Little Richard.

Hendrix hated the concept of band uniforms and making movements on cue, but he was not alone in that. When he and another guitarist Glen Willings bought coloured shirts and wore them on stage, Richard told them, 'Brothers, I am Little Richard and I am the king of rock'n'roll and I am the one who has to look pretty on stage. If you wear those shirts again, you will be fined.' He also fined Hendrix $5 for not having his hair cut.

When he wasn't hassling Hendrix over his wardrobe, Richard was trying to get the guitarist's clothes off altogether. Rosa Lee Brooks, a girlfriend of Hendrix, said, 'When I first met Jimi, he was under so much stress from being chased by Little Richard.' When Hendrix made it clear that his jimmy was off limits, Richard asked to watch Hendrix and Brooks make love. That, too, was refused.

Jimi Hendrix left Little Richard in June for Ike and Tina Turner, but that was short-lived. He returned for a few more gigs but finished playing with him in July 1965. It is said that Jimi Hendrix was fired for his indiscretions, but it's not true. In a postcard to his father, Hendrix wrote, 'Richard didn't pay us for five weeks and you can't live on promises when you're on the road, so I had to cut loose.'

Musically, Hendrix may not have learned much from Richard but he had learned about presentation – that is, the 'show' aspect of show business. In 1966 Jimi Hendrix was brought to the UK by Chas Chandler of the Animals and we all know what happened next. Jimi Hendrix said, 'I want to do with my music what Little Richard can do with his voice.' And would Jimi Hendrix have had that little moustache if it wasn't for Richard?

There is a postscript to the Little Richard and Jimi Hendrix story. In 1976 an album appeared in the UK called *Friends from the Beginning* and featuring Little Richard and Jimi

Hendrix. If the LP was suspect in 1976, it was even dodgier in 1998 on its CD release and I am confident that Jimi Hendrix isn't on any track and I rather doubt that Richard is on the insipid instrumentals, 'Belle Stars', 'Funky Dish Rag' and the instrumental version of 'Long Tall Sally', here called 'Tutti Frutti'. Richard's workout of Hank Williams' 'Why Don't You Love Me' can only have been an early rehearsal. *Caveat emptor.*

In October 1965 the Merseybeats wanted to set a world record for non-stop playing, and it would be at the Cavern in Liverpool. They played a gig in Bridlington first and drove back for the all-night session, hardly the best way to prepare for such an ordeal. They managed to play for eight hours before the drummer John Banks collapsed, so they didn't quite make it. However, their set included a half-hour version of 'Long Tall Sally'. Surely 'Long Tall Sally' should be a short quick burst.

II. Richard Meets Monty

Monty Lister presented the very popular *Tune Tonic* on BBC Radio Merseyside every Sunday morning. He was a superb broadcaster, full of compassion and totally genuine. Before that, he had worked in hospital radio on the Wirral and he had a collection of interviews with American stars who visited Liverpool during the golden years of rock'n'roll. Tape recorders were a rarity then and the performers must have been surprised as Monty stumbled in with his not-so-portable equipment. They invariably agreed to the interviews even though they would only be heard on a hospital radio station in the Wirral.

In 1995 I was finishing a series about Monty's interviews for the rock'n'roll magazine, *Now Dig This*. 'What's left?' I asked. 'Well,' he said, 'how about Winifred Atwell?' 'Not *Now Dig This*,' I told him. I thought we'd reached the end of the line but then he added, 'I've got Little Richard, but I didn't like him very much. He seemed very big-headed.'

I couldn't believe my luck. Here is Little Richard with Monty Lister backstage at the Plaza Cinema, Birkenhead on 15 May 1964. Strange isn't it, that so many rock'n'roll stage-shows took place in cinemas? The bill for this one included the Undertakers and the Pete Best Four. The Undertakers' lead singer Jackie Lomax could do a mean Little Richard.

MONTY: I'm very delighted to say hello to the star of the show at the Plaza Theatre, Birkenhead this evening. It's the most dynamic person in show business today, Little Richard. Welcome to our programme, sir.

LITTLE RICHARD: I'm very glad to be here and I am always glad to come to Liverpool. Such wonderful entertainment comes out of Liverpool, so much dynamics that sometimes I feel that I am not dynamic at all.

MONTY: You've have been dynamic for a long, long time - about seven years, I would think.

LITTLE RICHARD: No, about fifteen years.

MONTY: Fifteen years? What is the secret of your success? How do you manage to stay at the top?

LITTLE RICHARD: When people come to see me, I work hard. If it's only for two people, I work hard. If it's three people, I work hard because I love what I'm doing. I enjoy it just as much as my audience does. I love it. I feel just like Lucille, that's the way I feel! By doing this I have become a legend over the world. I haven't had a record out in seven years and yet we had two sell-out houses last night. Most of the places we go are complete sell-outs, all over the world. I put everything I can muscle and bustle into my act.

MONTY: Don't you feel exhausted after all that?

LITTLE RICHARD: No, I feel good. I feel that I could stay out there a little longer. Sometimes the theatres tell me to come off when I want to stay on longer.

MONTY: And of course the audiences wish the same...

LITTLE RICHARD: Oh, yes!

MONTY: We sometimes read that you are going to give it all up. Is this true?

LITTLE RICHARD: I have just returned! It is not a comeback: a comeback is for an artist that has died out. I have returned to my rightful position in rock'n'roll or rhythm and blues - I like to call it rock'n'rhythm. I came back because so many artists are capitalising on my style, making millions. I thought I would come back and give them the original tunes and the original sound from Little Richard. My new recording is coming out in a few days which is 'Bama Lama Bama Loo' on London Records and it is going to be a worldwide success.

MONTY: Of the previous songs you have done, which one has given you the most pleasure?

LITTLE RICHARD: It is very hard to say. The one that made me happiest is the one that sold more than others. I have sold 32 million records and one of them, 'Long Tall Sally', sold five million. Pat Boone and Elvis Presley covered me. 'Rip It Up' was covered by Bill Haley and 'Good Golly Miss Molly' was covered by Jerry Lee Lewis.

MONTY: But still you came out on top.

LITTLE RICHARD: Oh yes, and I wrote all of them too.

MONTY: Is it a secret if I ask you what your name is. I only know you as Little Richard.

LITTLE RICHARD: My real name is Ricardo Wayne Penniman. I was called Little Richard when I was very small, and I never changed it. I'm not that small now. I feel small but I am not in stature.

MONTY: I would like to introduce to someone who is also not very little, in fact, he is 6 foot 2. He is Steve Heyes and he would like to ask you some questions from a teenager's point of view.

LITTLE RICHARD (obviously rolling his eyes, you might even think he was flirting) I would be very happy to talk to Steve. He seems to be a wonderful person!

STEVE: (very seriously) Thank you. Over your long career, you must have played in many countries. Which country do you like best?

LITTLE RICHARD: Well, England is so receptive and it is the one that I feel most gracious about. They speak English here and I can understand them. The people are so warm. I love all the countries I have been in but I love England best.

MONTY: That's very nice to hear.

STEVE: You've done films and you've done stage shows, which do you like best?

LITTLE RICHARD: I like television and I like recording and I am getting ready to make a film and I will be starring in this film, acting and everything. It will be my first and I think I deserve it for the years I have put into this business. I like everything about my career. I love entertaining.

MONTY: And we like being entertained by you. There is no point in me wishing you success because you are obviously going to get it, but on behalf of all the patients who are listening to this, I would like to wish you all the very best.

LITTLE RICHARD: I would like to say to all the patients - I hope you have a speedy recovery and may God bless all of you.

STEVE: Just one more question, Monty, please. When you do your act, you jump on the piano, is that right?

LITTLE RICHARD: Yes, I love to jump on the piano.

STEVE: Have you ever fallen through?

LITTLE RICHARD: No, because I have been doing this so long and I know how to balance myself. If I did fall, I would include it in my act anyway.

STEVE: But some of these old pianos must look like they are giving in on you.

LITTLE RICHARD: No, when I see them giving in, I give out!

MONTY: Thanks again.

LITTLE RICHARD: Thanks a million, Bye-bye.

CHAPTER 9
Get Down with It

Oh dear. I appreciate of course that Little Richard was unmanageable, that he was someone who followed his own whims and that if he agreed to do something one day, he might not do it the next.

Also, some of his career choices were absurd and they ridiculed all the wonderful recordings he had made for Specialty. What he did in 1966, 10 years on from his rise to fame, proves the point.

Little Richard signed with Modern Records, founded in Los Angeles by the Bihari brothers in 1945 and noted for its blues and R & B catalogue with Lightnin' Hopkins, John Lee Hooker, Etta James and Young Jessie. Little Richard and Modern Records should have worked well. However, the label had gone through hard times and was hoping to regain its status with Ike and Tina Turner ('Goodbye, So Long'), the Ikettes (Peaches 'n' Cream') and now Little Richard.

A live recording from the Domino Club in Atlanta was an unadventurous start. Little Richard and the Upsetters played there for a fortnight in December 1965 and I suspect that Richard told the Biharis that he had live tapes which they could release. The Biharis agreed because it would give them classic titles for the catalogue.

There was a drawback. The performances were so mannered and so bad that John Waterfield, the vice-president of Little Richard's UK fan club, resigned in disgust. Little Richard showed no feeling for his old hits, yelping his way through them and his introductions were ridiculous. They were end-of-the-pier performances.

'Slippin' 'n' Slidin'' is reasonable and I like the way the female vocalist encourages him in 'Baby, What You Want Me to Do'. There is some modern soul with 'Do You Feel It', but these are slim pickings. It's interesting to hear Larry Williams' 'Bony Moronie' in view of what happens next but Richard takes the song too fast.

What's more, these tapes have surely been doctored with applause overdubbed. Some performances may come from a soundcheck, which would explain why 'Baby, What You Want Me To Do' was only a minute long (and also mistitled for the record – nobody cared.) For all that, the album was called *The Incredible Little Richard Sings His Greatest Hits – Live!* They got a second LP from these tapes too, *The Wild and Frantic Little Richard!,* but in all cases, the original studio recordings are better: of course they are.

Bumps Blackwell returned as Little Richard's manager and he and Bumps promoted the two-part 'Do You Feel It' which they had written together. Bumps had produced a studio recording for Richard and the Upsetters. It's good contemporary soul on the lines of Wilson Pickett, but it isn't much of a song.

In the spring of 1966, Modern Records recorded Little Richard with soul musicians at the Sun Studios in Memphis, so it was Little Richard in a great studio with class musicians including Lowman Pauling from the "5" Royales, who was an ace guitarist and the writer of 'Dedicated to the One I Love'.

'Holy Mackerel' was a good, lively single. Little Richard is going to see his girlfriend and has trouble with her father who says, 'Holy mackerel' whenever he calls. 'Your father must think I'm a fish,' sings Richard, telling her dad that 'Richard is my name'. It's good fun but Richard was becoming a parody of himself. The B-side, 'I'm Back', is good with Richard declaring that he is now in a 'brand new groove'.

Richard continued with his preoccupation with 'Directly from My Heart' and there's a passionate 'I moan, I groan cause I'm so all alone.' Another favourite was 'Baby', which emanated from Count Basie but had been reworked by Lloyd Price. Richard sang 'Baby, don't you want a man like me' but in concert it might be changed to 'Baby, don't you want a man like Little Richard'. Richard covered Sam Cooke's 'Bring It on Home to Me' (obviously, you can't top Cooke's vocal) and 'Do the Jerk', which would be reworked as 'Get Down with It'.

Little Richard was only with Modern for six months and then he moved to one of the oldest Black labels, OKeh. It had been started in the 1930s as a subsidiary of Columbia Records whose singles would only be 35 cents. It developed an important roster of blues, gospel and R & B acts including the Treniers, Chuck Willis, Big Maybelle and Screamin' Jay Hawkins. They took Little Richard as a package – he would be produced by Larry Williams and the lead guitarist would be Johnny 'Guitar' Watson. The arranger, Arthur Wright, would have a stellar career with Motown, working with Diana Ross and Marvin Gaye. What's not to like?

There were four sessions at the CBS in Hollywood and they started with the excellent 'Poor Dog', written by Larry Williams and Johnny 'Guitar' Watson. It was a poor dog that couldn't wag its own tail and it was in the wry vein of 'Holy Mackerel' but better and with a homespun message: 'Look after yourself'. The other side was the song Sam Cooke had written for Little Richard, 'Well'.

Both sides of the second single were written by Larry Williams. 'I Need Love' was a homage to Smokey Robinson's 'You Really Got a Hold on Me', a good song and performance, if derivative. 'The Commandments of Love' followed the Moonglows' doo-wop hit 'Ten Commandments of Love', and although dated, it worked fine.

Otto Preminger was making the film *Hurry Sundown* starring Michael Caine and Jane Fonda with Hugo Montenegro writing and conducting the music. Preminger wanted something folkier for the credits and commissioned a song elsewhere: he did not use it but it was recorded by Peter, Paul and Mary and released somewhat confusingly as a single. Meanwhile, Hugo Montenegro had turned one of his themes into the title song and although it was not heard in the film, it was recorded by Little Richard and intended for publicity. It's a good record with Richard showing his vocal range. Preminger was hoping for another *Gone with the Wind*, but the film was criticised for racial stereotyping. To be fair to Preminger, it was set in 1946 and a lot had happened in those intervening years. In 2017 Little Richard's 'Hurry Sundown' had a surprising revival when Jimmy McGill was arrested in 'Sunk Costs', an episode of *Better Call Saul*.

The other side of Richard's single, 'I Don't Want to Discuss It', was one of his best contemporary soul performances, but not as strong as the frantic version by Delaney & Bonnie with Eric Clapton. The song has also been recorded by Amen Corner and Rod Stewart.

The fourth single was Chuck Willis' excellent blues ballad 'Don't Deceive Me', which Richard performed to perfection. This is why Richard is so frustrating: he could weave magic if he wished. The wistful blues on the flip, 'Never Gonna Let You Go', was good too.

The fifth and final OKeh single 'A Little Bit of Something' was another Larry Williams song, this time with the sermonising slant of Joe Tex's 'Hold What You've Got'. On the flip was a good performance of Barrett Strong's 'Money', famous now for its outing with the Beatles.

Other studio tracks were Chris Kenner's 'Land of a 1,000 Dances', which had been a big hit for Wilson Pickett. Richard is not as controlled as the wicked Pickett and this sounds like frenzy for its own sake. 'Function at the Junction' was written by Shorty Long, a compère of Motown stage shows. Overall, Larry Williams had produced the best results for Little Richard since he left Specialty, although Richard was to say that he was the worst producer he had experienced. He did qualify the remark: 'He wanted me to copy Motown and I was no Motown artist.' Also, by then, he had fallen out with Williams in a big way.

The Northern Soul movement found favour around Wigan and Manchester in the mid '70s and the DJs loved turning obscure soul 45s into dance classics. Little Richard was very popular with 'A Little Bit of Something', 'I Don't Want to Discuss It', 'Talkin' 'bout Soul' and' Get Down with It'. 'Do the Jerk' was a favourite at the Twisted Wheel in Manchester. Most unexpectedly, the Upsetters' instrumental, 'Jaywalking' from 1960, was heard on the dance floors.

The UK promoter Roy Tempest promoted a string of dubious acts. A former Coaster, Cornel Gunter was encouraged to bring some musical chums to the UK as the Original Coasters. They did club dates and Gunter told the punters that he was prettier than Cassius Clay and Little Richard.

In November 1966 Little Richard came to the UK for three weeks of dates for the promoters Barry Clayman, Maurice King and Colin Berlin. There would be a brief trip to the Paris Olympia too. Richard didn't bring his band but he came over with the mother, Leva Mae, his aunt Roberta and his cousin, Roy Chester. Roy had hopes of a professional career and he opened for Richard.

Richard was backed by Johnny B Great (actually Johnny Goodison) and the Quotations and they mostly played ballrooms including the Wigan Casino, albeit long before Northern Soul. He was billed alongside the ballad singer Vince Hill at Wigan Casino.

At the press conference on 21 November, Richard said he endorsed the Love Generation as his music was about love, the universal language. He announced that he was a rock'n'roll singer and no longer a church minister, so what happened there?

Richard wore a gold lamé jacket for an appearance on ITV's *Ready Steady Go!* and when he performed 'I Need Love' and 'Good Golly Miss Molly', Ben E King could be seen applauding. He was also on BBC-TV's *Top of the Pops* singing 'I Need Love'; so the record company was definitely trying to get it away.

On 11 December, Richard topped the bill at Brian Epstein's Saville Theatre in Shaftesbury Avenue in the West End of London, supported by the Alan Price Set and Bluesology (with Elton John). Eric Burdon of the Animals was asked to introduce Richard, but some Welsh Teddy Boys regarded Burdon as the enemy and barracked him. Burdon told me, 'Welsh Teds weren't just rock fans. For them, it was a way of life.' The audience included Mick Jagger, Lionel Bart, Cilla Black, Georgie Fame and Dave Clark, and Dave Clark must have been worried sitting alongside those Welsh Teds.

When Burdon went on stage, the Teds hurled missiles and the speakers went off before he had time to say anything. Burdon went back in the wings while the sound was repaired and when he returned, he wore a World War II helmet that Chris Farlowe had just given him. The missiles continued and he shouted, 'All right, you fuckers, you fuckin' asked for it and now you're fuckin' gonna get it. Here's Little fuckin' Richard!' It was the best introduction that Richard ever had – indeed, it was possibly the best introduction that anyone has ever had anywhere in the world, and it worked a treat.

Little Richard cut out his showbiz antics, knowing he had a diehard rocker audience. He performed well but he had a cold and used an inhaler when his voice gave out on 'Long Tall Sally'. The Teds and their girlfriends were continually rushing the stage and some danced while Richard was playing. His voice again gave out in his closer, 'Whole Lotta Shakin' Goin' On', but everybody was well satisfied. After the show, Brian Epstein offered Little Richard a management contract – another 'might have been' situation for both parties.

While Richard was in London, there was a session at Abbey Road for OKeh, which worked out extremely well with Norman 'Hurricane' Smith producing. Smith had worked with the Beatles and Pink Floyd. Richard had sorted out 'Get Down With It' by now and his opening spiel about this being his own beautiful hair and not a wig was hilarious, especially when it was so obviously a wig. Richard was speaking so fast that he forgot what he was saying. There may have been a better, cleaner take but this works fine. It is the best rock'n'roll record to have been made in the UK, so how's that for praise?

Although it referred to an obsolete dance, the Jerk, it didn't stop Slade having their first hit with it in 1971. The song had been written and recorded by the New Orleans performer Bobby Marchan in 1964 and picked up by Richard. When Slade released it, Polydor listed a songwriting credit for Slade with Little Richard – wrong on both counts. Legal action had to be taken.

Dave Hill of Slade: 'We liked entertaining people in clubs and pubs and we found this rock song where people could stamp their feet and clap their hands during that song. That Little Richard record had a great atmosphere and you didn't get that in records at the time. We added the idea of a band stomping and the audience being in on it. The radio stations like it and then we got on *Top Of The Pops* which was our breakthrough.'

As for Bobby Marchan, he had a drag identity as Roberta and had been an influence on Little Richard, and when Chas White first met Roberta, he didn't realise it was Bobby in drag.

'Rosemary' was a brassy performance of a charming Fats Domino song for his wife. His 'Hound Dog' was really intended for a live audience as he pointed "You', 'You' and 'Not You'. There are too many yelps, although, to be fair, the song is called 'Hound Dog'. 'Rockin' Chair' is Richard's little tribute to England but there's no real song there.

Richard's final shows in the UK were a double-header of two clubs in Manchester, the Princess and the Domino. At the end of his first number at the Princess, he shouted, 'The piano isn't loud enough', which was quickly sorted. The audience loved him and he said, 'Even if I'm dead and in my casket, I would still sing if the fans wanted me too.'

Larry Williams had come to the UK in 1965, doing some shows with Johnny 'Guitar' Watson and working with a local band, the Stormsville Shakers, led by Phillip Goodhand-Tait. He recorded an album of new songs, *The Larry Williams Show* for Decca and *Larry Williams on Stage* for Sue, where the select audience included Screaming Lord

Sutch and Screamin' Jay Hawkins. Tait described Watson's playing as 'Chuck Berry and Jimi Hendrix combined into one'.

On 23 January 1967 Larry Williams produced a live album for Little Richard at the main CBS Studio in Hollywood, which was generally used for symphony orchestras. It was renamed the OKeh Club for the event but it is the same old, same old: OKeh simply wanted his hits in their catalogue. It could have, it should have, worked with Johnny 'Guitar' Watson. Billy Preston is said to be with him too, though I can't hear any organ.

Around this time, Frank Zappa acknowledged the influence of Johnny 'Guitar' Watson on his guitar parts for the Mothers of Invention's album, *Freak Out!*

Little Richard's album has a playing time of 28 minutes and a set list of 12 songs. The songs are even shorter than that implies as the timing includes Little Richard's rants – 'I am the most beautiful man in show business', 'Sock it to me, baby' and a claim that he isn't wearing a wig, which is on a par with President Trump's assertion on his own barnet. With all his yelps, Richard sounded like a children's entertainer. The band played way too fast and going too fast doesn't necessarily mean more excitement. Still, 'The Girl Can't Help It' worked as a pounding blues: if only it were longer. They could have slowed it down, worked out some fresh arrangements, and got Richard and Larry to perform together on something, say, 'Justine'.

Although I criticise the album, this is the first album that gives us Little Richard as he was on the stage in all his barking glory. Wherever you've gone, I've been there, and now I'm back. I am what I am – oo, oo, oo, my, my, my! My music is the healing music that makes the blind see, the lame walk and there's a whole lotta shakin' goin' on.' Cue for song.

The album, *Little Richard's Greatest Hits*, didn't sell because it was sub-standard but Richard saw it otherwise. 'It didn't sell at all because it was on OKeh which is an R & B label. It was originally meant to come out on Epic and it would have done a lot better because I am not primarily a black artist. A lot of the jocks in South couldn't forgive me for giving up the ministry.'

There's worse. In 1967 Richard made a guest appearance in a beach party movie, *Catalina Caper,* which promised 'wild adventures and international intrigue' on a cruise ship which sailed from Long Beach to Catalina Island. It starred Tommy Kirk, a decent actor whose career had been stalled when he was arrested for homosexuality. Most of the passengers were of retirement age but suddenly, teenagers appeared and danced frenziedly on the deck. Richard came down a staircase and joined them for 'Scuba Party' backed by the Cascades who were known for 'Rhythm of the Rain'.

This dreadful film was made by Lee Sholem, known as Roll' em Sholem. This industrious man directed 1,300 films and TV episodes, including *Tarzan, Ma and Pa Kettle* and *Bronco.* He also directed *The Adventures of Superman* (1952) and when Phyllis Coates, who was playing Lois Lane, got hit in the face by accident, Sholem ordered her to finish the scene before her face swelled up.

So come on, Richard, what are you playing at? The Beatles are making *Sgt Pepper*. The whole film is waterlogged and forgettable except for one thing – look at Richard in his tight, gold lamé trousers; don't you think that Prince must have seen this film?

In the summer of 1967 Little Richard moved to Brunswick, a major label which wanted to establish him as a soul performer. The first two singles were produced in New York City by Nat Tarnopol with arrangements by Bert Decoteaux. Don Covay wrote the first single, 'Try Some of Mine', which has a Stax sound and Richard declaring, 'I'm a soul man, baby'. It's a good record, but I'm not sure people buy songs that start 'You've one foot in the grave'. Richard and Don wrote the B-side 'She's Together' together,

The second single, 'Baby, Don't You Tear My Clothes', is a typical Little Richard rant and indeed written by him and J W Alexander. It is about the importance of brand names, and though it features Richard on piano, it isn't much of a record. For the B-side, Richard recorded an Esquerita song, 'Stingy Jenny'. It has a wild vocal but the backing is restrained and goes nowhere.

Brunswick took Richard to Chicago for some Chicago Soul, produced by Carl Davis and Willie Henderson. 'Soul Train' is an exhortation to dance crossed with James Brown's 'Night Train'. Good but not great. Tony Matthews' song, 'Can I Count on You' lacks originality but Richard, no doubt inspired by Aretha Franklin, sings, 'I want to be your do right man,'

Richard was disillusioned as his time with Modern, OKeh and Brunswick hadn't been very productive, certainly not financially. He toyed with starting his own label like Sam Cooke, but that was hard work. Larry Williams convinced Richard to focus on his live shows. By 1968, he had ditched the Upsetters for his new backup band, the Crown Jewels, run by Eddie Fletcher, and performed on the Canadian TV show, *Where It's At.*

Both Bumps Blackwell and J W Alexander shared his management. He was placed with the ABC agency, which had Lou Rawls. If a promoter booked Little Richard now, he had to pay half the fee in advance.

There was a revival in old rock'n'roll records in the mid-1960s, which had prompted record companies to revitalise their old catalogue. Art Rupe repackaged his Little Richard recordings for Specialty with the cartoonish but knowledgeable DJ, Dr Demento. The new Little Richard compilation had the logo 'Plays on all phonographs' – industry talk for 'Rechannelled stereo', so 'No, thank you'.

Pete Kirkham discussed the reissue of the original 'Good Golly Miss Molly' with the jukebox owners in *World's Fair*: 'Little Richard lives! This vigorous entertainer is to my mind the greatest of all rock artists. Absolutely hysterical. Fabulously exciting piano, rich colourful sax and pounding relentless beat. As a discotheque sound, it has few equals. And if anything from the rock era merits renewed popularity, I think this is it. This and the flip 'Lucille' were massive in their day, and with sufficient exposure and the rock revival gaining momentum, it has chances. Be prepared.'

In June 1968 Richard was booked into the prestigious Aladdin Hotel & Casino in Las Vegas for a fortnight. It took place just before Elvis and the Colonel decided that Vegas was a career move. The casino owners didn't mind paying top dollar for their attractions because much of it came back via the roulette wheel anyway. Fats Domino was in a spiral and had to play free shows to repay his debts. In June 1969 Ray Charles, Solomon Burke, Gladys Knight and the Pips, Aretha Franklin, Little Richard and poor ol' Fats were all within a few blocks of each other on the strip. Quite a change from ten years earlier when the big attraction was Liberace and invariably white.

Richard's dates were successful, and he did the same in Atlantic City, telling an audience: "Lucille' always wins for me. There's something about that riff that is electrifying.' He played before 10,000 at the Woolman Skating Rink in Central Park where his forty-minute set only contained three songs. He did arena shows including Madison Square Garden. When asked if he was making a comeback, he would say, 'No, the world is making a comeback.'

In 1968, Jack Good thought he could combine his passions for rock'n'roll and the Bard with a rock version of *Othello* called *Catch My Soul* and with some outrageous casting.

Jack Good: 'I was trying to persuade a producer who was staging *Catch My Soul* in Los Angeles that he should have Little Richard as Othello and Jerry Lee Lewis as Iago. He didn't agree and I thought I'd better get Richard involved with Shakespeare and see what he would be like. I took him to a cinema to see Laurence Olivier's *Othello*. Richard and I got very good seats in the front of the the circle, but he was wearing a very high wig and I felt terribly embarrassed because the people behind him couldn't see anything. I said, 'Richard, could you take off your wig as the lady behind you can't see.' He was very nice about it: he took it off and he put in a brown paper bag. After we saw the film, he said, "Hey, man, that was cool. I thought I'd seen all the black actors, but I hadn't. This dude is good." I said, "But Laurence Olivier isn't a black actor," Richard said, "He ain't a black actor! Well, what does he do for a living?" He stared at me with his great saucer eyes and he said, "Tell me, man, where did he get all that action from?" We went back to my place and I tried to get him to say a few lines but it was pretty impossible, although I do think we could have made something out of it. However, when he left my flat, he forgot his wig, which was still in the brown paper bag. My daughter came in and said, "Daddy, that man has left his fish and chips" and that's because the bag was all greasy.'

On 2 August 1969, a few weeks before Woodstock, he closed the open-air Atlantic City Pop Festival, following a set by Janis Joplin and performing to an audience of 60,000. It was raining and the band was wary of electrocution. They were dressed for night club appearances, but Little Richard was wearing his new jacket of flashing mirrors. The hippie audience loved him as he declared, 'I am the only one left. I am the King of Rock'n'Roll.'

Before Richard sang 'Joy to the World', he spoke of the healing power of his music: 'We got everybody here tonight. We got black folk. We got white folk. We got red folk. We got brown folk. We got yellow folk. We got real folk. We got love folk. I want you all to know that I am here tonight, and I've been talking about love for a *long* time, because, honey, I'm the man who started it all – the Emancipator of Soul and the King of Rock'n'Roll from Macon, Georgia. I want you all to know that the Beauty is still on duty. Let it all hang out with the *beautiful* Little Richard from down in Macon, Georgia. I want you all to know that I *am* the Georgia Peach. A man walked up to me yesterday and said, "Richard, don't you know that James Brown can beat you at dancing?" I said, "Beat me dancing? Maybe but have you ever thought that he don't look like me?" Shut up! I am the star. And don't you *ever* forget it.'

In order to be seen in larger venues, he worked on lavish outfits, usually to his own designers. His mirrored jerkin over white top and trousers was a ridiculous idea and even worse in practice. Richard later said his mirror jacket weighed 10 pounds and wasn't suitable for throwing into the audience. Then he had a lighter, and hopefully less dangerous, version made. The cost of each jacket was $600.

In order to promote his concerts, Richard would appear loudly and brashly on American chat shows. He never gave much away and if he got a question he didn't like, he'd shout 'Shut up!', not an approach a politician could take. It didn't matter – it sold Little Richard the package, Little Richard the brand.

However, it went horribly wrong when Richard appeared on Dick Cavett's syndicated show with Erich Segal, a university professor who had written *Love Story*, the Broadway critic John Simon and the actress Rita Moreno. Richard, colourfully dressed, was quiet when Segal and Simon disagreed over the merits of *Love Story*, but after 10 minutes Richard was bored from the inattention and told them to 'Shut up!'.

After criticising Simon, Segal was confronted by Richard, who said he had never read any book but the Bible. Richard said there was no point in writing love stories as everybody's idea of love was different. Segal could have responded that the same could be said of love songs. Richard said his own book was going to be called *He Got What He Wanted But He Lost What He Had.*

In January 1969 Little Richard was set for a profitable European tour with large shows in six countries. His concert at the Royal Albert Hall was going to be filmed by Yorkshire TV after the BBC had turned it down; there is a curt 'No' from Bill Cotton Jr in the BBC's Written Archives.

Richard was featured with Fats Domino and Jerry Lee Lewis on a TV special with the Monkees. Peter Tork recalled, 'There was a TV special *33 1/3* and we had Jerry Lee Lewis, Little Richard and Fats Domino on top of each other playing their pianos. Four pianists actually, as Brian Auger was on the very top. They were banging away together and it was fabulous. I got to meet Little Richard who could have been a great blues singer but he is the greatest rock'n'roll singer of all-time. He is to rock'n'roll singing what Jimi Hendrix was to rock guitar. 'Lucille' gets me every time.'

'I hated that show,' said Richard told *Rolling Stone* in 1970, 'They were really trying to rebuild the Monkees and they had me and Fats and Jerry Lee to build them up. We knew what they were doing but we went on and did the show.'

When Little Richard and Jerry Lee Lewis were booked for the Cobo Arena, Detroit, there was the expected disagreement as to who would close. Jerry Lee won but he didn't really because when he started performing, Richard came out for photographs and autographs.

When Richard was on the same bill as Ike and Tina Turner in San Diego, he was less sure that he could top her because she could dance sensationally. Not to worry – during his performance, he climbed a twenty-foot lighting rig and bopped around during a wild saxophone solo. He also did well at the Coconut Grove in Los Angeles.

But perhaps the merger of the talents came when both Chuck Berry and Little Richard were booked to play at the same school hall in Connecticut. Chuck was top of the bill but Little Richard was still calling himself the King of Rock'n'Roll. 'It meant nothing to me,' said Chuck in his autobiography, 'as long as I was satisfied with the fee.' This, according to the book, was the first time they had met. Richard said, 'Chuck, I've wanted to perform with you since the first time I saw you on television.' Chuck said, 'You mean to make love?' Richard smiled, 'You'd love it. It's like no other performance in the world.' Chuck made his excuses and left.

Little Richard joined Delaney and Bonnie for a funky version of his old B-side, 'Miss Ann'. Delaney was taking the vocals, but Richard was hitting the 88s incorporating a solo.

On 13 September 1969 a rock'n'roll festival featuring the 1950s legends was held at the Varsity Stadium in Toronto which could hold 20,000 fans. The day-long festival starred Chuck Berry, Bo Diddley, Bill Haley, Jerry Lee Lewis, Little Richard and Gene Vincent with Bumps Blackwell being one of the organisers. As well as those legendary rock'n'rollers, there were the Doors, Alice Cooper, Tony Joe White and unexpectedly, Screamin' Lord Sutch. The festival was filmed by D A Pennebaker and released as *Sweet Toronto* in 1971.

It was an admirable objective to gather these rock'n'roll legends together, but as the organisers needed contemporary acts for ticket sales, it led to an incongruous mix. The

'50s had been the bedrock for '60s music but this was now a world of prog and psych and recreational drugs. The next generation had built upon it in a way that the originators didn't understand. Little Richard was not so much a cutting-edge pioneer as a vaudeville sideshow. I would love to know what Little Richard thought of the Jimi Hendrix Experience – but publicly at least, he didn't pass judgment. Richard had created the '60s but was no longer part in it. He was now selling nostalgia.

Nevertheless, this mix of the old and new wasn't bringing in big sales and with a week to go, the promoter John Brower called the Beatles at Apple and asked John Lennon if he would like to watch his heroes as a celebrity guest. John said that he would do more than that – he would perform. He put together a band with Eric Clapton, Klaus Voormann, Alan White and, of course, Yoko Ono.

It was said to be his first show since 1966 though that wasn't entirely true: he'd had a few one-off performances at small venues with Yoko Ono, which usually ended with Yoko screaming inside a bag. *Musique concrète* is the correct term for it, but most people found it a total turn-off. However, when the organisers announced that John Lennon was going to perform in Toronto, the event sold out.

Meanwhile Little Richard had negotiated his spot on the festival. If he closed the show, that would mean following the Doors and he rightly assumed that many rock'n'roll fans would go through the doors once they started. So, he had wanted Little Richard, then the Doors and goodnight. Now it was to be Little Richard, the Plastic Ono Band and then the Doors.

Little Richard was wearing his mirrors and a bouffant wig which added four inches to his height. The moment he stepped onto the stage he was fully in control but also, being Richard, he hadn't planned his half-hour set. It was 30 minutes of mayhem.

He started as always with 'Lucille'. He sat at the piano and it worked fine. Then he told the lighting team to cut the lights and have the spotlight on himself. He only played the piano for another minute or so and then he stood on it – 'Rip It Up', 'Good Golly Miss Molly', 'Tutti Frutti', 'Keep-a Knockin'' (accompanied in Pennebaker's film by a lad trying to undo a bra) and then his 'You! You! You!' accusations before he got into 'Hound Dog'. He invited two dancers on stage for 'Jenny Jenny' and took off his top for his closer 'Long Tall Sally'.

John Lennon had stage fright and Yoko asked for some coke to calm him. She meant cocaine and the bottles of Coca-Cola weren't appreciated. It was getting dark and the audience lit matches to welcome them. The Plastic Ono Band included Eric Clapton and in keeping with the 50s acts, they included rock'n'roll standards – 'Blue Suede Shoes', 'Money' and 'Dizzy Miss Lizzy'. The audience didn't appreciate Yoko Ono's contribution. Her screaming matched Little Richard's, but was very non-musical.

There were rumours of a similar rock'n'roll show at the Empire Pool, Wembley on 17 October featuring Chuck Berry, Jerry Lee Lewis, Bo Diddley and Little Richard, but the promoter Phil Lubman couldn't pull it off.

Filmed in the UK, Tom Jones' US TV series was drawing larger audiences than Andy Williams' or Dean Martin's. Tom said, 'ABC wanted me to be like them but then I would do something different, something harder than the usual stuff of the time and I would get great people to come on the show like Little Richard and Jerry Lee Lewis. Back then, no one else would let these guys on television.'

Little Richard filmed his guest spot at Elstree Film Studios on 28 October. He wore orange slacks with a cloak and had long black hair. He performed 'Lucille' and then he and Tom did a medley of 'Tutti Frutti', 'Jenny Jenny' and 'Rip It Up' before finishing with 'Good Golly Miss Molly' and 'Send Me Some Lovin''. There was also a barroom scene where Richard in a beige suit and red bow tie played 'As Time Goes By'. Richard had a good time but commented that Tom Jones was not so good on the long notes. Nevertheless, Lee Angel saw Little Richard on the show and could see that he was looking lost. She realised that he must be on drugs.

The director of *The Mike Douglas Show* had a good sense of humour because he booked Little Richard and Liberace for the same show, alongside Laurence Kaye from Christian Dior introducing the new fashion lines. Richard said he could wear them all. Richard talked about the dangers of getting cut on his mirror suit and told American youth not to take heroin or speed. He said, 'All you need is a love injection from God.' He had recently been on a plane and thought it would crash, but God heard his scream and saved him (and of course the rest of the passengers). Liberace was calm and collected alongside Richard and said, 'I've never told anyone in the audience to shut up.'

Richard had met Keith Winslow at Oakwood College when he was a boy because Keith's mother had taught there. In 1969, Winslow joined Richard as his valet, and worked his way up to be road manager. 'We got high and did orgies every night after the show – never during the day or before the show,' Winslow told Dr Rock. 'We stayed up all night and did most of our sleeping during the daytime.'

Richard wasn't alone in being out of place in the '60s. Elvis Presley, after all those dire films, reinvented himself as the ultimate star in Las Vegas and particularly with 'In the Ghetto', which showed his concern for the world today. Presley told Richard that his music was an inspiration to him and that he was the greatest.

Jerry Lee Lewis, never far from country music in the first place, had repositioned himself as a country star and preferred to forget about his rock'n'roll past. Likewise, Rick Nelson drew a line under rock'n'roll and had become a cutting-edge country/rock artist with a brilliantly chosen band.

Chuck Berry had opened a leisure venue, Berry Park, and all but given up writing songs, particularly ones that highlighted adolescence in America. Bo Diddley was in repeat mode; and Bill Haley's Comet had run out of gas. Gene Vincent was a grouchy ghost of himself, shuffling from one pitiful gig to another. The Everly Brothers, who should have known better, let their personal relationship ruin their magnificent partnership.

Little Richard was maintaining he was the King of Rock'n'Roll when he should have been moving on. His excursions into soul music were often very good but he hadn't won the audience over. Ten years earlier, he had felt his future was in gospel music and now he was recycling. His outlandish outfits owed much to Liberace and they diminished his songs.

The only two rock'n'roll stars with unblemished records were Buddy Holly and Eddie Cochran, who both died in their early twenties.

We were moving into the 1970s. A time for bad fashions and cheesy Hammond organs. What would Richard do next?

CHAPTER 10
Second Coming

I. Reprise or Renewal

Specialty was back making records and promoting an album by the blues-based white psychedelic band, Kingdom. They often toured with other acts and became part of the Little Richard Revue. Their lead singer was Jim Potkey, who wrote most of the songs: 'Everybody has been used, Everybody's lost their shoes'. Yes, well…

Richard had his brothers Marquette, Robert and Peyton working with him in a company called Bud Hole Inc, so it was named after their father (in a way). Richard's manager J W Alexander wanted to ensure that the entourage wasn't soaking up the expenses. Old friends were back too. Angel joined Richard for wild parties. The old team was back in business.

But Richard's next move was astonishing. He joined Reprise, the label founded by Frank Sinatra in 1960 when Sinatra had angrily left Capitol Records and established his own company, Reprise. He would record extensively for Reprise and he brought in his friends, Dean Martin and Sammy Davis Jr. It was a launch pad for his daughter, Nancy Sinatra, who gave the label a contemporary touch. The label had an extensive roster including at different times the Chiffons, Dorsey Burnette, Gordon Lightfoot, Randy Newman, Tom Lehrer, Jimmy Witherspoon and the Jubilee Four. Rock wasn't for Sinatra although the label would have major success with Neil Young after Sinatra had sold the label to Warners.

When Reprise signed Little Richard in 1970, he still had enormous potential but he was not used to making albums of new material, especially if he were producing himself

And what Reprise expect from Little Richard? By 1970, he was a talk show attraction, dressing loudly and telling guests to 'Shut up!' The evidence is on YouTube.

The first session was at Rick Hall's FAME Studio in Muscle Shoals, Alabama. Richard brought with him Eddie Fletcher (bass) and Wade Jackson (tenor sax) from the Upsetters but mostly used the Muscle Shoals rhythm and horns.

Richard had been writing with Esquerita and they wrote about an old haunt in 'Dew Drop Inn' as well as the repetitive 'Freedom Blues', which became the first single as well as the opening cut. Esquerita's original 'Dew Drop Inn' had the same words and only listed Esquerita as the writer.

In June 1973 Little Richard told *Rolling Stone* that he had spent $20,000 of his own money to put 'Dew Drop Inn' into the charts 'and Warner Brothers didn't pick it up from there.' I'm sure he's joking: no one would admit to such behaviour and anyway, with that amount of money, you could simply purchase the single in the record shops and get in the charts that way.

Richard wrote 'Spreading Natta, What's the Matter?', with Maybelle Jackson, known for 'Heeby-Jeebies' and in case you're wondering, Spreading Natta was a girl. It's a good track but Richard sounded hoarse.

'Greenwood, Mississippi' was written by Muscle Shoals guitarist Travis Wammack, a cool dude who had a snakeskin guitar strap and he had killed the snake himself. When he played Richard the song, Richard said he wanted to record it. Travis already had the backing track and Richard sang over that. Tom Jones was visiting the studio and was blown away by the song, releasing his version in 1976.

Knowing he was recording for a major label, Richard wanted to reach as wide an audience as possible. He had a fortnight at the exotic Cocoanut Grove within the Ambassador Hotel in Los Angeles, supported by Freddy Martin and his Orchestra, the bandleader who had been involved with Elvis Presley's début in Las Vegas in 1956. Richard wore an elegant blue and silver cape, talked about his beauty, compared himself to Liberace, and said to one audience member, 'Sorry about that sweat, honey. That's just holy water.' On racial issues he said, 'We don't hate each other, that's just talk. We're all part of God's bouquet – the white, the black, the brown, the yellow' and then he burst into 'I Can't Stop Loving You'.

In April, two tracks from that session were released as a single, 'Freedom Blues' backed by 'Dew Drop Inn'. *Billboard* liked 'Freedom Blues' and said, 'This rock item should bring him straight to the charts.' And *Billboard* was right – 'Freedom Blues' was No.28 on the R & B chart and No.27 on the pop chart. Not the big time, but promising.

Richard was on fine form for an interview by Chuck Pulin in *Melody Maker,* saying 'I'm teaching love and peace and goodwill to all mankind. That is as much as Billy Graham is doing.' Also, 'I don't like to say the word 'hippie'. I call them 'the real people because I was the first hippie. I've been wearing my hair long and fancy all my life.'

Richard praised Janis Joplin: 'God didn't give all the soul to the black man, and this woman is singing from the heart.'

However, Richard wasn't routinely attracting big audiences. Mike Gormley reported only 150 attending the Music Hall Theatre in Detroit. Richard, wearing an ankle-length glass suit and silver pants, stopped the show after a few bars as 'he immediately realised the sound system was useless.' Once again, Richard was opting out of sound checks. He persevered so that he could collect his fee and his repertoire included Aretha Franklin's 'Chain of Fools'.

Rolling Stone wanted a lengthy feature about Little Richard, but Richard's management wanted money. The editor, Ben Fong-Torres, pointed out the publicity value and that it would probably be the cover story. In May 1970 the feature written by David Dalton appeared. When he saw Richard after it was published, Richard had hundreds of copies. He papered his living room with its cover. The feature was called *Little Richard, Child of God,*

Little Richard told *Rolling Stone*: 'I don't like James Brown giving credit to other people, when I started him in the business.'

After the chaos and tragedy at a free Rolling Stones festival in Altamont, California, the police were wary of large gatherings for rock events. Little Richard was part of a big show with Country Joe and the Fish at the Olympic Auditorium in May 1970. The stadium in downtown LA was not as grand as its name: it had been used for boxing and wrestling but now it was a rock venue. Richard invited the fans onto the stage to dance. 'Come on up! Come on up!' he called and 200 came. The stage collapsed. No one was killed but something fell on Little Richard and he was out of action for a few days, though he played

Boston a fortnight later.

Richard was working hard on the road undertaking live dates before the recording session to finish his first Reprise album. He had short seasons at Al Hirt's Supper Club in New Orleans and the Seven Seas Hotel in Miami.

In June, Richard was back in Muscle Shoals with a new song of his own, 'Somebody Saw You', a vocal *tour de force*. Inspired by Wilson Pickett, Richard was using his voice to enhance the song rather than the other way around. 'Two Time Loser' by Nashville songwriter Larry Lee had a catchy riff but it needed more Little Richard and less harmonica.

Richard had taken the 'Whoo!' on the Beatles' 'I Saw Her Standing There' as a tribute to himself and he said thanks by recording the Lennon/McCartney song. There was a clavichord in the studio and Little Richard wanted to try it. This prompted a 10-minute instrumental, 'The Rill Thing', but it sounds like it was there to fill out the album.

Richard Nader had promoted a *Rock'n'Roll Revival Show* at in the Felt Forum at Madison Square Garden in 1969 with Bill Haley, Chuck Berry, the Coasters and the Shirelles. He sold the full complement of 4,500 tickets and so he opted for the main arena for a second event in October 1970, selling 20,000 tickets this time. Little Richard and Chuck Berry topped the bill with the Coasters, the Shirelles and Hank Ballard in support. You might expect Richard to stick to the hits at such an event, but he included Leadbelly's 'Midnight Special' and the Beatles' 'I Saw Her Standing There'. In the second show, he had his band dancing in the aisles, an idea taken from Fats Domino who did it nightly with 'When the Saints Go Marchin' In'. *The New York Times* concluded that Richard had the best sound of the night and gave the best performance. Over the years there would be 25 such concerts at Madison Square Garden with Richard as a regular performer.

Creedence Clearwater Revival integrated the old and new forms of rock and in 1970 their leader John Fogerty wrote 'Travellin' Band', a witty song about touring. Little Richard was in two minds about their record, one day praising it and the next dismissing it as a steal from 'Long Tall Sally'. It wasn't a direct crib but it was certainly in Richard's style and he could have recorded a great version himself.

The Rill Thing was released in 1970 and Richard recorded two wacky promotional spots for radio, calling it his best work. The renowned critic, Robert Christgau said, 'Little Richard produced this alleged comeback in Muscle Shoals. He wrote most of the songs including the title track, a slow, ten-minute funk instrumental on which he doesn't even seem to play piano (very rill). I continue to value his singing.' Exactly – if you buy a Little Richard album, you want to hear him singing. ('Rill' incidentally is not in my dictionary of slang, so I assume it is Richard's own term and as no one else has used it, it didn't make the dictionary.)

In 1971 the James Gang with guitarist Joe Walsh had a jam session with Little Richard. They recorded 'But I Try', though it was not released until the 2012 album *Analog Man*. It's a good song about how we should live together and it contains a great guitar solo. Richard sounds like Otis Redding and there is a good interplay of vocals at the end. 'I'm here with the truth,' says Richard. Six minutes of fun.

In January 1971 Little Richard had a session with the engineer Tom Dowd and the producer Jerry Wexler at the Criterion Studio in Miami. They recorded a fine version of one of Richard's favourites, 'Shake a Hand'. This was an attempt to give him a hit single but even though it's a fine recording, nobody bought it.

Not to worry. At the same time, a Wolverhampton group, Slade, which had been performing since 1966, had their first UK hit with a revival of Little Richard's 1966 single recorded in the UK, 'Get Down with It' and now called 'Get Down and Get with It'. Jim Lea of Slade recalls, 'Chas Chandler came to see us and he said that we were the greatest live band he had ever seen. We would finish with 'Get Down and Get with It' and we recorded that for a single.' Noddy Holder's rasps sounded like Little Richard after a night on the tiles. This barnstorming record took them to No.16.

Also in the UK charts and climbing to No.3 was 'Resurrection Shuffle' by Ashton, Gardner and Dyke. Tony Ashton recalled, 'We started recording in Dean Street and we would have a few pints in the Crown first and I asked Roy Dyke to give me a Little Richard rhythm like 'Rip It Up' and it all fell into place. I left spaces for the vocal and we did some other tracks. That night I wrote the most ridiculous lyrics, and we booked a trombone and a sax, which was played by Howie Casey. I did the vocal and we went on tour with Deep Purple. A couple of months later Kid Jensen had 'Resurrection Shuffle' on Radio Luxembourg, and it took off. Everybody has done it now, Tom Jones, Clarence Clemons, Lulu and Brian Conley.'

The San Fernando earthquake in southern California in February 1971 was unexpected and caused 58 deaths with vast structural damage. Once again Little Richard took it as a message from God that he should change his ways and devote his life to his ministry. But that didn't last long.

In July 1971 Little Richard was making his second album for Reprise, this time in Hollywood and audaciously called *King of Rock'n'Roll.* Richard had a producer, H B Barnum. Barnum had worked with Richard both on the studio and on the road and knew what to expect. These were studio recordings, but the musicians had to act like an audience from time to time, so that it is not clear what you are listening to.

Once you get over the braggadocio, this is a fine album. It began with a deep male voice intoning, 'And it came to pass in the year of rock and superstars, King Richard returned from exile to claim his throne and from around the world, the cry was…'. Cries of 'Long live the King' are then followed by Richard singing, 'Good golly, Miss Molly, gonna tell everybody, Every Johnnie, Joe and Jack that the King is back.' During the song, he dismissed Elvis Presley, Aretha Franklin, Ike and Tina Turner, Three Dog Night and Sly and the Family Stone – an eclectic bunch to be sure.

As if that wasn't enough, there's a sermon before Hoyt Axton's 'Joy to the World' where Richard calls himself 'The Emancipator of Soul' and adds, 'The beauty's still on duty'. There are rants before John Fogerty's 'Born on the Bayou' and Martha and the Vandellas' 'Dancing in the Street'. On his best behaviour, Richard sang another Motown song, Smokey Robinson's 'The Way You Do the Things You Do'.

Instead of the Beatles, Richard turns to the Rolling Stones for a power-packed 'Brown Sugar' and it's back to the Hank Williams songbook for 'I'm So Lonesome I Could Cry' and 'Settin' the Woods on Fire', which contains a line he must have loved, 'You look swell but I look sweller'. Leadbelly's 'Midnight Special' had a fine treatment although there were too many 'Whoos!' (of course) as Little Richard imitated the train, the midnight special.

Richard's own soul song 'In the Name' makes good use of his voice alongside female vocalists as well as a narrated verse. Also, H B Barnum wrote a good song about the importance of money, 'Green Power', giving Richard a Tony Joe White-styled arrangement.

The cover for *The King of Rock'n'Roll* showed Little Richard sitting on a throne. Chas White: 'When Richard did *The King Of Rock'n'Roll*, they took him up to Mulholland Drive where they filmed *Rebel Without a Cause* and they sat him on a throne and put a huge crown on him. He liked it so much that when the album came out, he had six lackeys carrying him on this throne with his sceptre and crown. He would be carried into a restaurant to the amazement of the guests. He lived up to his image of being such an outrageous character.'

Although Little Richard wasn't having the best of luck in getting attention for his new albums, one good thing fell into place. Warren Beatty and Goldie Hawn were starring in *$,* a film about a bank heist, which was renamed *The Heist* for the UK. Quincy Jones was writing, arranging and conducting the score, and the cast album would be on Reprise. It featured Roberta Flack, at the time the hottest of hot names, and Little Richard. The musicians included Billy Preston and Doug Kershaw.

Richard was given 'Money Is', a top dollar song that was old-style Richard with '70s funk. It was the first time he'd had to record an intricate and witty lyric and he did it exceptionally well; one of his best-ever tracks. His second song, 'Do It – Do It', was a straight-ahead rhythm song where he could just be Little Richard. It would have been good if Quincy Jones had suggested a full album with Richard but Q had other priorities. The film paved the way for the blaxploitation films of the early '70s: *Super Fly* (Curtis Mayfield), *Shaft* (Isaac Hayes) and *Trouble Man* (Marvin Gaye). Little Richard wouldn't have wanted to be aligned to films about Black cops taking on the white establishment but with the right project, he could have been a good fit. Two songs from the period that would have been ideal for him were on Willie Dixon's 1971 album, *Peace* – the title song ('Don't make sense if you can't have peace') and the opening song, 'I'm Wanted'.

In March 1972 the psychedelic blues band Canned Heat recorded a tribute to Little Richard, 'Rockin' with the King', which they had recorded with him on piano. It's hard to tell who is doing the yelping but clearly everybody was having a good time. More problematically, Richard played piano on Jefferson's Airplane's song about police brutality, 'The Man (Bludgeon of a Bluecoat)', but Jack Cassady from the band was against the track being released as he thought Richard was inappropriate for the song.

On 27 March and 12 April 1972, Little Richard recorded his third album for Reprise, which would be called *The Second Coming.* This time there were only nine tracks and one was a relaxed instrumental, 'Sanctified Satisfied Toe-tapper'. The album was produced in Los Angeles by Little Richard with Bumps Blackwell and the musicians included Lee Allen (tenor sax), Jim Horn (baritone sax), Sneaky Pete Kleinow (pedal steel) and Earl Palmer (drums): an A-team if ever there was one. The tenor saxophonist Bill Hemmons wrote 'Nuki Suki' which was 'Yakety Sax' with Richard shouting 'Nuki Suki' from time to time; to each his own. It is less frenzied than the second Reprise album.

There's a tremendous 'When the Saints Go Marching In' which pitted a *Shaft*-type rhythm against New Orleans horns plus that 'Yakety Sax' again. Richard's vocal was a cross between himself and Sly Stone. Top marks!

All the other songs are Little Richard's, but sometimes in collaboration. 'Second Line', based on a Mardi Gras dance, had Richard talking about his new girlfriends and we could expect individual songs about them soon: a neat idea but they never came. One of his new girlfriends, 'Thomasine', was a good song with a strong vocal and arrangement. 'Rockin' Rockin' Boogie' lived up to its title: Richard had done it before but it's still fun.

That song was co-written by Candy Hunter, who said, 'I used to open the show for Richard in the 70s and I knew just what he could with his God-given voice. Richard produced 'I Saw What You Did' on me. We shopped a record deal, first with Warner Bros, but the master was lost while we were travelling. Richard used to tease me and the audience by playing a few bars from it on stage spontaneously while resting between songs, but not much of it because we hadn't completed our deal and that was the first release planned.'

'Mockingbird Sally' was typical Little Richard, but I can't decipher the words. I've looked at lyric sites and the compilers are as confused as me. 'Prophet of Peace' found Richard preaching about someone else's washtub: maybe it's best when you don't know the words. Oddly, 'It Ain't What You Do, It's the Way that You Do It' was a variation on Richard's old favourite, here given a disco arrangement and a clean-up.

There was talk of a fourth Reprise album, *Southern Child,* which would have used tracks left over from the earlier sessions. However, Reprise had lost money on Little Richard and it was time to move on.

Some tracks have emerged but there is no quality control with bootlegs and they may not have been intended for release. For example, 'Puppy Dog Song' is a joke in which Richard mimics one breed of dog after another. 'Ain't No Tellin'' can't be complete because Richard says, 'Everybody sing' and nobody does. 'Sneak the Freak' is a studio jam but it could simply be musicians warming up. Richard's piano is to the fore in 'Under the Red Sea' and I know the title's right because he shouts it out.

'California (I'm Comin')' is a good ballad about somebody on the move, and then there are the romantic ballads, 'If You Pick Her Too Hard' and 'Burning Up with Love'. 'Over Yonder' is country, while a folk song in updated in 'Still Miss Liza Jane'.

'Southern Child' has Richard looking back to Macon and his voice is similar to what he used on 'Send Me Some Lovin''. The best of the tracks is the bluesy 'Last Year's Racehorse' with the witty couplet, 'Last year's racehorse can't run in this year's race, / Since you've been gone, somebody has taken your place.' Richard himself must have felt like last year's racehorse, but he would never have admitted it.

Joining Reprise should have been part of an overall plan on relaunching Little Richard to a new generation without alienating old fans. When Geoffrey Cannon reviewed Little Richard at the Electric Circus in New York for the *Guardian*, the poor organisation around Richard's gigs was still evident. Here, the band didn't get on until 1 a.m. and even then they played for an hour without Richard. When Little Richard finally appeared, he was wearing African robes and giving the audience so many double peace signs that it became boring. He was ignoring his new album and only playing his old hits. A reboot was necessary.

II. Own Goals at Wembley

The brothers Ronnie and Ray Foulk had presented the Isle of Wight Festivals with Bob Dylan (1969) and Jimi Hendrix (1970). Ray Foulk recalls, 'We didn't make an approach to Simon & Garfunkel for the Isle of Wight but we suggested Wembley Stadium in 1972 and we got close to it. We agreed to pay first-class airfares for them to come from New York to look at the stadium. I came back to England feeling that I had achieved something, that once they saw it, they wouldn't be able to resist it, but they pulled out before that and decided that they wouldn't waste our money. They were splitting up.'

Knowing that Wembley Stadium was available, the brothers thought of a rock'n'roll festival instead, akin to what Richard Nader was doing successfully at Madison Square Garden. Ray Foulk continued, 'We didn't think it was realistic that Elvis would agree to play the festival, but had he done so, I am sure he would have done the business. We ended up with Chuck Berry, Little Richard, Bo Diddley, Bill Haley and Jerry Lee Lewis. We would have been limited by what the event could afford and any artists or their management would have to agree with that. If someone asks for too much, it won't happen. Artists know their own drawing-power.'

Ray Foulk flew to America and signed Chuck Berry (who was in Las Vegas), Bo Diddley (New Mexico) and Jerry Lee Lewis (Memphis). Richard, being Richard, kept him waiting for a week. Fats Domino was unavailable, but when Bill Haley agreed they had five US headliners plus Billy Fury, Joe Brown, Emile Ford, Gary Glitter, Heinz and Screaming Lord Sutch. The Houseshakers with Graham Fenton would perform their own set as well as accompanying Chuck Berry and Bo Diddley. In addition, MC5 would be telling us to kick out our jams.

Sutch, a master of self-promotion but little else, got some busty strippers and took them to Downing Street where he handed out leaflets for the show while the girls undressed. They were arrested and fined, but Sutch, wanting maximum publicity, opted for a jury trial which would lead to a larger fine but more publicity.

Little Richard came over with Bumps Blackwell (manager), Steve Woods (attorney), his brother Peyton (sound engineer), Candy Hunter (valet), road manager and four musicians, including Lee Allen (saxophone), Eddie Fletcher (bass), George Davis (guitar) and Robin Russell (drums). Richard said he was being paid $43,000 (not so much after paying the entourage) and he needed the lawyers to get it out of the country. How extraordinary to have a performer admitting that tax avoidance was his No.1 priority.

His No.2 priority was his place on the bill, although Chas White says, 'They didn't really bother too much about who topped the bill. In 1972 Richard said, "I am the King of Rock'n'Roll and Chuck Berry is only an old blackberry, and why should be above me on the bill." It is like a boxer talking. Whether it is Cassius Clay or Mike Tyson, people want to see the fights because of all the publicity. Little Richard may have seen the braggadocio of the American wrestler Gorgeous George in the 1940s and 1950s.

But Richard's administrative skills weren't great: he'd overlooked the requirement for UK work permits. The lawyer proved his worth and the band could join him on stage. Whatever, it meant that there was a lot of action in Richard's rooms at the Great Cumberland Place Hotel in Marble Arch: no time to party at all.

The day before the concert Richard agreed to a 10-minute interview for BBC2's arts programme, *Late Night Line-Up*. Richard, sat at a piano and said he was 'going to let it all hang out with the beautiful Little Richard from down in Macon, Georgia'. Ray Connolly came from Ormskirk and had been a reporter for *Liverpool Daily Post.* He had to overcome a stammer and now here he was doing his first TV interview and it was with Little Richard, who had flown into London that day.

Richard, wearing a pink outfit with an outrageous wig, demonstrated that he had an operatic voice. He was playful and sang a little bit of 'Mockingbird Sally' a cappella even though the piano was in front of him. He praised his mother's blackberry wine and said, 'I'm a little Jewish boy from Macon, Georgia.'

The next morning Little Richard was not happy as half of his intended fee, now said to be $35,000, had not been deposited. He said that he would not be playing the concert. Ray Foulk recalled that the chairman of the bank told him to collect the money from a casino in Edgware Road and it would be sorted out later.

As this rock'n'roll festival was attracting hundreds of Teddy Boys, there must have been questions over Little Richard's appearance anyway. Would they approve of Little Richard's outrageously campy performance, or would they think he was betraying his younger self? That campness had always been always there but now it was up front.

Quite fortuitously, Little Richard was falling in line with the new Glam era. Indeed, Malcolm McLaren had a stall at the event and Marc Bolan was there in a Chuck Berry T-shirt, so there were mixed messages all over the place. His T. Rex single, 'By the Light of a Magical Moon' was surely inspired by Little Richard's 'By the Light of the Silvery Moon'.

A large stage had been erected at one end of Wembley Stadium and the audience of thousands would be on the pitch and in the stands.

The Houseshakers performed a Gene Vincent set in tribute to the pioneer who had died in 1971. Similarly, Emile Ford paid tribute to Buddy Holly. Screamin' Lord Sutch was carried on stage in a coffin and should have stayed there as he sang out of tune versions of 'Til the Following Night' and 'Jack the Ripper', which included mock strangulations: desperate stuff. Possibly Sutch knew this, as he had brought along strippers to entertain the crowd.

The audience gave Gary Glitter a hard time for 'Money Honey' and 'Rock'n'Roll (Part 2)'.

And how extraordinary that Wizzard should choose to make their live debut on a show like this and performing Little Richard's 'The Girl Can't Help It'. Their leader Roy Wood referred to it as 'the rot'n'roll concert'.

After the British acts, Bo Diddley added much-needed gravitas with 'Mona', 'Road Runner' and 'Bo Diddley'. Jerry Lee Lewis' band, the Memphis Beats, played 'Hey Jude' (possibly deliberately antagonising the diehard rock'n'rollers) and then his sister, Linda Gail, did some songs. Jerry Lee was rock'n'roll all the way – ditching his country hits, he sang 'Down the Line', 'Mean Woman Blues', 'Whole Lotta Shakin' Goin' on' and 'Great Balls of Fire'.

Bill Haley and his Comets, including saxophonist Rudy Pompilli, dressed like a show-band but performed very good versions of 'See You Later Alligator', 'Shake Rattle and Roll' and naturally, 'Rock Around the Clock, which they encored. Their set bizarrely was less than 30 minutes.

Little Richard had refused to perform until the sun went down because somebody might want to assassinate him. He wore a yellow suit covered in mirrors. Still, he did keep moving.

It was past 10 p.m. and time for Little Richard. I know that sounds incredible because all that has gone before doesn't sound like seven hours of music but there were endless delays at 70s festivals including this one. Little Richard with his hair piled high performed 'Lucille', 'Rip It Up' and an excellent 'Good Golly Miss Molly'. So far so good, but then the microphones went wrong during 'Tutti Frutti'. While technicians were correcting the fault, Richard climbed on his piano and began removing his clothes. The band played 'When the Saints Go Marchin' in' on repeat as he tore his clothes into pieces and threw the pieces, along with his boots, into the audience. This, you'll have realised by now was standard Little Richard fare; no wonder he demanded such large fees, as he was constantly replenishing his stage wear. By way of contrast, Bill Haley could have been wearing a suit from the 1950s.

This did not sit well with the audience. There were no big screens then, so the audience in the stands wondered what was going on. Richard himself should have realised this and performed straightforward versions of his biggest hits. Instead, he blew it. He finished with

'Long Tall Sally' and Chuck Berry might have been at the side of the stage thinking, 'And he calls himself the King of Rock'n'Roll?'

Roy Brown, the US blues singer from the 1940s, saw Little Richard at Wembley and recalled, 'Bill Haley had got the crowd moving and for the first five minutes, Richard was okay. Then he started his strip act, tearing off his jacket and his trousers and this went on for some time. It was terrible.'

The audience was more annoyed with Richard than the British acts because they knew what he could deliver if he had a mind to do so.

Chuck Berry had received his money but had to pay £20 expenses to cash his cheque. He demanded that from the promoters – and got it. Once they'd started, Chuck told Terry Clemson of the Houseshakers not to play his guitar too loud. In Wembley terms, he could be getting a red card. Chuck was in his '70s get-up of paisley shirt and white trousers. He did his hits ('Roll Over Beethoven', 'Let it Rock', Carol', 'Little Queenie') and some blues ('Mean Old Frisco' and 'Wee Wee Hours'), ending inevitably with 'Johnny B. Goode'. It was dark and the lighters were glowing. Unlike Little Richard, he had had the good sense not to include his recent No.1, 'My Ding-a-ling'. On this showing, Chuck Berry was the king of rock'n'roll.

Next day the newspapers covered the event and Screaming Lord Sutch and Little Richard took the headlines with their use of striptease.

Little Richard and his entourage did a few European dates and came back to the UK for a gig at the Intercon, Nottingham five days later, possibly arranged by Emperor Rosko who had compèred the Wembley festival and was the DJ at this event. Richard didn't get on stage until midnight, giving the audience peace signs and saying his band was drunk. He played 'Lucille' to his own piano accompaniment. He was wearing a white mirrored suit and he borrowed a red jacket he liked from someone in the audience. When they went into 'Keep A-Knockin'', it became clear that the band was indeed drunk. It didn't faze Richard, who performed Chuck Berry's 'Rock and Roll Music', Otis Redding's '(Sittin' on) The Dock of the Bay' and 'Miss Ann'. The audience loved him.

When Richard was back in the US, he took part in another rock'n'roll festival, this time at the Nassau Coliseum, Long Island and the Cobo Hall, Detroit with Bill Haley and his Comets, Fats Domino, Bo Diddley, Chubby Checker, Danny and the Juniors, the Shirelles, the Coasters and the 5 Satins. It was released as a film and double-album called *Let the Good Times Roll*. Richard's contribution was 'Lucille', 'Good Golly Miss Molly' and 'Rip It Up'. We are shown backstage tantrums and he strips on top of a speaker column and throws clothes to the audience: his agility can never be questioned. The filmmakers had asked him to perform 'In the Midnight Hour' but he declined.

There was talk of Little Richard returning to the UK for three appearances in clubs own by the Sundown company with a TV concert as well, but Richard changed his mind before the contracts were signed.

Also in 1972, the Rolling Stones recorded 'Rip This Joint', the title an obvious nod to Little Richard. Keith Richard wrote in his biography, *Life*, that 'in terms of beats per minute, it is something of a world record. Maybe Little Richard has done something faster, but, in any case, nobody was looking to beat the world record.'

CHAPTER 11

The Heritage Years

Richard Penniman was 40 years old and had led an eventful life. He had overcome challenges (being poor, Black, gay and part of a minority religion), but he had also fallen down on several occasions, the setbacks often of his own making. Little Richard did what he wanted, but he wasn't always sure what that was.

We now come to the second half of his life where he is playing Little Richard the celebrity, which could be very lucrative, alongside Little Richard the evangelist. Most of the time, he wasn't interested in doing anything new and he got work simply through being Little Richard.

Take January 1973. Little Richard was about to go on tour when he received an offer from a small label, United Records. Richard was no longer with Reprise, so would he like to record for them, preferably something modern and funky? Richard asked Bumps Blackwell to negotiate, and he secured $10,000. Richard took his touring band into a studio and with Bumps producing, they made the album, *Right Now!* in one night – and it sounds like it.

'(Sittin' on) The Dock of the Bay' was among Richard's favourite tunes but he hadn't considered what he could bring to the party apart from a few whoos and a scream. The song fizzled to an end and where was the whistling?

Don Covay's 'Chain of Fools' had been a hit for Aretha Franklin, and Richard's interplay with the girl singers worked well. Inspired by this, Richard wrote 'Chains of Love' on the spot. He worked with another vocalist who said, 'Sing it, Little Richard!' at one point in case listeners had forgotten that this was Little Richard's album.

In the early 1930s there was a spate of innuendo-packed blues songs and among the dirtiest (and funniest) was 'Get 'em from the Peanut Man' by Lil Johnson. Richard half-remembered this and made up the rest for his own 'Hot Nuts'. Over in the UK around the same time, George Melly saw the comic potential in the song and revived it with panache.

Although Richard had recorded 'In the Name' for Reprise, he repeated it here when you are meant to leave a five-year gap between recordings of the same song for different companies. He probably thought no one would notice. For the rest of the album, the band was playing with blues licks and if these lasted six minutes, so much the better. Richard filled out 'Geraldine Jones' with a reference to Jerry Lee Lewis, and the album was a waste of time, not least for the listeners.

Charles Greene, who had written 'Baby Don't Go' for Sonny and Cher and produced 'For What It's Worth' for Buffalo Springfield, was starting his own label, Greene Mountain. Richard was given 'In the Middle of the Night' and 'Where Will I Find a Place to Sleep This Evening', both written by Jimmy Holiday, the writer of 'How Can I Forget?' (Ben E King) and 'Put a Little Love in Your Heart' (Jackie DeShannon). It was a fine record made to help tornado victims.

On 16 August 1974, the American late night music show *Midnight Special* devoted much of the programme to Little Richard and his garish jumpsuits. He and a funky eight-piece band did fine versions of 'Greenwood, Mississippi', 'Midnight Special' (naturally) and 'Ooh Poo Pah Doo' which would have suited him fine in his Specialty days.

Little Richard was admired by the Glam rockers in the early 1970s. Music writer Paul Du Noyer: 'David Bowie liked talking about the artists he loved and admired and like Paul McCartney, he had first wanted to be Little Richard.'

At the time, Little Richard told *Rolling Stone,* 'I've heard David Bowie is some type of homosexual. I don't believe that a man who is homosexual would declare that he is homosexual. That's something to draw people to him, a gimmick. I wish him the best, but I really believe he is straight.'.

David Essex recalled, 'My first influence was Little Richard and then on the blues front, Buddy Guy. I heard Buddy Guy sing and thought it would be good to be a singer. Before that, I had wanted to be a jazz drummer, so Buddy Guy was influential in me opening my gob and shouting, and Little Richard just had a brilliant voice. I have only ever been nervous of meeting one person in my life and that was Little Richard at Radio City Music Hall in New York. He was an extrovert and his priority at the time was getting one of his roadies to get him a bottle of bourbon.'

Chris Norman, the raspy vocalist from Smokie, reflects, 'When I started my voice was much smoother but with straining it in pubs and clubs with Little Richard songs, it changed, and that croaky voice with the harmony was what Smokie was all about.'

In 1975 Little Richard had a single released on ELP's label, Manticore, which was made with Billy Preston. 'Call My Name' had an exciting rhythm track, much in keeping with his early hits, but what is the significance of that much repeated line, 'If the boogaloo gets you, call my name.' The other side lives up to its strange title, 'Steal Miss Liza (Steal Liza Jane)'. Clearly it had its origins in the folk song, 'Lil Liza Jane' but who knows where they are taking it? Who is the intended audience? Whoever they are, they didn't buy it.

Keith Winslow, his road manager, had written 'Try to Help Your Brother' which was in keeping with the times, and he asked Richard and the band to record it. The instrumental B-side of the Mainstream 45, 'Funk Proof', was good background listening, but there was no promotion.

Little Richard played piano on two tracks on a gold album, *Head On,* by Bachman-Turner Overdrive. 'Take It Like a Man', which was also a US hit single, was sung by Fred Turner, who says 'Play it, Richard' and he plays a frantic solo. 'Stay Alive' is more restrained with Richard down in the mix.

In the US, K-Tel was leading the way in TV promotion with special albums which were not available in the shops. They asked Little Richard to record his 20 best-known titles at Jack Clement's studio in Nashville and film a TV ad. They followed the original arrangements but added audience reaction to make it seem like a concert. A single from the album combining 'Good Golly, Miss Molly' and 'Rip It Up' even found its way into the UK charts.

Little Richard had not been to the UK since the Wembley fiasco, largely because of an unsettled tax bill for £4,000 and he would have to sort that out with the authorities. In June 1975 Richard took a chance and was brought over by John Martin and Patrick Malynn, who didn't appreciate how demanding he could be. The flights had to be changed as Richard was setting off from California and not New York. He had a seven-piece band and two backing vocalists and Richard stipulated first-class accommodation. Furthermore, he had excess baggage.

The tour started on the Continent and Little Richard, who was contracted for an hour's performance at each show, only did 30 minutes in Brussels and 40 in Gothenburg. In Marseille, only 320 turned up to see him when the hall held 5,000. The show at Theatre de la Bastille was cancelled and the promoters were thinking that Richard deserved the Bastille as expenses were running high. Malynn said, 'At one soundcheck in Munich, he was incredible. He played the whole range, from gospel, blues, early '50s rock 'n' roll, everything. He's the most exciting performer ever.' There has to be something wrong when the best performance was only heard by the road crew.

The first UK show was at Lewisham Odeon on 20 June 1975 and Richard refused to join the band for a soundcheck. He wanted an evening meal at the Hilton. He didn't arrive at the theatre until half-past nine.

Melody Maker called it 'an evening of mounting chaos and absurdity'. The show began with holiday camp entertainment, the Wild Wax disco in which two rockers on stage mimed to rock'n'roll tracks while two girls danced.

The Wild Angels, an experienced UK rock'n'roll band noted for their work with Gene Vincent, performed for 45 minutes but the balance was poor and there was a long delay in moving equipment and testing microphones before Little Richard appeared: twenty minutes of 'Testing, one, two, three, four'.

Richard's band opened with funk instrumentals which did not sit well with the audience. Little Richard entered, sporting a huge Afro, a tight-fitting scarlet catsuit cut to the navel with white platform shoes and giving peace signs: not what your average Ted wants to see.

Little Richard had been so disappointing at Wembley that many fans gave up, thinking further performances would be similar. The venue was half-full, but there was no self-doubt with Little Richard. Wembley hadn't been a wake-up call: the audiences were wrong, never him.

Even if the sound had been perfect, nobody wanted funky guitars: audiences wanted the beefy saxes from the early records with Richard playing piano. After 'Lucille', Richard complained about the sound, which caused another delay. In the end, Richard told the band to turn down their sound as the sound crew couldn't turn him up further.

When the show restarted, Little Richard stood on the piano, which meant that your average Ted could see him – and take aim. Richard gave out peace signs and the audience gave him two fingers back but pointed the other way.

Richard could have won them round by doing his classics properly but no, he considered that the best course of action was to rush through them and get off as quickly as the contract allowed. 'Long Tall Sally' began incredibly fast and then got faster – and dafter. As he sang 'Be-Bop-A-Lula', a bottle smashed onto the stage. There was applause but also a chant of 'Bring back Jerry Lee'. That must have hurt.

Patrick Malynn told a disgruntled reporter, 'His voice is still as good as ever. His piano playing is great. He could have been marvellous.' Of course he could, and it's your job to sort it out.

The next morning the touring party was booked on the train to Newcastle for a performance at City Hall, but Richard insisted on making the 480-km (300-mile) journey by limousine – more expenses. The show passed without incident and it was back to London for the Hammersmith Palais and 40 miles north for Dunstable, where the sound was dreadful, the tenor saxophonist was missing, and the audience booed. At first Richard refused to appear at Studio La Valbonne in the West End, a night club associated with porn star Mary Millington, as he said he had been underpaid.

What must have disappointed the promoters is that this tour could have cleaned up. There was a tremendous audience for the old rockers as Chuck Berry, Duane Eddy and Charlie Rich were riding on current hits and coining it. With straightforward common sense, Richard could easily have some of that, but he never put things into perspective.

Before he left, Richard had a hearing with the Registrar regarding his unpaid tax. Until it was settled, he was an undischarged bankrupt. Little Richard was contrite and blamed everything on Bumps Blackwell's poor accounting. Richard was ordered to return to court for a full hearing in August but he went home and wouldn't return to the UK for nearly 10 years.

Because of Little Richard's touring expenses, the promoters refused to fund his tickets home, so they had some revenge. Back home, Richard sued Backwell, alleging that he had refused to hand over documents that would substantiate his expenses. Blackwell's defence was that he knew where the money was going (drugs) but how could he account for it? The trick, as the Pretty Things will tell you, is to invent a roadie called Charlie who needs to be paid.

But if there wasn't Little Richard in the UK, there was the aptly named Tony Conn. He was a 50s rocker from Boston Massachusetts, who had made a real raver 'Like Wow!' in 1959. He was brought to the UK and was billed as 'the white Little Richard'. He wasn't but he did okay.

As well as the diehard fans, there was also an interest in rock'n'roll that never left the British public. Brian Protheroe starred in *Leave Him to Heaven,* a light-hearted rock'n'roll musical which included some of Richard's hits.

Little Richard was drinking heavily and snorting cocaine, despite his entreaties to audiences and congregations not to take drugs. One of his suppliers was Larry Williams.

Williams visited Little Richard and told him that there would be no more cocaine until he paid for the last lot. Seems reasonable, but in true *Superfly* fashion, Larry threatened him with a gun, which was a wake-up call for Little Richard.

Forever contradictory, Little Richard then declared that everyone should follow and obey all Ten Commandments. Richard in full confessional mode said, 'If the Lord can save an old drug-taker like me, He can save anyone.' Richard criticised Pat Boone for playing Las Vegas on a Sunday when he should be worshipping, though if you were looking for somebody who needed saving, the best place to start would be Vegas on a Sunday.

Richard's brother, Tony was a schoolteacher married to another teacher. In 1976, when he was 33, he asked Richard for $200 for a station wagon. Richard said yes but he was going to a cocaine and sex party first. There was a girl in a Hollywood hotel who would cover her naked body with cocaine and her guests would flock around her and snort it off.

Richard planned to give Tony the money in the morning but during the night, Tony had a heart attack and died. Richard said, 'God permitted this thing as a warning to me.'

So in 1976, Little Richard decided to retire again, physically and mentally exhausted. Also, Richard's voice had been affected by drug and alcohol misuse and he sounded worn out: he didn't record again until the gospel album, *God's Beautiful City*, in 1979.

When Elvis died in August 1977, Little Richard said, 'He was a rocker. I was a rocker. I'm not rockin' anymore and he's not rockin' anymore.'

In 1977 Richard preached in churches, sang gospel and offered the public *The Black Heritage Bible*. The book revealed how many people in the Bible were Black – well, probably Jesus for a start.

But was Little Richard ordained? After his death, a leading Adventist said that Richard was not ordained but preached in churches. The Adventists' creed was for a clean-living life and they opposed homosexuality, so it is unlikely with his back history that he was ordained.

At ordination, a bishop lays his hands on the head of the new clergy and thereby passes the holy spirit to them, so it could be said that every member of the clergy was ordained by the Holy Spirit. Richard in interviews stated that he was 'ordained by God'. He may have meant this process, but more likely, he was referring to his own relationship with God; that is, God himself had ordained him.

Certainly, Richard did conduct weddings and funerals, but they could also have been a registrar in attendance, which is the crucial factor. As Richard was the best-known Adventist by a long way, the church did not want to lose him.

Chas White: 'I saw Richard preach at Morris Park in the Bronx in 1979. He was immaculately dressed and there were lovely families all around him. He said, "Look at you all here today but at home some of you don't even talk to each other. I want you women to know that if you don't give your man what he wants, he is going to go round the corner and find himself a Jezebel." Everyone went "Hallelujah! Praise the Lord!" Then he went down the aisle to the men and said, "I want you men to know that your wife just ain't a rollercoaster." Complete lunacy, but lovely stuff.'

In 1978 Tim McIntire starred as Alan Freed in a film about the disc jockey's triumphs and travails, *American Hot Wax*. Although 'Tutti Frutti' was on the soundtrack, Little Richard didn't appear but Chuck Berry tells Freed he will do a show for free: so much for realism. Other guests are Screamin' Jay Hawkins, Jerry Lee Lewis and Frankie Ford. When Alan Freed goes into a studio, he sees a pile of singles marked 'Don't play' and picks up the top one. 'I'm Alan Freed,' he says over the airwaves, 'And this is rock and roll.' The record: Little Richard's 'Tutti Frutti'.

At the end of the film, after a rock'n'roll riot, the camera pans to the street where a Black lad is banging an upturned dustbin and singing Little Richard songs. The message presumably is 'You can't stop rock'n'roll', although it could be 'You turned us down, Richard, this is where your music belongs.'

Larry Williams did oldies shows, wearing silk suits and shades and including an impersonation of James Brown. Larry Williams was found by his mother on the 10 January 1980 dead on his garage floor. He had been shot in the head. A coroner ruled it had been self-inflicted.

Larry's funeral was attended by Johnny 'Guitar' Watson, Joe Tex, Bobby Womack and Little Richard, who was all forgiveness, singing 'Take My Hand, Precious Lord'. Chas White: 'I wasn't at that funeral but I did see Richard at the funeral for Bumps Blackwell's mother. He sang 'It's Real' in his beautiful tenor voice. There were lots of people there and lots of flowers. He said, 'How many of you brought her flowers while she was alive? How many of you came round to talk to her?' He really let them have it.'

Oddly enough, Martin Allbritton from Bobby Bland's band developed an act and went out as 'Larry Williams', leading to a request from the family to desist. He said he would in future work as 'Big Larry Williams'

In 1979 Little Richard recorded gospel tracks in Nashville, although the album, *God's Beautiful City*, would not be released until 1981. It included gospel favourites like 'It Is No Secret' and 'I Surrender All', sung with quiet sincerity. 'What Am I Supposed to Do Without Jesus' is his most restrained performance ever and yet it has an undoubted passion. The title song is about Paradise and around this time, Richard was performing this song and 'One Day at a Time', which was recorded but not released.

Richard recorded 'There Is Someone Worse Off Than I Am.' Although it aims to spread the gospel, this is appalling songwriting. According to the song, you should be grateful for all that you have but you should also thank God because there is always somebody worse off than you.

The album includes 'Little Richard's Testimony' in which he talks for 10 minutes about what religion can do for you. On the web, you will find an interview with Richard by James Robison at the North Phoenix Baptist Church in 1979. Richard talks about his drug habits – he was taking cocaine which cost $1,000 an ounce (really?) and it was destroying his septum. Then he would mix heroin and cocaine for speedballs. He talked about playing the Magic Mountain amusement park in LA and waiting for Little Gus who got shot. Another of his friends, Curly Knight, was cut up with a butcher's knife.

Another story is that Little Richard gave up drugs when a dealer said to him, 'Take care of yourself, old man.' Richard was so horrified that someone thought of him as an old man that he changed his ways.

Richard took part in crusades such as *Your Bible Speaks* in Oakland, California and he told the congregation at the Calvary Tabernacle Church in Brooklyn, 'I used to be a flaming homosexual from Macon, Georgia until God changed me. If your brother's a homosexual, you must protect your little boy from him because homosexuals are sick. And lesbians are sick too. What real woman would want another woman to touch her?'

Faith and tolerance were an uneasy mix for Richard. 'God gave me the victory,' he said on a David Letterman appearance in 1982. 'I'm not gay now, but I was gay all my life. I was one of the first gay people to come out. But God let me know that he meant Adam to be with Eve and not Steve. Now I'm a man for the first time in my life.'

Whatever he was doing, Richard liked praise. Starting in the early 1980s he realised that long-standing performers could get lifetime awards at prestigious events that attracted publicity around the world – and he wanted some of it. He could get his name everywhere and all he had to do was say, 'Thank you. I don't deserve this.' Well, Richard would never say that, but you know what I mean.

When Ray Charles was honoured at the 1982 Grammys, he was joined by Little Richard and Jerry Lee Lewis for 'What'd I Say'. Little Richard was having trouble singing secular lyrics as he wanted everything to be dedicated to God. He wrote a new verse for the song, 'I found God in Seven-Four, I don't sing rock'n'roll no more.' The *Washington Post* said that only the pencil-thin moustache remained from the old days.

On New Year's Eve 1982 Steve Van Zandt from the E Street Band and Maureen Santoro were married in New York City with Bruce Springsteen as best man. The service was conducted by Little Richard. 'I'd read about Little Richard becoming a preacher,' says Steve Van Zandt, 'We called him and said, "Come and marry us." Percy Sledge sang 'When a Man Loves a Woman' when we walked down the aisle. We had the band from *The Godfather* movie and it was a crazy rock'n'roll wedding. Little Richard was hilarious as he went off into some crazy Little Richard thing. We were laughing the whole time.' Little

Richard also married Bruce Willis and Demi Moore in 1987.

In September 1983 Dick Clark hosted a TV special, *Salute,* which paid tribute to Jerry Lee Lewis with several star guests (Mick Fleetwood, Keith Richards, Emmylou Harris). The show ended with Jerry Lee and Little Richard performing the gospel song, 'I'll Fly Away' and then everyone comes on for 'Whole Lotta Shakin' Goin' On'.

In 1983 'The Payoff Mix' by Double Dee and Steinski sampled a version of 'Tutti Frutti' by Rufus Thomas. The track did not get much airplay because of strong language.

Wherever David Bowie recorded, he put a framed photograph of Little Richard on the studio wall. Nile Rodgers, who produced 'Let's Dance', remembers Bowie showing him a picture of Little Richard wearing a red suit and getting into a red Cadillac and David told him that was how he wanted the album to sound, whatever that might mean.

His influence on the artists of the '80s was just as clear: Prince built his image around Richard's pompadour, moustache and androgynous wild freedom. Long before Michael Jackson put on a sequined glove, Richard performed in a mirrored jacket, a living disco ball; and Madonna could have taken 'Vogue' straight from Richard ('It makes no difference if you're black or white, if you're a boy or a girl".)

With twin themes of sexuality and religion, the 1984 film *Purple Rain* can be seen as Prince's take on Little Richard. Indeed, one of Prince's musicians, Morris Day, is a dead ringer for the young Richard. One song, about bondage and female masturbation, 'Darling Nikki', ends with an unlikely comment about the Lord, an indication that Prince like Richard struggled with religion.

Prince's narcissistic album, *1999*, was a record, a tour and an event. Prince's look was becoming more like Little Richard's. He discusses bondage, orgasms, the sexuality of female cab drivers and self-love.

Prince had been raised as a Seventh-day Adventist and he said, 'I like to believe that my inspiration comes from God. I've always known God is my creator. Without God, nothing works.' Prince switched to Jehovah's Witnesses in 2003. Even though he was a world star, he would knock on doors with copies of *The Watchtower.*

Chas White, a chiropodist from Scarborough, was an ardent rock'n'roll fan and devoted to Little Richard. He knew Bumps Blackwell and they persuaded Richard that he should tell his story.

While working on the book, he met a couple who were going to be married by Little Richard that Saturday. 'About midnight, everybody was well killarnied and I was dancing with Jan Rooney, who was Mickey Rooney's eighth wife. About 1a.m., Little Richard hadn't arrived. I'd have been worried if I was getting married, but the couple said, 'Hey Dr Rock, will you marry us if Little Richard doesn't make it.' I don't know how to marry people and I wouldn't have dared do that – marriage is a sacred thing. Little Richard didn't turn up and some other guy did the wedding. Such is Hollywood lunacy.'

The Life and Times of Little Richard: The Quasar of Rock was published by Pan in 1984. Melvyn Bragg devoted an episode of *The South Bank Show* to the book. Leva Mae died just before its publication. The book was launched at the Red Parrot Disco in New York City. Pan Books brought Little Richard to London and put him up in Hilton Hotel. He was now managed by his brother, Robert. The book launch was at the Hippodrome.

Suddenly Little Richard was everywhere. Anne Diamond said on *TV-am,* 'I didn't realise you were so big.' Richard rolled his eyes and said, 'Honey, everything about me is big.'

On this stopover, Richard said he was a minister with the Remnants of the Church of

God. They are of an offshoot of the Seventh-day Adventists and are a fundamentalist sect who believe strongly in the Ten Commandments. It is possible that this was to give him more scope to work as a minister.

Parts of Little Richard's life were kept private. His former wife Ernestine married McDonald Campbell in Santa Barbara, California, in March 1975 and she died in the year 2000. While he and Ernestine had been married, they befriended another family through the church – the husband had died and their tenth child, Danny, was born in 1959. The mother, Creola, asked Richard to adopt Danny when he was 14. No papers were signed but he accepted the adoption. Danny was to move in with Richard during his rather erratic lifestyle, often living in hotels, and he ended up his manager. He has been called a rap artist, but there is no evidence of any records being released.

CHAPTER 12

Lifetime Friend

Little Richard's authorised biography with Chas White was a game-changer. There had been books which told of sex and drugs and rock and roll before but this was Little Richard himself telling the stories and revelling in them. As Chas says, 'I remember talking to him at this restaurant in Hollywood where he spoke about his sex life like most people talk about their chrysanthemums. I was amazed and embarrassed, but it is all part of being Little Richard.'

As the book was raising his profile, Richard thought that the time was right for some new music, and one of Chas' closest friends was the UK record producer Stuart Colman. Stu was at his best when he gave a contemporary feel to 1950s music. He had produced hit records for Shakin' Stevens and in 1983 he had a Top 10 single with 'She Means Nothing to Me', a song he had found for Cliff Richard and Phil Everly. In 1986, he would make the No.1 charity single, 'Living Doll' with the Young Ones and Cliff Richard. Stu and Chas persuaded Richard to make an album in the UK. Nevertheless, they were surprised when Richard agreed and WEA was prepared to finance it.

Stuart Colman: 'I met Little Richard when he was promoting his book and he was funny and volatile in the most lovable way. He had all the emotions you could wish for. He is hypnotic. He agreed to make an album for Warners and I knew it had to be as user-friendly for him as possible. I gathered the songs and he flew into Gatwick with his musicians, some of whom I knew. He had with him Travis Wammack, who was wonderful, and Jesse Boyce, who had written 'Operator'. We cut the tracks in a studio just outside Gatwick, and Richard III had stayed in one of the buildings, which amused him. It was all going swimmingly, but I thought something could go wrong.'

This was in October 1985 and something did go wrong, but it couldn't have been predicted. Stuart Colman: 'I shut the session down on Friday at 7 p.m. because he wanted to observe the Sabbath. He had the weekend to himself. Come Monday morning, I was at Eden Studio in Chiswick at 8.30 and I was told that Little Richard had had a car crash in California. I called Radio 1 and they said the report had come from Reuters. Richard had gone straight to Heathrow on Friday night and got a flight to LA for Rock Hudson's memorial service. He was doing a walk-on part in *Miami Vice* on Sunday for $50,000 and he would get the last flight out and be back for the session. When he got in his car to come back, he fell asleep at the wheel and crashed into a telegraph pole. He nearly killed himself. He did it outside the NBC building so they brought out a film crew. This was shown live and he was getting more publicity than he had had in years!'

Richard even held a press conference from the hospital. He was wheeled into a conference room at Cedars-Sinai Medical Centre in Los Angeles on a hospital bed with his head in a turban. Dr Edwin Gromis said his recovery would take six months. Gromis had to reconstruct the singer's leg, which was fractured in several places. Richard needed 36 pins in his leg.

Stuart Colman: 'The fire chief was a Mexican called Jesus, so Richard was telling people, 'Jesus pulled me from the wreckage. It was meant for be. The great Lord had chosen him for my safety.' He had broken his right leg and had pins inserted and he was left with a permanent limp. I was unable to do anything for three or four months to finish the record. He wouldn't come back to England, so I flew to him and we finished it in LA.'

Richard proclaimed, "I've never been at death's door before. I believe it was meant to happen to turn me around and to show other people there's going to be a brighter day and that God still works miracles.'

In January 1986 the first 10 inductees were received into the Rock and Roll Hall of Fame: they were James Brown, Chuck Berry, Ray Charles, Sam Cooke, Fats Domino, the Everly Brothers, Buddy Holly, Jerry Lee Lewis, Little Richard and Elvis Presley. They are all pioneers, it's true, but that list would never be permitted today as there were all men. The choices are a little odd but it all depends what you mean by rock'n'roll. There was a Survivors show at the Waldorf-Astoria. Richard wasn't fit enough to attend but he did send a 'Whoo' by videotape.

In another way, Little Richard was on top of the world. In 1985 Michael Jackson bought the Beatles' catalogue for $47 million, but the parcel included many other copyrights including Little Richard's. Michael Jackson gave them to Richard as a gift. Maybe he was repaying his debt for Richard's influence: there are certainly shades of Richard in the song, message and video for Jackson's 1979 million-seller 'Rock with You'.

But Richard hadn't got his money yet and he approved of Bumps Blackwell making a fun record, 'Pay Little Richard'.

His first session after the accident was on 6 March 1986 in Los Angeles and involved Jackie Kelso and Plas Johnson. Billy Preston and Dan Hartman recorded a new, gospel-slanted arrangement of 'Great Gosh A'mighty' for the film *Down and Out in Beverly Hills*. Although the girls sing 'Great Gosh A'mighty', Richard sings 'Great God A'mighty'. Fair enough: like the other songs on the Warner Music album, *Lifetime Friend,* it had been pitched to Little Richard as a religious song. For example, Travis Wammack's 'One Ray of Sunshine' could be a tribute to Ray Charles or it could be about the Lord. Travis had the measure of Little Richard and his four songs all contain that ambiguity.

Chas White: 'Richard didn't get the airplay he should have done for the album because there was too much competition from George Michael and Van Morrison. He did a Christmas song on the album, 'Somebody's Comin'', written by John David who often worked with Stu. Richard did a great vocal and Ken Bruce thought it could have been a Christmas hit.'

Richard played the flamboyant Orvis Goodnight (that is, himself) in a major Hollywood comedy, *Down and Out in Beverly Hills* with Nick Nolte, Bette Midler and Richard Dreyfuss. Chas White: 'They were filming a party sequence for *Down and Out in Beverly Hills* and Richard was supposed to be playing the piano while everybody was falling into the pool. Everybody was there and the director Paul Mazursky said, "Where's Little Richard?" He was in his hotel because he was observing the Sabbath. Richard is changing his mind constantly and is very difficult to deal with.'

When Richard was on set, he was fine and the filming went well. There was a promotional video with Richard at the piano where he appears to be the sanest person in the room.

The film was a double whammy for Richard as 'Great Gosh A'mighty' was a successful theme song, written by Richard and Billy Preston. 'A spiritual message in the rip-roaring style of his 1950s classics,' said *Billboard* and, lo and behold, Little Richard did reasonably well on both the Hot 100 and the R & B charts.

And how bizarre is this? To promote the new album, Little Richard appeared on British TV with the comedians Cannon and Ball. First he sang 'Somebody's Comin'' with some lifeless accompaniment but things livened up when Cannon and Ball appeared and they did 'Great Gosh A'mighty' with the three of them at different pianos. The number worked very well.

In 1987 an all-star concert was created around Chuck Berry for the feature film, *Hail! Hail! Rock'n'Roll,* directed by Taylor Hackford with a band directed by Keith Richards. Chuck was a logistical nightmare and Keith was to say, 'I'm never going to complain about Mick again.' Little Richard arrived too late to take part in the concert, perhaps deliberately, but he was filmed in conversation with Chuck and Bo Diddley for a DVD extra. It's a rambling affair with no new insights but you sense the tensions between them. 'I did get arrested for long hair,' Richard confirmed, 'They said, "Why did you put all that stuff on?" They didn't know it was natural beauty underneath.' When Richard cackled at his own joke, Chuck said, 'You've been laughing since 1955.'

With his induction into the Rock and Roll Hall of Fame, with his new album and with his much-publicised biography, Little Richard should have realised that he could become of the world's leading entertainers, particularly as there were so few 1950s rock'n'rollers performing with any real credence.

Consider how Tina Turner had been repackaged and remodelled for the 1980s without losing her integrity. Richard didn't have the application or dedication to rebrand himself and the next 20 years, as you will see, is very hit and miss - sometimes it worked, but mostly it didn't.

It is a shame that nobody got hold of Little Richard and said, 'You've got to preserve your legacy and you've got to do it right', but presenting a game plan to Little Richard would have meant nothing. Somebody else would come along with a worthless project and Richard would have said, 'Give me the money. I'll do it.' The factor that was holding back Little Richard's legendary status was Little Richard himself.

Little Richard made a guest appearance on the Beach Boys' 'Happy Endings', a fine ballad written by Terry Melcher and Bruce Johnston. It should have been a hit single but although it was featured in a Whoopi Goldberg film, *The Telephone*, neither the film nor the song went anywhere.

Philip Bailey from Earth, Wind & Fire got together with Richard to perform the title song for *Twins*, a comedy about a genetic experiment that went wrong with Arnold Schwarzenegger and Danny DeVito as twin brothers. It was a good disco number and the soundtrack album included an a cappella version, though there's percussion on the track. Five years later, Richard was given a cameo as himself in Schwarzenegger's *The Last Action Hero* (1993).

Richard played a hairdresser Alphonso in a TV movie, *The Goddess of Love*, the film being a vehicle for Vanna White, the hostess from a long-running TV quiz series, *Wheel of Fortune*.

In 1987 Little Richard was asked to present the award for Best New Artist at the Grammys. He opened the envelope and said, 'And the winner is me!' He should have left the joke at that but he added, quite seriously, 'I have received nothing. You never give me no Grammys and I've been singing for years. I am the architect of rock'n'roll. I am the originator.'

In 1989 Little Richard was at it again when presenting an award to Mariah Carey at American Music Merits. He asked the audience, 'Don't you think it's about time for me to win one?'

Maybe Richard's remarks did some good. In 1993, the Grammys gave him a Lifetime Achievement award and in 1998, he received a Grammy Hall of Fame Award for 'Tutti Frutti' and in 1999, for 'Long Tall Sally'.

During the Beatles' induction into The Rock and Roll Hall of Fame in 1988, George Harrison commented, 'Thank you all very much, especially the rock'n'rollers, and Little Richard there, if it wasn't for (gesturing to Little Richard), it was all his fault, really.'

More significantly, Little Richard had become a cultural reference. In an episode of the ITV series *Minder* called *A Star is Gorn*, Arthur Daley says of a current singer who has allegedly died, 'He's going to be up there with the immortals like the Big Richard and Little Bopper.'

Woody Guthrie and Huddie Ledbetter (Leadbelly) had both recorded for the Folkways label, and the Smithsonian Institute asked Columbia Records if they would make an album of established performers recording their songs, which would also be filmed for a documentary. The result was a terrific album with Bruce Springsteen, Bob Dylan, Willie Nelson, Emmylou Harris and Brian Wilson. Little Richard was twinned with the LA rock band Fishbone, and they recorded a fine version of Leadbelly's 'Rock Island Line'.

Rock Around the Mouse in which Disney cartoon favourites performed rock'n'roll was sold to a TV shopping channel. Little Richard merged his talents with Goofy in 'Gawsh Golly Goofy', but the middle section with Goofy is unlistenable. Otherwise, it's rapid-fire lyrics – and who does that better than Richard?

At the end of 1988, Little Richard appeared on a US TV special hosted by Dennis Miller called *A Rock and Roll Christmas.* He sang 'Santa Claus is Comin' to Town' in Bruce Springsteen's arrangement. He did it very well in a smart, red leather jacket but there's a sense that he wanted to let rip at the end and had been told to hang fire.

'Purple People Eater', a 1958 novelty hit by Sheb Wooley, had been adapted for a film written and directed by Linda Shayne. Richard isn't listed in the opening credits with Shelley Winters and Chubby Checker, but he's there, coming on in the final minutes as the town's mayor and getting a special credit at the end.

The Purple People Eater had come to earth to join a children's rock'n'roll band and when they performed Sheb Wooley's song, Little Richard adds a variation of 'Awopbopaloobop'. There's seriousness too as the mayor stopped senior citizens from being evicted. The residents weren't surprised when they saw the Purple People Eater because they're used to Little Richard.

A cartoon series prompted by the film *Bill & Ted's Excellent Adventures* still used Alex Winter and Keanu Reeves' voices. In the episode *The Birth of Rock'n'Roll,* Bill and Ted failed their musical appreciation class at school but Little Richard helped them out.

Richard recorded the theme for *Grand Slam*, starring John Schneider and Paul Rodriguez as bounty hunters. It was funky soul produced by Bill Conti and had many whoops and hollers. Richard released an album which featured the song plus his old hits.

And then there's Jive Bunny.

In 1989 Les Hemstock, a DJ from Doncaster, had the idea of making disco singles from samples of previous hits and his first attempt used rock'n'roll standards including Little Richard's 'Tutti Frutti'. It was developed into a single by the father-and-son team of John and Andy Pickles. Andy created the name Jive Bunny and the Mastermixes and the video for 'Swing the Mood' showed the cartoon bunny imposed on newsreel footage. 'Swing the Mood' went to No.1 not only in the UK but in several other countries as well. It was included on the huge-selling *Jive Bunny – The Album*, so Little Richard with a stuttering 'Awopbopaloobop' was in the charts.

Rock critic Greil Marcus on Jive Bunny: 'They trivialise every piece of music that they get. Chuck Berry and Elvis Presley have now advanced on the nostalgia scale – they're now as safe as the music our parents liked. Somebody should sue the motherfuckers for crimes against history.'

There is a report in *Now Dig This* of the chaos surrounding *The Legends of Rock,* the opening concert at the Skydome in Toronto in July 1989. Jim Newcombe, the reporter, was frustrated by the whole event and undoubtedly if I'd been there, I'd have been similarly annoyed. However, as an outsider, I can see its comic potential. The key players are like animals claiming their territory. The show's impact was ruined by long delays, probably caused by backstage wranglings. The audience was banned from taking photographs of Richard wearing a black suit with silver studs on the shoulders. He had 'the Little Richard Dancers' on stage during 'Good Golly, Miss Molly', an unnecessary distraction. After his closer 'Great Gosh A'mighty', he said, 'Stay close to God, we need Him more than ever.' Chuck Berry wanted the TV screens off, even though there were 35,000 there. Jerry Lee Lewis didn't appear because he had flu, or so they say, but the audience did see Bo Diddley, Ronnie Hawkins and the Four Seasons amidst long, long delays.

By the time Richard spoke with *Rolling Stone* in 1990, he was performing rock'n'roll again. 'I will always love God, and I feel that I'm a messenger for him. To me, rock'n'roll music is the only way I know how to make a living. I'm making people joyful, and I still spread my love for God.'

In 1990 Little Richard was used to good effect in the music video for the rock band Cinderella's 'Shelter Me'. Richard takes charity calls on an outsize phone and he ends by repeating the title line and then saying, 'Shut up!' The other guest stars are Pamela Anderson, Shelley Duval, Harry Shearer and Dweezil Zappa. With a slight change to the 'Bible' line, the song would have suited Richard perfectly.

Although the organisers of USA for Africa included Quincy Jones and Michael Jackson, Little Richard was not part of the 'We Are the World' single and video, but six years later, he took part in Voices That Care, a similar concept to help Desert Storm survivors. Among the participants were Randy Travis, Peter Cetera, Garth Brooks, Luther Vandross, Will Smith and Mark Knopfler. It made No.11 on the *Billboard* Hot 100.

Richard was honoured with a star on the Hollywood Walk of Fame in 1990. Soon afterward, he returned to his hometown of Macon for the unveiling of the Little Richard Penniman Boulevard.

Bob Dylan said he converted Little Richard to Judaism in less than an hour. Often you have to take what Dylan says with several more grains of salt than even Little Richard's outpourings.

The Specialty catalogue, now run by Art Rupe's daughter, Beverly, was sold to Fantasy in 1990 – Little Richard's recordings being the jewel in the crown. This meant that Little Richard's catalogue would be repackaged properly for the CD age as well as being marketed and licensed for compilations, TV and films, hopefully not more Jive Bunny. A genuine band Funkdoobiest featuring B-Real sampled 'Tutti Frutti' in 'Wopbapalubop'.

The group Living Colour was into sound collage and they recorded 'Elvis Is Dead' in 1990 with a guest appearance from Little Richard preaching about Elvis. He was telling the listeners not to exploit him: 'Be my guest and let him rest' and 'How do you sleep, don't you feel the shame?'

In 1989, U2 recorded 'When Loves Comes to Town' with B.B. King. There are various mixes and the *Live from the Kingdom* mix includes a fiery sermon from Little Richard. He was in his element – 'I don't care how much money you got, You need love, Whoooooooooooooo!'

After writing 'Blaze of Glory' for the western *Young Guns II,* Jon Bon Jovi wanted to record a suite of songs inspired by the film. He needed a barroom piano for 'You Really Got Me Now', and who better than Little Richard? When Richard died, Jon Bon Jovi issued this statement: 'In 1990 when I wrote the *Young Guns* record, I had the chance to ask some of my heroes to record with me – Elton John, Jeff Beck, and an all-star cast came together to have fun and make music. I reached out to Little Richard and he made all of us feel like little kids. He played, he sang, he laughed and he told us stories. He blessed us with his smile and with his talents. I'll never forget him. I pray, there's a heaven and that Richard is at the piano.'

There was money to be made from jukebox musicals, especially ones with highly danceable hits from the '50s and '60s. These musicals have been widely criticised and the plots are creaky, but providing the old hits are performed competently, they do well. The big winner was Bob Charlton's *Return to the Forbidden Planet*, which started in 1985 and was in the West End and UK theatres for many years.

Bob Eaton had success with *Good Golly Miss Molly* and he explained, '*Good Golly Miss Molly* came about because of the New Vic in Stoke. Peter Cheeseman developed the concept of a musical theatre documentary which took local subjects and turned them into shows. In 1989 he asked me if they could do my show *Lennon* at the New Vic but I didn't have the rights to the songs – I lost them when Michael Jackson bought the catalogue. I said, "I can do you a new show based around rock'n'roll songs and with some local story." I happened upon this story of people fighting to save their street and I put the two things together. It was a jukebox musical but it had what I hoped was an interesting story.'

In 1990 Little Richard was given a star on Hollywood Boulevard and a Little Richard Day was announced. Arnold Schwarzenegger said he had always admired Richard's beautiful body. David Bowie, Jon Bon Jovi and Michael Jackson sent goodwill messages. A passer-by was disappointed to find he was Little Richard and not Lionel Richie.

The event was followed by a TV appearance on Arsenio Hall's show, performing 'Lucille', 'Good Golly Miss Molly' and 'Tutti Frutti'.

In 1991, Richard's performance of a rock 'n' roll version of the children's tune, 'Itsy Bitsy Spider', was a stand-out track on the star-studded Disney Records' benefit album, *For Our Children.* Even the rappers Casanova and Nate enhanced his performance. Richard made the track with bass player, King Charles Glenn. It opened with a rap about spiders and the performance contained his longest yell and some rock'n'roll piano. For the same album, Bob Dylan sang 'This Old Man', James Taylor 'Getting to Know You' from *The King and I,* and Bruce Springsteen 'Chicken Lips and Lizard Hips'. The record went gold and earned millions for the Paediatric AIDS Foundation.

Richard had a spot on a Jim Henson album, *Kermit UnRigged* on which he guested on the all-star song and video for a remake of 'She Drives Me Crazy',

Richard appeared on TV in a rock'n'roll pantomime, *Mother Goose Rock'n'Rhyme,* directed by Jeff Stein, in which order must be restored in Nursery Rhyme kingdom as characters have gone missing. The production starred Jean Stapleton (Mother Goose), Shelley Duvall (Little Bo Peep), Cyndi Lauper (Mary who had a little lamb), Debbie Harry (The Old Woman who lived in a Shoe), Art Garfunkel (Georgie Porgie) and Little Richard (Ol' King Cole). Van Dyke Parks wrote a song for Richard, 'Waiting for the King'.

As a result of the successes of the *For Our Children* CD and the *Mother Goose* show, Disney asked Little Richard to record an album for children and the result was the delightful *Shake It All About,* again made with King Charles Glenn, but with Shepard Stern as the main producer. The cover shows Richard happily singing and playing with children of different ages, one looking too old for this kind of thing. There are plenty of musicians around but the key component is synths and programming. This should have been a lively album of real music, thereby ditching the synths.

The CD included a frantic 'Hokey Pokey' but not even children could dance that fast. Richard sang a comic 'On Top of Old Smokey', now called 'On Top of Spaghetti'. For a short while, Richard included 'On Top of Spaghetti' in his stage act. The knock, knock jokes added to 'Keep-a Knockin'' are surely the oddest reworking of a hit single by any artist anywhere. 'Knock, knock.' 'Who's there?' 'Amos.' 'Amos who?' 'A mosquito just bit me.'

With a Bo Diddley beat, 'Twinkle Twinkle Little Star' has a verse for racial equality, which has nothing to do with the original poem. Why not sing the original words by Jane Taylor in 1806 which are rarely heard? 'Old MacDonald' has a 'Bony Moronie' workout with Richard rockin' his piano like no tomorrow and plenty of animal noises: get yelping, Richard! The album ends with a plaintive, 'Oh Where, Oh Where Has My Little Dog Gone'.

Chas White: 'Little Richard was excellent on that album. He has done two films with Arnold Schwarzenegger and several TV commercials, even one for lipstick and he does one for some cream which 'makes me feel just like Tutti Frutti'. He is a great showman and he can still play. The kids are crazy about his 'Itsy Bitsy Spider' and it was on the Disney channel every day and he has done voiceovers for cartoons. This shows what a great artist he is.'

Full House (1994), a TV series directed by John Tracy, was a family sitcom and Richard played an uncle who helped their school have a successful rally. It starred John Stamos and Bob Saget and he performed 'Itsy Bitsy Spider' in the family house and then 'Keep-a Knockin'' with a pile of rock'n'roll musicians at the rally. Everyone was having a great time and what other rock'n'roll star was making cameos like this?

From 1994 to 1997, a popular children's cartoon series in the US was *Magic School Bus*. It won awards for its educational content and the voices belonged to Lily Tomlin (Ms Frizzle), Elliott Gould, Dolly Parton, Rita Moreno and Eartha Kitt. The theme song was sung by Little Richard with his usual embellishments.

With his garish outfits and forthright personality, Little Richard was a perfect children's entertainer. *The Muppet Show* didn't use him as much as they could but he was featured in the hilarious, all-star music video for 'She Drives Me Crazy' from Kermit and Miss Piggy in 1994. Three years later he was briefly in an episode called *The Cameo Show*.

In 1994 he was on *Sesame Street,* describing how he loved his Rubber Duckie in the bath and singing 'Rosita' to another puppet. In both items, Hoots the owl played sax.

Children's songs can be notoriously difficult to get right, so top marks for Richard in all this. Less successful was another singer/pianist, Neil Sedaka, with Waking Up Is Hard To Do.

Columbo and the Murder of a Rock Star (1991) has Lt Columbo (Peter Falk) going to a club to see Little Richard and question his drummer, who is being framed for murder. Richard has a brief chat with Columbo, but just one more thing – where does that song 'Boogie Woogie' come from?

In 1992 Richard was one of several guest starts in *The Naked Truth*, a feeble crime caper with Robert Caso and Kevin Schon playing the main characters, both called Frank: how stupid is that? Richard is cast as Airborne Mustard Lover. It was written and directed by Nico Mastorakis. Other guest appearances came from Yvonne de Carlo and Zsa Zsa Gabor.

Rather tougher was *Sunset Heat*, also called *Midnight Heat*, a 1992 film directed by John Nicolella in which a drug dealer is looking for his money. As the dealer is Dennis Hopper, you know this is not going to be a walk in the park. The first person to die is a drugs runner played by Adam Ant.

In November 1992 Little Richard was on a European *Giants of Rock'n'Roll* tour with Jerry Lee Lewis, Duane Eddy, Lloyd Price, Bobby, Chris Montez and Johnny Preston with UK appearances at Wembley, Manchester and Birmingham. Richard had a seven-piece band led by Travis Wammack. Richard wore a black Charles II wig at Wembley Arena and was given a piano-styled cake for his sixtieth birthday. He threw jewellery to the crowd. He performed eight songs in 45 minutes with plenty of chat, mostly of the 'Don't I look pretty?' variety. As well as hits, he did 'Blueberry Hill', 'Rock and Roll Music' and 'Baby, What You Want Me To Do' and at Wembley, had Dr Rock dancing on stage with him.

Travis Wammack commented on working with Richard: 'I have everybody more or less watch me. He does certain little things or he gets me to hit him with a certain chord right before he does the song, and from that I pretty much know basically what he's fixing to do.' Wammack is best-known for his 1964 feedback-drenched instrumental, 'Scratchy', based around Mel Tormé's 'Comin' Home baby'.

In 1993 Paul Mazursky, who made *Down and Out in Beverly Hills,* directed the satire *The Pickle*. It was about a Hollywood director who longed to make a classic but had turned out three turkeys in a row. To make some cash, he directs a ridiculous money spinner called *The Pickle*. It is about kids who find themselves transported to another galaxy by a flying pickle. Its President is Little Richard but as everyone on the planet dies when they are 49, Richard has only six months to live. Maybe you're wondering why you've never heard of this film, but I doubt it.

In 1992 Little Richard made what would be his final album, *Little Richard Meets Masayoshi Takanaka.* For this album, he and his band were reworking their hits with a Japanese guitarist associated with the Fender Stratocaster in the 1970s. In a way, it is Little Richard meets Jimi Hendrix again. The album received minimal publicity outside Japan, so sadly most westerners do not know of it.

Little Richard played a Star-Club reunion concert in Hamburg for Horst Fascher. By way of contrast, Richard also performed at the inauguration of President Clinton. In 1993, he took part in tribute in front of Clinton for the gospel singer, Marion Williams.

In 1993 Elton John released the album *Duets* where he sang with 15 music stars. Elton and Bernie Taupin had written a gospel ballad, 'The Power', which he and Little Richard recorded with Andraé Crouch Singers. The song trod familiar ground but it was a powerful performance.

In 1994 Richard was on an album which united country music and rhythm and blues called *Rhythm, Country and Blues*. Little Richard and Tanya Tucker duetted on Eddie

Cochran's 'Somethin' Else'. They recorded a video and appeared together on the CMA Awards. They matched each other very well, having a great time together.

You can see a pattern emerging with guest appearances which would benefit both parties. The first generation rock'n'roll stars were now around 70 years old and they looked cool by working with the whippersnappers. The stars of the day were adopting old codgers to acknowledge the trailblazers. You know, Norah Jones and Ray Charles. U2 and B.B. King. David Bowie and Bing Crosby.

Perhaps by working with younger performers, Little Richard realised the benefits of merchandising. Rock'n'roll music was Richard's one sure of making a living, and so he continued to play shows. Guitarist Kevin Holly joined Richard's band in 1994 and stayed with him for 18 years. Gigs came in short bursts: fly out on a Friday, play a weekend show, usually a package deal with Jerry Lee Lewis, Fats Domino, Chuck Berry or B.B. King, fly back on Sunday. They played arenas, casinos, clubs and tycoon's birthday parties. Richard got paid before the show, preferably cash, or he didn't perform. Holly remembers a casino show where the money was slow in arriving. 'We waited and waited and the crowd was getting unruly,' he told *Rolling Stone*. 'They came back with a cart full of one- and five-dollar bills and rolls of quarters, and the band went on.'

In 1995 *Baywatch* featured Richard in the episode *The Runaways,* directed by Lewis Stout. The other guest star was Richard Branson, who rather impressively, wanted to achieve a water-skiing record for the *Guinness Book of World Records.* Pamela Anderson was not in this episode, which is a pity as they could have had a rerun of *The Girl Can't Help It* scene with Jayne Mansfield. Richard was the owner of a beach café. He spoke to customers in his song titles: 'This is my Specialty, my Tutti Frutti' At the end of the show, there was a beach party where he performed 'Good Golly, Miss Molly'.

Also in 1995 the Rhythm & Blues Foundation gave Little Richard a Pioneer Award, not before time. The UK promoter Jeffrey Kruger recalled meeting Richard on a table with Johnny Otis and it was a familiar complaint. Kruger told me, 'Little Richard was talking even faster than he sang. He said, "I'll teach these people for honouring James Brown before honouring me." He was playing it for laughs but I was sure he meant it. He told the band to follow him and he did a six-minute 'Lucille'. At the end he said, "I hate you for not recognising me before James Brown. Now you know who is the best!"'

Holly Johnson from Frankie Goes To Hollywood mentioned Little Richard in his song 'Legendary Children', 'Little Richard is definitely queer in the original sense of the word. In my opinion, he created rock'n'roll. We can thank him for the androgyny, the make-up, the glamour and the general outrageousness. He said, "Elvis is the king but I am the queen of rock and roll." There is a queer aesthetic – a colourfulness and a fastidiousness – and it can affect your work and the things that you are influenced by.'

In 1995 Little Richard and Chuck Berry had UK dates with Fats Domino but Fats caught an infection in Sheffield. Richard and Berry played Wembley Stadium.

BBC Radio Merseyside did toy with the idea of presenting a Little Richard concert at the Liverpool Empire, but the cost was prohibitive. Richard and his band charged £22,000 a night.

Little Richard had played the Montreux Jazz Festival. In 1996 he was booked to close the Atlanta Olympics with Celine Dion, B.B. King and Gloria Estefan. Richard performed 'Good Golly, Miss Molly' and 'Long Tall Sally' with a full band and madcap balloons representing 20-foot skinny people. It looked shambolic although Richard in a regency wig acquitted himself well.

When Richard did Channel 4's *The White Room*, which was hosted by Mark Radcliffe, he had his brother Peyton with him. Richard said he was making an album with Solomon Burke. He said, 'It's bad enough that Pat Boone took my songs and made them hits but Frankie Ford's still doing my act.' He performed 'All Around the World' with Ronnie Wood joining his band.

The Drew Carey Show was a comedy sit-com, and in a 1997 episode, *Drewstock,* Drew and his friends have a piss-up in a brewery as they invite everyone to a brewery that is closing down. The celebrities attending this party as themselves included Joe Walsh and Little Richard, and Richard is at the piano for Joe Walsh's 'Rocky Mountain Way'.

A rock'n'roll saxophonist who obtained superpowers was the theme of the comic *Night Man,* which became a TV series in 1997. It was part-action, part-comedy and the guest stars included Donald Trump and Little Richard, unfortunately not in the same episode.

The Streatham Megabowl opened in south London with 36 lanes and a photograph of Little Richard on the wall. He signed it, 'Lots of love, Megabowl, Little Richard'. The Megabowl is now demolished.

In 1997 Little Richard received the American Music's most distinguished award of merit, but oddly he was effectively homeless at the time. He was living in the Hyatt Hotel on Sunset Boulevard while having a house built in Nashville. He loved Sunset Boulevard because it is all about vitality and energy and neon signs.

The film director John Water went to see him regarding a retrospective that would include *The Girl Can't Help It.* He said, 'The thing that shocked me the most is he lived in this normal hotel room. It wasn't fancy. It was just a single room. It wasn't a big suite or anything. I thought, 'Really, this is where Little Richard lives?' But it was great to meet him.'

In 1998 there was a *Legends of Rock'n'Roll* concert at Wembley Arena where a low-key Jerry Lee Lewis was followed by a barnstorming Little Richard who cut short every one of his hits. Seventeen songs in 40 minutes was the order of the day as he kept asking the audience if they were having a good time. He brought along *Steps to Christ* to give away.

In 1999 Richard was part of a film *Mystery Alaska* starring Russell Crowe, Burt Reynolds and Colm Meaney. It's about an ice hockey game and to place the New York team at a disadvantage, Little Richard is required to sing the National Anthem over and over again so that they remain immobile on the ice. Instead of his familiar 'Shut up!', Richard is saying, 'I'm cold!' You may wonder why you've never heard of these films: I wonder how they ever got made.

The tragic story of the teen star Frankie Lymon was brought to the screen in *Why Do Fools Fall in Love.* Little Richard did 'Keep A Knockin'' on the soundtrack but it was the only true rock'n'roll performance on the album. Lymon's original hits with the Teenagers were knocked into touch as Lymon's wives were arguing over his money. Richard played himself when he was in his twenties but that's Hollywood for you and the *New York Post* and the *Village Voice* said he was the best thing about the film, but that wasn't difficult.

A Little Richard biopic was obviously a good idea and Chas White wanted it to be based around his book, Although a script was written with Barry Hampshire, nothing came of it. There was a biopic, *Little Richard,* in 2000, directed by Robert Townsend, but it was a made-for-TV movie with Little Richard acting as an executive producer. It was not based on Chas White's book and doesn't show the complex nature of Richard's personality.

Leon Robinson is fine as Little Richard but he is miming to Ali Woodson's singing.

Tamala Jones is his girlfriend Lucille (who's she?) and his homosexuality is suggested rather than shown. We share his delight in dressing up and using Pancake 31. The film starts with Little Richard on stage in Sydney in 1957 and seeing the Sputnik as a sign from God and then goes into the back story. The film ends with Don Arden seeing Little Richard preach and offering him a gospel tour of the UK. The final scene is in Doncaster in 1962, where Sam Cooke is going to upstage him so he goes into 'Good Golly, Miss Molly.' The best (and the funniest) sequence is the edit of both Pat Boone and Little Richard recording 'Long Tall Sally'. On *IMDB*, the film is described as a 'costume drama': I like that.

In 1999 Chas White was at the funeral of Don Harris from Don and Dewey with Little Richard officiating. Chas commented, 'Little Richard was wearing so much make-up that it was hard to tell which one was the corpse.' At the time his musical partner Dewey Terry was living on Johnny Otis' estate outside Pasadena, so everything goes round in circles.

For me, 1999 ended with Paul McCartney at the Cavern promoting his album of oldies, *Run Devil Run*. Among the songs were 'Shake a Hand' and 'She Said Yeah'. Blues musician Al Peters says, 'That night was Paul McCartney at his best, singing good old rock'n'roll. People like myself who are very much into R & B are very choosey about which bands to watch. We saw the Beatles a few times at Hambleton Hall and the Cavern and we followed them because like Little Richard, they had the rock'n'roll edge.'

A charity connected to the late composer, Leonard Bernstein, organised a new score for *West Side Story*, produced by David Pack with entertaining spins on these great songs. Little Richard combined self-mockery with self-aggrandisement for 'I Feel Pretty'. It's amongst his best recordings.

CHAPTER 13

Goin' Home

An excellent revival in roots music was taking place with Bill Wyman's Rhythm Kings, often with Albert Lee, Georgie Fame and Gary Brooker. 'We don't just bash out rock'n'roll songs,' said Bill Wyman. 'We want to do them excellently. Gary Brooker does the New Orleans stuff like Little Richard or Fats Domino and he can do them like they did with the horns. That is true to Little Richard and it is not how most bands do it. Even the Stones did them like that in the early days – we just whacked it out and I think that we should have done them a bit better than that. We do it better now because we've got the musicians who know how to do it. There's a feel and an atmosphere and a rhythm that you should get right and we really do that.'

The National Association for the Advancement of Coloured People, which was established way back in 1909, put Little Richard in their Hall of Fame, so he was clearly doing something right. By now the awards were coming at regular intervals: BMI awards, Songwriters Hall of Fame, Louisiana Hall of Fame, the Georgia Music Hall of Fame and so on.

In a rare case of humility, Little Richard said, 'Rock'n'roll is something I created. It's all I know how to do. I'm not a minister, and I'm not what you'd call a gospel singer, even though I've made gospel records. I'm just an old rock'n'roll singer from Macon, Georgia.' (Note that, 'I'm not a minister': you see how confusing this guy is.)

An old rock'n'roll singer charging £20,000 a show. Unfortunately, the plans for Richard to play an old ballroom, the Olympia, in Liverpool fell through as the organisers realised that they would have to charge £40 a ticket. Maybe it would be safer to put your money on another Little Richard, a racehorse that was making a name for itself, albeit Little Richard's, in the UK. Come to think of it, wouldn't Get Down With It be a perfect name for a racehorse?

Even when Little Richard came to London to appear for the Make a Wish charity, the organisation had to pay his fee. They thought that by inviting Chas White to compère the show, disruptions would be minimal. What could go wrong? Well, he didn't arrive on time at the Truman Brewery and Boiler House in London's east end and would leave if the money didn't turn up. It did and he performed a fine set that included 'I Got a Woman', 'Pledging My Love' and 'I Saw the Light'.

In 2001 Little Richard sang 'Louie, Louie, Louie' for the animated film *The Trumpet of the Swan*, based on a story by E B White, who wrote *Stuart Little*. The swan is mute, so his father steals a trumpet for him and he becomes famous, the parallel being with Louis Armstrong.

During the 1980s and 1990s, Richard officiated at celebrity weddings. In 2006, Richard married 20 couples who had won a contest in one massive ceremony. He preached at the funerals of Wilson Pickett and Ike Turner.

From time to time, Richard also officiated at funerals, one of them being for Ike Turner, whose musical ability had been overshadowed by his drug use and mistreatment of his former wife, Tina. Richard, speaking at his funeral, said, 'Stop holding his mess whatever it is against him. Even Jesus forgives."

Richard made a guest appearance on the daytime soap *The Young and the Restless*. A couple in Vegas were being married by a Liberace impersonator, but he was ill and so the real Little Richard stepped in and also sang a wedding blues. In the *Mr Rogers* TV show, he played a vet's assistant: is there no end to this man's versatility?

Little Richard took up residence at the Hilton in Nashville shortly after moving out of Los Angeles in 2003 to be near his sister Peggie. In time, he bought a house in Nashville but he still liked the comfort of the Hilton.

Little Richard became embedded in showbiz, appearing frequently on American television, in roles and as himself, including being a judge on Simon Cowell's *Celebrity Duets* in 2006.

Little Richard was animated for an awards ceremony in *The Simpsons*. He was asked to pick the best teacher and said he is a teacher himself because he taught Paul McCartney to go 'Whoo!' Homer Simpson barracks him with 'Purple Rain' and Richard tells him to 'Shut up!'. Homer believes he was being put down by Michael Jackson.

When he appeared at the Royal Festival Hall in 2005, Richard announced from the stage that signed posters were available for £20. He included the Rolling Stones' 'It's Only Rock'n'Roll (But I Like It)' as well as one of his earliest songs, 'Directly from My Heart'.

In 2006 when he played in the *Eat to the Beat* concert series at Walt Disney World in Florida, he was carried onstage in a throne that doubled as a piano stool. He had difficulty singing 'Long Tall Sally' and he said, 'Jesus, please help me, I can hardly breathe.'

Little Richard recorded 'I Saw Her Standing There' with Jerry Lee Lewis for Lewis' album *Last Man Standing* (2006), although by having Little Richard and Willie Nelson on the album, Lewis clearly wasn't the last man standing. Stuart Colman used to say, 'Never have too many guests on an album as the main artist can get lost.' This is a supreme example: there are 21 tracks and 21 guests and not enough thought has gone into the arrangements. Richard and Jerry Lee bring nothing new to 'I Saw Her Standing There'.

Key industry people were admitted into the Rock & Roll Hall of Fame, but its founder Ahmet Ertegun of Atlantic Records was not keen in allowing his competitors the honour. Art Rupe's induction was blocked, but after Ertegun's death in 2006 the way was clear and he was inducted by Lloyd Price. Art Rupe survived to a magnificent age, 104: he died on 15 April 2022, the date for filing tax returns in the US.

Marty Stuart, once Johnny Cash's son-in-law, was putting together a tribute to his songwriting, *Kindred Spirits*. It was a high-level tribute with Dylan and Springsteen in the guest list. Little Richard recorded one of Cash's rockabilly songs for Sun Records, 'Get Rhythm', and it was given a pounding arrangement with Marty Stuart on piano and Richard rapping at one point.

The insurance giant GEICO ran a series of ads with real customers and celebrity translators, a brilliant one being with Denise Bazik and Little Richard in 2007. She tells her story and Richard translates in his madcap manner. How did she manage to keep a straight face? Someone on *YouTube* then put Little Richard's outbursts alongside a speech by President George W Bush for true comic potential.

In 2007 Richard developed sciatica in his left leg, requiring him to use crutches. In

November 2009, he had replacement surgery on his left hip. Despite returning to performing in 2010, his hip problems continued and from then on, he was brought onstage in a wheelchair and played sitting down.

He had needed hip replacement surgery for years but was wary of the consequences. In the event, he had left it too late and surgeons were unable to replace the broken bone. From 2008, he spent most of his life in a wheelchair and in constant pain. He occasionally made an appearance, such as singing 'Tutti Frutti' in Washington for a July 4 celebration in 2011, which put him back on national TV.

Little Richard loved Nashville and when he moved there, he found that its music industry was wide-ranging, but still with country at its core. Richard settled in Nashville and he was welcomed by the magazine, *The Tennesseean*. He said, 'I came to Nashville to see my sister Peggie. I bought a home for me and her in the hills. I went in for surgery on my hip. I was walking on the way in but I couldn't walk out. I haven't walked since.'

In 2008 Little Richard did a relatively sane interview with Sarfraz Manzoor for BBC Radio 4, and the most interesting part was the writer's passion for Richard's work.

Also in 2008, he appeared on an Imus Ranch album made in New Mexico for the radio host and comedian Don Imus. He performed a country song Webb Pierce's 'I Ain't Never'. It's a sad, seemingly endless version.

He had to cancel a UK tour with Chuck Berry in 2008 because of heart trouble which involved surgery in addition to his problems with mobility.

In 2009, Ace Records released Tony Rounce's compilation, *Holy Mackerel!* of artists trying to sound like Little Richard. This 25-track CD had a playing-time of 55 minutes, so they've got that right: if you're imitating Little Richard, don't outstay your welcome. A single should be a fiery ball of energy that leaves you wanting more.

In June 2010, Richard recorded a gospel track for a tribute album to the songwriter, Dottie Rambo, but this album has not been released. It was probably Little Richard's final studio recording. Tom Jones called Little Richard and asked him to join him for 'Footprints of Jesus', a gospel song associated with Sister Rosetta Tharpe. Richard said he wasn't up to it and suggested Tom took her voice from the recording and did the duet with her instead.

In 2011 the Rock and Roll Hall of Fame recorded a meeting between Chuck Berry, Fats Domino, Little Richard and Jerry Lee Lewis in New Orleans. Little Richard said that God had brought them together. In a rare burst of humour, Jerry Lee said no, a plane had brought him here and Little Richard had come by bus.

In 2012 Little Richard opened *Wrestlemania X* at Madison Square Garden. I presume that they didn't want a piano in the ring and so Richard stood up to perform 'American the Beautiful' with a gospel choir around the ringside. He was taking a chance: who knows what those wrestlers might have done to him in the name of entertainment?

Richard was 79 when *Rolling Stone* spoke to him backstage at the Howard Theater in Washington DC, in 2012. He was brought on with a throne which was a necessity, not a gimmick. Richard said, 'I don't like being photographed in a wheelchair. I don't like anyone seeing me like this, but I'm in pain 24 hours a day,' Still, he played his songs, though he stopped during 'Tutti Frutti', again having difficulty with his breathing.

Richard performed a full 90-minute show at the Pensacola Interstate Fair in Florida in 2012 at the age of 79 and headlined at the Orleans Hotel during the *Viva Las Vegas Rockabilly Weekend* in March 2013. He played for 80 minutes including 'Every Night about This Time', 'Directly from My Heart' and 'Miss Ann'. It was his final performance, as he hadn't the strength to do it anymore. He said, 'I don't perform like I used to but I still have my singing voice. I've had hip surgery, but I am healthy.'

When Richard appeared at a fundraiser for the Recording Academy, clearly he was having a Sputnik moment. He said, 'God talked to me the other night. He said He is getting ready to come. The world is getting ready to end and He's coming.' Somebody laughed and Richard responded, 'When I talk to you about God, I am not playing.' Nevertheless, he presumably thought his old stage suits would endure as he sent them to the Smithsonian.

In May 2013, Richard returned to Macon, where he was awarded an Honorary Doctorate of Humanities from Mercer University. Around this same time, his childhood home on Fifth Avenue was acquired by the Department of Transportation and the process began to relocate it and renovate it. On September 2013, he suffered a heart attack at his home and stated he had taken aspirin and told Danny to turn the air conditioner on, which the doctor confirmed had saved his life. His heart was not strong enough to take any more surgery.

Richard announced his retirement. He received a Distinguished Artist award at the 2019 Tennessee Governor's Arts Awards in Nashville.

In 2014 Brandon Mychal Smith received acclaim for his portrayal of Little Richard in the James Brown biopic *Get On Up*. Mick Jagger was a producer.

In the same year Richard was involved in a car accident in Murfreesboro, Tennessee when somebody came out of a parking lot carelessly. There was damage to Richard's Cadillac SUV but nobody was injured.

In June 2015, Richard appeared in sparkly boots and brightly coloured jacket at the Wildhorse Saloon in Nashville to receive the Rhapsody & Rhythm Award from the National Museum of African-American Music. He was carried in on a wheelchair by four tough guys in suits and shades, so it looked like a kidnapping in reverse. Richard's bodyguards were handing out *Finding Peace Within*, an updated version of *Steps to Christ.* He reminisced about working in Nashville nightclubs.

Richard moved into a penthouse suite at the Hilton Hotel in Nashville. After Prince's early death in 2016, he became obsessed with Prince because all the obituaries referred to Little Richard. William Sobel commented, 'I used to represent Prince, and Richard engages me in all sorts of Prince conversations.' Obviously, Richard saw himself in Prince. I hope that Richard saw Tim Minchin before he died. You may think that the comedian has nothing in common but there are the manic eyes, the attacking piano and the fast and furious novelty songs. Richard must be an inspiration.

In May 2016, Richard was a special guest at the Celebration of Legends Luncheon in Nashville which was honouring Shirley Caesar, Kenneth Gamble and Leon Huff. He appeared at a charity event with Brenda Lee in October 2017.

That year he also appeared on the Seventh-day Adventist television network, Three Angels, to offer his testimony. He sat in a wheelchair, dressed smartly with an ornate jacket and sequinned boots. He was a practised and confident speaker and he said, 'In times like these, we need a Saviour. We need Jesus. There's never been a time in our life where we need God so much. Get on your knees and talk to Jesus. Don't you go to bed another night without giving your commitment to God. The world is getting ready to end. Jesus is getting ready to brush the clouds away. Please, please give your life to Jesus.'

Then again, 'Everybody wants to win the Lottery but God wants to make a deal with you. That is Everlasting Life and he has a mansion that he has built for you. There will be no racism in heaven.' The gathering had equal numbers of Black and white believers. Back in the 1960s, it had been largely Black.

Little Richard was an unpredictable as ever. 'My friend Hugh Hefner passed away. We represent the Bible and he represented another book. I am so glad that I know Jesus and I am 84 years old.' And again, 'The Lord has put me in a wheelchair to save me. I would like to walk to the bathroom on my own as that is a very private thing.'

And his current take on sexuality: 'Jesus made men, men, Jesus made women, women, you know? You gotta live the way God wants you to live.'

Wikipedia estimated Little Richard's wealth at $40m, largely due to Michael Jackson's generosity in giving him the publishing rights on his songs. Little Richard acknowledged this with humour: 'A guy rang me and said, "You are worth over $40m", and I said, "What bank is it in?" (Laughs) Someone has been putting money away and not telling me.'

Little Richard's last years were spent largely at the Hilton in Nashville. With the assistance of Danny, he'd come down the elevator every morning in stage makeup, wig, and spangly costume. Sometimes, he'd play the lobby piano on the way to his gold Cadillac Escalade.

Little Richard was filmed praising Motown musicians in *Hitsville* (2019) and wearing a strange suit where the sleeves had nothing to do with the rest of the jacket. No doubt it was fashion at its most expensive and stylish.

In early 2019, Maggie Gonzalez from Macon began an online campaign proposing that a statue of Richard be erected in downtown Macon, taking the place of a Confederate memorial. It hasn't happened yet.

Bob Dylan's 'Murder Most Foul' included a host of cultural references to the rock'n'roll era including 'Lucille' and 'Dizzy Miss Lizzy' and namechecks for Etta James and Guitar Slim.

After a two-month illness, Little Richard died on 9 May 2020 at the age of 87 at his home in Tullahoma, Tennessee. Although he had heart and mobility problems, Richard's cause of death was cancer. His agent, Dick Alen, said Richard succumbed to bone cancer. 'He was battling this for a good while, many years.'

Both John Prine (April 7) and Little Richard (May 9) died in the Nashville area in 2020, and Bob Dylan commented. 'They don't need anybody doing tributes. Everybody knows what they did and who they were. And they deserve all the respect and acclaim that they received.' Nevertheless, the many tributes included Elvis Costello, John Fogerty, Paul McCartney, Elton John, Mick Jagger, Quincy Jones and clearly, Bob Dylan. 'It is not an ephemeral thing. I can listen to Little Richard forever,' said Lou Reed and we hope he can.

In 2023 *Little Richard: I Am Everything*, a new film directed by Lisa Cortéz, was first shown at the Sundance Film Festival and then released in the UK at selected cinemas for one-day showings. I saw it at The Light in New Brighton with 40 other people, nearly all male but some in their twenties.

The film got off to a cracking start as one short clip follows about another to show us how great Little Richard was, both as a performer and as a guest on a talk show. The pre-credits sequence has pace and life and it says, 'Enjoy the ride!'. However, from that point on, the film is disappointing.

There is little interest in Little Richard's musical legacy. Apart from a couple of gospel songs, there is nothing from his work after 1958. Nothing about Jimi Hendrix or Northern Soul and nothing about his film appearances (*Down and Out in Beverly Hills, The Last*

Action Hero) or his work for the Disney channel.

The man next to me was an expert on American cars and he was tut-tutting over the captions: how can a car from 1962 be in a scene that is dated 1950s?

My favourite moment was Mick Jagger talking about being with the Rolling Stones on a nationwide tour with Little Richard in 1963. He said, 'It was 30 dates, so I saw Little Richard 30 times.' And the Stones got paid for it too.

Acknowledgments

My thanks to Tim Adams, Trevor Cajiao, Stuart Colman, Andrew Doble, Graham Knight, Ulf Krüger, Manfred Kuhlmann, Norman Killon, Anne Leigh, Mark Lewisohn, Jana Russakoff Sultan and everybody that I have quoted directly in the text for this story.

I have consulted back issues of *Disc, Melody Maker, New Musical Express, Record Mirror, Record Retailer* and *World's Fair* as well as the US magazines, *Billboard* and *Rolling Stone,* and the British Newspaper Archive at British Library.

Now Dig This, the rock'n'roll magazine, is a treasure of information with numerous features on Little Richard. I was particularly glad to find a 1988 edition featuring Seamus McGarvey conducting a frank interview with Charles Connor, drummer with the Upsetters and Little Richard's brother-in-law. Charles died in a hospice in 2021. I wrote features on the Everly Brothers–Little Richard–Bo Diddley tour of the UK for *Now Dig This* from September 2013 to January 2014,

Credits also to *The Life and Times of Little Richard* by Charles (Dr Rock) White (Omnibus 2003), *Rocking the Closet* by Vincent L Stephens (University of Illinois Press, 2019), *American Rock'n'Roll: The UK Tours 1956–72* by Ian Wallis (Music Mentor 2003), and scores of other rock books that have Little Richard in the index.

Shout, Sister, Shout! by Gayle F Wald is an engrossing study of one of Little Richard's key influences, Sister Rosetta Tharpe, and how the most unlikely people became rock'n'roll trailblazers.

As for travel books, you can't do much better than *Music USA* (Richie Unterberger (Rough Guides, 1999) and *Blues Highway – New Orleans to Chicago* by Richard Knight (Trailblazer, 2001). A big shout-out to my old pal Roy Kerridge, the author of an extraordinary travelogue, *In the Deep South* (Michael Joseph, 1989). Roy was one of the UK's great eccentrics and a lovable and thoughtful guy, who really got you thinking.

There is a mass of material on the internet – over 7 million hits if you Google 'Little Richard' – and what I've seen is mostly repetitive. However, there is a very informative account by Dr DeWitt S Williams of his time at Oakwood College studying theology with Little Richard.

I've been writing and broadcasting on popular music since the 1970s and so have amassed hundreds of interviews, which I suppose has some cultural significance. Some of my programmes are online with the British Library and Liverpool Records Office. Chas White (Dr Rock) was one of my regular guests and so I have many fascinating comments as to how he ghosted Little Richard's autobiography.

Joe Ankrah was a member of the Liverpool doowop group, the Chants.

Tony Ashton was part of Ashton, Gardner and Dyke.

Pete Best played drums for the Beatles and then formed the Pete Best Four.

Peter Bogdanovich was the director of *The Last Picture Show* and *Paper Moon.*

The Merseyside academic **Mike Brocken** could be the most opinionated critic in the area. It is always stimulating to listen to him.

Eric Burdon was the lead singer of the Animals, the Newcastle band.

Roger Chapman was the lead singer of Family.

John Collis has written biographies of Chuck Berry, Eddie Cochran, Van Morrison and Gene Vincent. He is also a noted cricket writer.

Stuart Colman was a record producer who worked with the Crickets, Phil Everly, Shakin' Stevens and Cliff Richard as well as making an album with Little Richard.

Tony Crane is the lead singer of the Merseybeats.

Marshall Crenshaw has released several albums and wrote the book, *Hollywood Rock* (1994).

In the 1980s **Kid Creole** led the hitmaking Coconuts.

Geoff Davies founded Probe Records in Liverpool.

For rock'n'roll with attitude, you can't beat **Bo Diddley**.

For years, I've telling **Andrew Doble** to write *The Names in Brackets*, the history of '50s and '60s songwriting.

If the history of New Orleans music can be embodied in one man, it is **Dr John**. He is my default position on Spotify.

Paul Du Noyer began writing for the *NME i*n the 1970s and founded both *Q* and *MOJO*. His history of Liverpool music is called *Wondrous Place*: I agree.

Theatre director **Bob Eaton** is acclaimed for musicals, including *Good Golly Miss Molly*.

Throughout all the Hollies' line-ups, **Bobby Elliott** has been the drummer and they worked with Little Richard on their first US dates.

David Essex was a major '70s music star and film actor.

Ron Ellis is known for his Johnny Ace series of crime novels.

Brill Building songwriter **Paul Evans** wrote 'When' (Kalin Twins) and had his own hits with 'Seven Little Girls' and 'Hello, This is Joanie'. His autobiography *Happy Go Lucky Me* is published by McNidder & Grace.

Frankie Ford is a New Orleans singer/pianist known for 'Sea Cruise'.

In 1972 **Ray Foulk** promoted the Wembley Rock'n'Roll Festival with Little Richard, Chuck Berry, Jerry Lee Lewis and Bill Haley: a logistical nightmare.

Clarence Fountain was the leader of the gospel group, the Five Blind Boys of Alabama.

Andrew Gold is an American singer/songwriter best known for 'Never Let Her Slip Away'. (1978).

Oxford graduate **Jack Good** was the pioneering rock'n'roll producer of British TV with *6.5 Special* and *Oh Boy!* and he worked with Richard on the US series *Shindig*.

British singer **Julie Grant** toured with Little Richard in 1963.

Michael Gray is known for his authoritative books on Bob Dylan and the blues. He saw Little Richard in the early' 60s.

Sid Griffin is an American singer/songwriter strongly influenced by the Byrds and Gram Parsons and the author of several music books.

Granada producer **Johnny Hamp** made a TV special with Little Richard and the Shirelles.

Sam Hardie was the pianist with Kingsize Taylor and the Dominoes and worked with Little Richard in Hamburg.

Jet Harris played bass guitar for the Shadows and had a No.1 with Tony Meehan on 'Diamonds'.

Billy Hatton was a member of the Fourmost, who covered 'The Girl Can't Help It' and 'Heeby-Jeebies'.

Dale Hawkins wrote and recorded the rock'n'roll classic 'Susie-Q'.

Noted for his studies on Bob Dylan, **Clinton Heylin** wrote about 'fake' songwriting credits in *It's One for the Money* (Constable, 2015). He describes Art Rupe as 'a thief amongst princes'.

Herbert Hildebrand of the Rattles toured with Little Richard in 1963.

Dave Hill was a member of Slade who had their first hit by covering Little Richard's 'Get Down with It'.

Michael Hill was educated at Quarry Bank with John Lennon.

Chas Hodges was half of Chas & Dave.

In the 1960s **Chris Hutchins** was a noted *NME* journalist.

Holly Johnson fronted Frankie Goes To Hollywood.

Paul Jones is the front man for Manfred Mann and the Blues Band and a blues aficionado.

Norman Jopling was a staff writer for *Record Mirror* in the 1960s.

John Jorgenson was the guitarist with the Hellecasters and Desert Road Band and is a great solo performer.

Dave Kelly is part of the Blues Band with Paul Jones.

Who better to ask about rock'n'roll films than the eminent film critic **Mark Kermode**?

B B King has influenced a whole generation of blues-orientated guitarists.

Billy Kinsley played bass with the Merseybeats and Liverpool Express.

Graham Knight was a close friend of Little Richard's. I am so grateful that he read over my draft text and made comments.

Jeff Kruger was a UK impresario.

Jim Lea is a founder member of Slade and produed many of their records.

Hollywood songwriter **Joe Lubin** wrote new words for 'Tutti Frutti'.

Tom McGuinness was part of Manfred Mann and the Blues Band.

UK theatre impresario **Laurie Mansfield** has been involved with many rock'n'roll musicals.

Gerry Marsden led Gerry and the Pacemakers and worked with Richard at the Star-Club in Hamburg.

Songwriter **Bill Martin** won the *Eurovision Song Contest* with 'Puppet on a String'.

Juan Martin is a Spanish classical guitarist.

Hank Marvin was the distinctive lead guitarist for the Shadows.

Bill Medley was one-half of the Righteous Brothers.

Drummer **Trevor Morais** made his name in the 60s club band, the Peddlers.

In the early 1960s, **Pete Morris** was a Liverpool jazz musician.

Chris Norman was the distinctive lead singer of Smokie.

Since the 1950s, **Mick O'Toole** has been an ardent rock'n'roll fan.

Folk musician **Tom Paley** was a member of the New Lost City Ramblers.

Al Peters is a Liverpool rock musician best known for his band, Almost Blues. Travels everywhere with his harmonica as he never wants to miss an opportunity to jam.

When I interviewed **Slim Jim Phantom** of the Stray Cats, he got a call from Harry Dean Stanton who was struggling with the crossword in the *LA Times*.

The American session singer Jim Smith established a new career for himself in the UK as **P J Proby**.

Very excitingly, **Bonnie Raitt** merged blues with rock in the 1970s.

Tim Rice has been knighted for his services to musical theatre.

In 2004 **Tim Riley** wrote a definitive study, *Fever,* on how rock'n'roll transformed gender in America. He wrote, 'Little Richard's gibberish was really code for God knows what.'

Red Robinson was a Canadian DJ who interviewed Little Richard in the 1950s.

Sing if you're glad to be gay with **Tom Robinson**.

Chris Smither is a noted blues performer with a fine catalogue of his own songs.

John Stafford was a music writer and researcher, best known for a biography of Ricky Nelson.

Bob Stanley is among the UK's best-known rock writer and a member of Saint Etienne.

John Steel played drums for the Newcastle band, the Animals.

Dicky Tarrach played drums for Gene Vincent's Blue Caps.

Peter Tork was one of the Monkees who featured Little Richard on a TV special.

The actress **Rita Tushingham** is best known for her roles in *A Taste of Honey* and *Dr Zhivago.*

Steve Van Zandt is famed as a member of E Street Band and was married by Little Richard.

The veteran of many pop tours, **Bobby Vee** sometimes worked with Little Richard.

Since the 1950s, **Steve Voce** has been a critic for the UK publication *Jazz Journal.*

Artist and bass player **Klaus Voormann** saw Little Richard at the Star-Club in Hamburg.

Loudon Wainwright is one of the quirkiest of all songwriters.

Session singer **Jennifer Warnes** is best known for her hits with Joe Cocker and Bill Medley.

Brian Wake has a wonderful tale about the Beatles and Little Richard.

All hail to **Chas White** for writing Little Richard's autobiography.

Bill Wyman has been both a Rolling Stone and a Rhythm King.

Roy Young worked with Little Richard and sang many of his songs.

APPENDIX 1

A Little Richard Discography

Little Richard only recorded around 250 different songs, not a substantial amount for someone who was on the scene for over 50 years. His full discography, however, would be vast as he often rerecorded his hits and his main recordings have been endlessly reissued, particularly in the UK where recordings went out of copyright after 50 years. From 2007, anybody in the UK could issue *Little Richard's Greatest Hits*, and frequently did. There's no point in listing all these reissues and what's more, it means you can't see the wood for the trees. Except for a few noted instances, the reissues are omitted from this discography.

UK chart placings are from *Guinness Book of British Hit Singles and Albums*. US chart placings are from *Billboard* magazine.

Little Richard – UK Discography

SINGLES

Rip It Up / Reddy Teddy (London HLO 8336, First UK release and not issued until November 1956, No. 30)

Long Tall Sally / Tutti Frutti (London HLO 8366, 1957, A-side No. 3, B-side No. 29)

The Girl Can't Help It / She's Got It (London HLO 8382, 1957, A-side No. 9, B-side No.15)

Lucille / Send Me Some Lovin' (London HLO 8446, 1957, No. 10)

Jenny, Jenny / Miss Ann (London HLO 8470, 1957, No. 11)

Keep A-Knockin' / Can't Believe You Wanna Leave (London HLO 8509, 1957, No. 21)

Good Golly, Miss Molly / Hey Hey Hey Hey (London HLU 8560, 1958, No. 8)

Ooh! My Soul / True Fine Mama (London HLO 8647, 1958, No.22)

Baby Face / I'll Never Let You Go (London HLU 8770, 1958, No.2, Richard's highest UK chart placing)

By the Light of the Silvery Moon / Early One Morning (London HLU 8831, 1959, No. 17)

Kansas City / She Knows How to Rock (London HLU 8868, 1959, No. 26)

I Got It / Baby (London HLU 9065, 1959)

He's Not Just a Soldier / Joy Joy Joy (Mercury AMT 1165, 1961)

He Got What He Wanted / Why Don't You Change Your Ways (Mercury AMT 1189, 1962, No.38)

Crying in the Chapel / Hole in the Wall (London HLK 9708, 1963)
Travellin' Shoes / It Is No Secret (London HLK 9756, 1963)
Blueberry Hill / Cherry Red (Fontana TF 519, 1963)
Bama Lama Bama Loo / Annie Is Back (London HL 9896, 1964, No. 20)
Whole Lotta Shakin' Goin' on / Goodnight Irene (Stateside SS 340, 1964)
Joy Joy Joy / Peace in the Valley (Mercury MF 841, 1965)
Holy Mackerel / Baby, Don't You Want A Man Like Me (Stateside SS 508, 1966)
I Don't Know What You've Got But It's Got Me (Parts 1 & 2) (Fontana TF 652, 1966)
Poor Dog / Well (Columbia DB 7974, 1966)
I Need Love / The Commandments of Love (Columbia DB 8058, 1966)
Dance What You Wanna / Without Love (Sue WI 4001, 1966)
It Ain't What You Do / Cross Over (Sue WI 4015, 1966)
Get Down with It / Rosemary (Columbia DB 8116, 1967)
A Little Bit of Something / Money (Columbia DB 8240, 1967)
I Don't Want to Discuss It / Hurry Sundown (Columbia DB 8263, 1967)
Whole Lotta Shakin' Goin' on / Lawdy Miss Clawdy (President PT 201, 1968)
Try Some of Mine / She's Together (MCA MU 1006, 1968)
Baby, What You Want Me To Do (Parts 1 & 2) (Action ACT 4528, 1969)
Freedom Blues / Dew Drop Inn (Reprise RS 20907, 1970)
Dancing in the Street / Green Power (Reprise K 14124, 1971)
Without Love / Talkin' 'Bout Soul (President PT 329, 1971)
Money Is / Money Runner (B-side by Quincy Jones, Reprise K 14150, 1972)
Rockin' with the King / I Don't Care What You Told Me (A-side with Canned Heat, B-side just Canned Heat) (United Artists UP 35348, 1972)
Mockingbird Sally / Rockin' Rockin' Boogie / King of Rock and Roll (Reprise K 14195, maxi-single, 1972)
Poor Boy Paul / Wonderin' (Specialty SON 5001, 1972)
Tutti Frutti / Keep A-Knockin' (Specialty SON 5002, 1973)
Long Tall Sally / Heeby-Jeebies (Specialty SON 5015, 1974)
Lucille / Good Golly Miss Molly (Charly CYS 1027, 1977)
Good Golly Miss Molly / Rip It Up / By the Light of the Silvery Moon (Creole CR 140, maxi-single, also available on 12-inch, 1977, No. 37)
Send Me Some Lovin' 1978 / King Sax (A-side with Tutti Frutties, B-side just Tutti Frutties, Creole CR 61, 1978)
The Girl Can't Help It / Good Golly Miss Molly / Rip It Up (Creole CR 191, 1980)
Long Tall Sally / Tutti Frutti (CBS A 4593, 1984)
Great Gosh A'mighty / The Ride (MCA 1049, 1986, No.62)

Operator / Big House Reunion (WEA YZ 89, 1986, No.67)

Happy Endings / California Girls (A-side with Beach Boys, B-side just Beach Boys), Critique B 7-99392, also available on 12-inch picture disc, 1987)

EXTENDED PLAYS

Little Richard and his Band, Part 1 (London REO 1071, 1957)

She's Got It / Heeby-Jeebies / I'm just a Lonely Guy / Slippin' And Slidin'

Little Richard and his Band, Part 2 (London REO 1074, 1957)

Rip It Up / Long Tall Sally / Ready Teddy / Tutti Frutti

Little Richard and his Band, Part 3 (London REO 1103, 1957)

Lucille / Jenny, Jenny / Send Me Some Lovin' / The Girl Can't Help It

Little Richard and his Band, Part 4 (London REO 1106, 1957)

Miss Ann / Baby / Can't Believe You Wanna Leave / Oh Why

Little Richard and his Band, Part 5 (London REO 1208, 1957)

Baby Face / By the Light of the Silvery Moon / Early one Morning/ She Knows How to Rock

Little Richard and his Band, Part 6 (London REO 1234, 1957)

Keep a Knockin' / True Fine Mama / All Around the World / Good Golly Miss Molly

Little Richard and his Band, Part 7 (London REO 1235, 1957)

Kansas City / Chicken Little Baby / Shake a Hand / Whole Lotta Shakin' Goin' on

Little Richard and Brock Peters (Summit LSE 2049, 1963)

He's Back (Atlantic tracks, London REK 1400, 1963)

Travellin' Shoes / Hole in the Wall / Crying in the Chapel / It is No Secret

Four Dynamic Numbers (Summit LSE 2049, 1963)

His Name's so Sweet / Sorrow Valley / Shilima Jiwe / Take My Hand, Precious Lord

Memphis Slim and Little Richard (Vocalion EP VEP 170-155, 1964) This isn't a magical session that nobody has heard before. It is an EP with separate tracks from Memphis Slim and Little Richard. Richard performs Directly from My Heart and I Love My Baby, both with Johnny Otis' Orchestra.

Do You Feel It (Stateside SE 1042)

Do You Feel It / Holy Mackerel / Baby, Don't You Want a Man Like Me

Little Richard (Reprise K 14343, 1974)

Rockin' Rockin' Boogie / King of Rock and Roll / The Saints / Mockingbird Sally

Little Richard (Specialty SON 5016, 1975)

I Got It / Rock And Roll Is Here To Stay / Keep A-Knockin' / Bama Lama Bama Loo

Little Richard and Larry Williams (UK Specialty SONE 1, 1977)

Long Tall Sally and Lucille plus Larry Williams with Bony Moronie and Dizzy Miss Lizzy

ALBUMS

Here's Little Richard (London HAO 2055, 1957)

Tutti Frutti / True Fine Mama / Can't Believe You Wanna Leave / Ready Teddy / Baby / Slippin' and Slidin' / Long Tall Sally / Miss Ann / Oh Why / Rip It Up / Jenny Jenny / She's Got It

Little Richard, Volume 2 (London HAU 2126, 1958)

Keep A-Knockin' / By the Light of the Silvery Moon / Send Me Some Lovin' / I'll Never Let You Go / Heeby-Jeebies / All Around the World / Good Golly Miss Molly / Baby Face / Hey, Hey, Hey, Hey, / Ooh! My Soul / The Girl Can't Help It / Lucille

The Fabulous Little Richard (London HAU 2193, 1959)

Shake a Hand / Chicken Little Baby / All Night Long / The Most I Can Offer / Lonesome and Blue / Wonderin' / She Knows How to Rock / Kansas City / Directly from my Heart / Maybe I'm Right / Early One Morning / I'm just a Lonely Guy /Whole Lotta Shakin' Goin' on

Little Richard (RCA Camden CDN 125, 1959)

The four US RCA singles with additional tracks from the Buck Ram Rock and Roll Orchestra

It's Real (Mercury MCL 20036, 1961)

It's Real / Joy, Joy, Joy / Do You Care / The Captain Calls for You / In Times Like These / Do Lord, Remember Me/ Ride On King Jesus / Peace in the Valley / He's Not just a Soldier / My Desire / He's My Star / It Takes Everything to Serve the Lord

Little Richard Is Back (Fontana TL 5235, 1965)

Hound Dog / Money Honey / Goin' Home Tomorrow / Lawdy Miss Clawdy / Short Fat Fannie / Only You / Groovy Little Suzie / Memories Are Made of This

The Incredible Little Richard Sings His Greatest Hits Live! (UK Polydor 236 202, 1967)

Tutti Frutti / Keep A-Knockin' / Rip It Up / Jenny Jenny / Lucille / Bama Lama Bama Loo / Long Tall Sally / Ready Teddy / True Fine Mama / Whole Lotta Shakin' Goin' On / Slippin' and Slidin' / Bring It on Home To Me / Bony Moronie / Do You Feel It (Parts 1 &2)

King of the Gospel Singers (Fontana SFL 13010, 1968)

Let's take the 1961 LP *It's Real*, remove the first track from each side and sell it at a budget price.

Little Richard Sings with Brock Peters (UK Summit ATL 4124, 1964)

Really Movin' Gospel (with Sister Rosetta Tharpe) (UK Ember NR 5022, 1965)

Little Richard and Roy Orbison (RCA Camden CDS 1077, 1970)

Little Richard and Sister Rosetta Tharpe (Marble Arch MAL 1319, 1970)

Four of the many examples of Little Richard tracks that are put with other artists in the hope some people will be taken in.

Little Richard's Greatest Hits (Fontana TL 5314, 1966)

Send Me Some Lovin' / Lucille / She's Got It / Keep A-Knockin' / Slippin' And Slidin' / Good Golly Miss Molly / Tutti Frutti / Long Tall Sally / Rip It up / Baby Face / The Girl Can't Help It / Ooh! My Soul

Little Richard Is Back (Joy JOYS 100, 1968)

Whole Lotta Shakin' Goin' on / Going Home Tomorrow / Money Honey / Only You / Hound Dog /Goodnight Irene / Lawdy Miss Clawdy / Groovy Little Suzy /Short Fat Fannie / Cherry Red/ Memories Are Made of This / Blueberry Hill

The Rill Thing (Reprise RS 6406, 1970)

Freedom Blues / Greenwood, Mississippi / Two Time Loser / Dew Drop Inn / Somebody Saw You / Spreading Natta What's the Matter / The Rill Thing / Lovesick Blues / I Saw Her Standing There

Although promoted as the new Little Richard album in the UK, they were imported copies and so had the US catalogue number.

King of Rock and Roll (Reprise K 44136, 1971)

Green Power / Settin' the Woods on Fire / Dancing in the Street / The Way You Do the Things You Do / In the Name /Midnight Special / Born on the Bayou / I'm So Lonesome I Could Cry / Brown Sugar / Joy to the World

The Heist (Reprise K 44168, soundtrack album with two Little Richard tracks. 1972)

Money Is / Do It – To It

The Second Coming (Warner WB K 44204, 1973)

Mockingbird Sally / The Saints / Sanctified Satisfied Toetapper / Nuki Suki / Thomasine / Rockin' Rockin' Boogie / It Ain't What You Do / Second Line / Prophet Of Peace

Lifetime Friend (WEA WX 72, 1986)

Great Gosh A'Mighty / Operator / Somebody's Comin' / Lifetime Friend / Destruction / I Found My Way / The World Can't Do Me / One Ray Of Sunshine / Someone Cares,/ Big House Reunion

Little Richard Meets Masayoshi Takanaka (Japanese album 1992)

Good Golly Miss Molly / Tutti Frutti / Miss Ann / Lucille / Long Tall Sally / Send Me Some Lovin' / Jenny, Jenny / Rip It Up / Kansas City / Ready teddy

The EP Collection (See For Miles SEECD 366, 1993)

The seven EPs above so 28 tracks on one CD but the playing time is still only 64 minutes.

The Best from the Star-Club (Outlaw OTB 1100031, 2CD, 1996)

Four familiar Little Richard studio tracks with added applause. Avoid.

Talking 'Bout Soul (RPMSH 217, 2001)

28 track compilation of Little Richard on Vee-Jay in the early 1960s.

Rock'n'Roll Radio Australia 1957 (Rockstar RSRCD 022, 2003)

Two radio shows hosted by Jack Davey in Sydney with US rock'n'roll stars. Little Richard and the Upsetters perform Lucille and Long Tall Sally and the Upsetters back Eddie Cochran on Whole Lotta Shakin' Goin' On. There's an interview with Little Richard.

The Girl Can't Help It (Fantastic Voyage FVTD 149, 3CD, 2012)

A triple-CD set of almost four hours music based around the soundtrack of *The Girl Can't Help It*. The first 16 tracks are all by Little Richard.

The Rill Thing / King of Rock and Roll / The Second Coming (BGO BGOCD 1235, 2CD, 2016)

The three Reprise albums spread over 2CDs with CD booklet from Stuart Colman

Cast a Long Shadow (Floating World FLOATM 6288, 2017)

22 track collection of tracks produced by Larry Williams on OKeh in 1966/7.

Little Richard – US Discography

SINGLES

Every Hour / Taxi Blues (RCA 4392, 1952)

Get Rich Quick / Thinkin' about My Mother (RCA 4582, 1952)

Ain't Nothing Happenin' / Why Did You Leave Me RCA 4722, 1952)

Please Have Mercy on Me / I Brought It All on Myself (RCA 5025, 1952)

Fool at the Wheel / Ain't That Good News (As the Deuces of Rhythm & Tempo Toppers), Peacock 1616, 1952)

Rice, Red Beans and Turnip Greens / Always (As the Tempo Toppers, Peacock 1628, 1954)

Tutti Frutti / I'm just a Lonely Guy (Specialty 561, 1955, Pop No.17, R & B No.2 for 6 weeks)

Directly from My Heart / Little Richard's Boogie (Little Richard with the Johnny Otis Orchestra, Peacock 1658, 1956)

Maybe I'm Right / I Love My Baby (Little Richard with the Johnny Otis Orchestra, Peacock 1673, 1956)

Long Tall Sally / Slippin' and Slidin' (Specialty 572, 1956, A-side Pop No.6, R & B No.1 for 8 weeks, B-side Pop No. 33, R & B No.2)

Rip It Up / Ready Teddy (Specialty 579, 1956, A-side Pop No.17, R & B No.1 for 2 weeks, B-side Pop No.44, R & B No.8)

She's Got It / Heeby-Jeebies (Specialty 584, 1956, A-side R & B No. 9, B-side R & B No.7, a mystery: why wasn't this on Pop chart?)

The Girl Can't Help It / All Around the World (Specialty 591, 1956, A-side Pop No.49, R & B No.7, B-side R & B No.13)

Lucille / Send Me Some Lovin' (Specialty 598, 1957, A-side Pop No.21, R & B No.1 for 2 weeks, B-side Pop No.54, R & B No.3)

Jenny Jenny / Miss Ann (Specialty 606, 1957, Pop No.10, R & B No.2)

Keep A-Knockin' / Can't Believe You Wanna Leave (Specialty 611, 1957, Pop No.8, R & B No.2)

Good Golly Miss Molly / Hey Hey Hey Hey (Specialty 624, 1958, Pop No.10, R & B No.4)

Ooh! My Soul / True Fine Mama (Specialty 633, 1958, No.31 for A-side, No. 68 for B-side, R & B No.15 both sides listed together)

Baby Face / I'll Never Let You Go (Specialty 645, 1958, Pop No.41, R & B No.12)

She Knows How to Rock / Early One Morning (Specialty 652, 1959)

By the Light of the Silvery Moon / Wonderin' (Specialty 660, 1959)

Kansas City / Lonesome and Blue (Specialty 664, 1959, Pop No. 95)

Shake a Hand / All Night Long (Specialty 670, 1959)

Maybe I'm Right / Whole Lotta Shakin' Goin' On (Specialty 680, 1959)

I Got It / Baby (Specialty 681, 1959)

Directly from My Heart / Most I Can Offer (Specialty 686, 1959)

Troubles of the Word / Save Me Lord (End 1057, 1959)

Milky White Way / I've just Come from the Fountain (End 1058. 1959)

I Found a God / Fly Away Jesus (Sensational Sounds 45-196, 1960)

I'm In Love Again / Every Night about This Time (Little Star 123, 1961)

He's Not Just a Soldier / Joy Joy Joy (Mercury 71884, 1961)

Do You Care / Ride on King Jesus (Mercury 71911, 1961)

He Got What He Wanted / Why Don't You Change Your Ways (Mercury 71965, 1962)

Crying in the Chapel / Hole in the Wall (Atlantic 2181, No.119, 1963)

Travellin' Shoes / It Is No Secret (Atlantic 2192, 1963)

Valley of Tears / Freedom Ride (Little Star 128, 1963)

Milky White Way / Need Him (Coral 62366, 1963)

Bama Lama Bama Loo / Annie Is Back (Specialty 692, 1964, B-side Pop No.82)

Whole Lotta Shakin' Goin' On / Goodnight Irene (Vee-Jay 612, 1964)

Blueberry Hill / Cherry Red (Vee-Jay 625, 1964)

Cross Over / It Ain't What You Do (Vee-Jay 652, 1965)

Dance What You Wanna / Without Love) (Vee Jay 665, 1965)

I Don't Know What You've Got But It's Got Me (Parts 1 & 2) (Vee-Jay 698, 1965, US R & B No.12)

Holy Mackerel / Baby Don't You Want A Man Like Me (Modern 1018, 1966)

Do You Feel It (Parts 1 &2) (Modern 1019, 1966)

Poor Dog / Well (OKeh 7251, 1966, No.121)

I Need Love / The Commandments of Love (OKeh 7262, 1966)

I'm Back / Directly from My Heart (Modern 1022, 1966)

I Don't Want to Discuss It / Hurry Sundown (OKeh 7271, 1967)

Don't Deceive Me / Never Gonna Let You Go (OKeh 7278, 1967)

A Little Bit of Something / Money (OKeh 7286, 1967)

Try Some of Mine / She's Together (Brunswick 55362, 1967)

Baby, Don't You Tear My Clothes / Stingy Jenny (Brunswick 55377, 1968)

Soul Train / Can I Count on You (Brunswick 55386, 1968)

Lucille / Whole Lotta Shakin' Goin' On (OKeh 7325, 1969)

Bama Lama Bama Loo / Keep A-Knockin' (Specialty 697. 1970)

Freedom Blues / Dew Drop Inn (Reprise 0907, 1970, Pop No.47, R & B No.28)

Greenwood, Mississippi / I Saw Her Standing There (Reprise 0942, 1970, Pop No. 85)

Poor Boy Paul / Wonderin' (Specialty 699, 1970)

Shake a Hand / Somebody Saw You (Reprise 1005, 1971)

Black Man – White Man / Midnight Man (ABC 11312, 1971, No. 80)

Rockin' with the King / I Don't Care What You Tell Me (A-side with Canned Heat, B-side just Canned Heat) (United Artists LP 50892, 1972, No. 88)

Goodnight Irene / Why Don't You Love Me (Ala 1175, 1972)

Money Is / Money Runner (B-side by Quincy Jones, Reprise REP 1062, 1972)

Good Golly Miss Molly / Lucille (Bell 1780, 1973)

In the Middle of the Night / Where Will I Find a Place to Sleep This Evening (Greene Mountain 413, 1973)

In the Name / Don't You Know (Kent 4568, 1973)

Call My Name / Steal Miss Liza (Manticore 7007, 1975, No. 106)

Try to Help Your Brother / Funk Proof (Mainstream 5572, 1975)

Great Gosh A'mighty / The Ride (Reprise 0907, 1986, No.42, R & B No.28)

Operator / Big House Reunion (WEA YZ 89, 1986, No.67)

Happy Endings (with the Beach Boys) (B-side California Girls by the Beach Boys, Atco B 9392, 1987) (also available as 12-inch picture disc)

EXTENDED PLAYS

Little Richard (RCA Camden CAE 416, 1957)

Ain't Nothing Happenin' / Why Did You Leave Me / Every Hour / I Brought It All on Myself

Little Richard Rocks! (RCA Camden CAE 446, 1958)

Taxi Blues / Please Have Mercy on Me/ Get Rich Quick / Thinkin' about My Mother

ALBUMS

Here's Little Richard (Specialty LP 100, then 2100, No.13.1957)

Little Richard (Camden LP 420, 1958)

*Little Richard (*Specialty LP 2103, 1958)

The Fabulous Little Richard (Specialty LP 2104, 1959)

Pray Along with Little Richard, Volume 1 (Golden LP-4001, 1960)

Need Him / Comin' Home / I'm Trampin' / Just a Closer Walk with Thee / Does Jesus Care / God is Real / Jesus Walked this Lonesome Valley / Take My Hand, Precious Lord

Pray Along with Little Richard, Volume 2 (Golden LP-4002, 1960)

Search Me, Lord / I Know the Lord / Every Time I Feel the Spirit / Certainly Lord / Tell God My Troubles / In My Heart / I'm Quittin' Show Business

Little Richard Sings Spirituals (United, UM 123, 1960)

The King of Gospel Singers (Mercury LP 60656, 1961)

Little Richard Sings Gospel (20th Century Fox 5010, 1963)

Little Richard Sings Freedom Songs (Crown 5362, 1963)

Clap Your Hands (Spin-O-Rama LP 119, 1963)

A reissue of the Crown LP, itself a reissue. It even has the Crown catalogue number in the run-off groove.

Comin' Home (Coral LP 57446, 1963)

Little Richard Sings (Summit 4029, 1963)

Little Richard's Biggest Hits (Specialty 2111, 1964)

Really Movin' Gospel (with Sister Rosetta Tharpe) (US Guest Star LP 1429, 1965)

Little Richard Is Back (US Vee-Jay 1107, 1964)

Hound Dog / Money Honey / Goin' Home Tomorrow / Lawdy Miss Clawdy / Short Fat Fannie / Only You / Groovy Little Suzie / Memories Are Made of This

Little Richard's Greatest Hits (Vee-Jay 1124, 1964)

Send Me Some Lovin' / Lucille / She's Got It / Keep A-Knockin' / Slippin' And Slidin' / Good Golly Miss Molly / Tutti Frutti / Long Tall Sally / Rip It Up / Baby Face / The Girl Can't Help It / Ooh! My Soul

The Incredible Little Richard Sings His Greatest Hits Live! (Modern LP 1000, 1966)

Tutti Frutti / Keep A-Knockin' / Rip It Up / Jenny Jenny / Lucille / Bama Lama Bama Loo / Long Tall Sally / Ready Teddy / True Fine Mama / Whole Lotta Shakin' Goin' On / Slippin' and Slidin' / Bring It On Home To Me (mistitled Bring It Back Home) / Bony Moronie / Do You Feel It (Parts 1 &2)

The Wild and Frantic Little Richard (Modern 1003, 1966)

Miss Ann / Good Golly Miss Molly / Send Me Some Lovin' / Groovy Little Suzie / Do the Jerk / Baby What You Want Me To Do (Parts 1 & 2)

The Explosive Little Richard (OKeh 14121, 1967)

Function at the Junction / Never Gonna Let You Go / Land of 1,000 Dances / Don't Deceive Me / Money

Little Richard's Greatest Hits – Recorded Live! (OKeh 14121, 1967)

Lucille / Long Tall Sally / The Girl Can't Help It / Send Me Some Lovin' / Jenny Jenny / Tutti Frutti / True Fine Mama / Whole Lotta Shakin' Goin ' On / Good Golly Miss Molly / Anyway You Want Me (actually Baby, What You Want Me To Do) / You Gotta Feel It / Get Down with It

The Rill Thing (UK Reprise RS 6406, 1970)

King of Rock and Roll (US Reprise 6462, 1971)

Friends from the Beginning – Little Richard & Jimi Hendrix (Ala 1972, 1972)

Right Now! (United 7791, 1973)

In the Name / Mississippi / Chains of Love / Don't You Know / Sittin' on the Dock of the Bay / Chain Chain Chain / Hot Nuts / Geraldine Jones

Let The Good Times Roll soundtrack (Bell 9002, 1973)

Lucille / Good Golly Miss Molly / Rip It Up + other artists

The Second Coming (Reprise MS 2107, 1972)

Talking 'Bout Soul (Dynasty 7304, 1974)

You Better Stop / Something Moves in My Heart

Little Richard Live (K-Tel 462, 1976)

Re-recordings of Specialty hits

God's Beautiful City (World 1001, 1979)

There is Someone Worse Off than I / If You Got the Lord on your Side / It Is No Secret / I Surrender All / What Am I Supposed to Do without Jesus / Come by Here, My Lord / God's Beautiful City/ Little Richard's Testimony (Parts 1 &2)

Down and Out in Beverly Hills (US MCA 6160, 1985)

Two tracks with Little Richard

Lifetime Friend (Warner 1-25529, 1986)

Mickey's Rock Around the Mouse (US Disneyland 62527, 1987)

One track from Little Richard

Grand Slam (Grudge 4758-7-F, 1989)

A Rage in Harlem (US Sire 9 22617-2, 1991)

Elevator Operator

For Our Children (Disney 60616-2, 1991)

Itsy Bitsy Spider

We're Back (MCA 10986, 1993)

One track in film, *Roll Back the Rock*

Casper the Friendly Ghost (US MCA D 1124, 1995)

Theme song!

Splish Splash (Sesame Street 72438 5544729, 1995)

Rubber Duckie

Songs from West Side Story (RCA 09026 62707 2, 1996)

I Feel Pretty

Why Do Fools Fall In Love (Warner 62765-2, 1999)

Keep A-Knockin'

Kindred Spirits: Tribute to Johnny Cash (Lucky Dog CK 86310, 2002)

Get Rhythm

The Complete Specialty and Vee-Jay Albums (Fantasy, 5CD, 2016)

Guest Appearances

James Gang (with Joe Walsh)

But I Try, 1971, but not released until Joe Walsh's *Analog Man* (Universal 46050 26711747, 2012). In 1997 Little Richard and Joe Walsh performed 'Rocky Mountain Way' on *The Drew Carey Show.*

Jefferson Airplane

The Man (Bludgeon of a Bluecoat), 1971, unreleased as the band released a version without Richard.

Delaney and Bonnie

Miss Ann on *To Bonnie From Delaney* (US Atco SD 33341, 1971)

Bachman-Turner Overdrive

Piano on Take It Like a Man and Stay Alive from the gold album, *Head On* (US Mercury SRM 11067, 1975)

Beach Boys

Additional vocals on Happy Endings (US Atco B 9392, 1987)

Fishbone

Rock Island Line on *Folkways: A Vision Shared* (US Columbia OC 44034, 1988)

Philip Bailey

Title song on soundtrack for *Twins* (US WTGP 45036-1, 1988)

Living Colour

Sermonising added to Elvis Is Dead (Epic single 49-73677, US Dance Hits, No.18, 1990

Jon Bon Jovi

You Really Got Me Now duet in *Young Guns II,* 1990

Elton John

The Power with Elton John for John *Duets* (US Rocket 518478-2, 1991)

Tanya Tucker

Somethin' Else with Tanya Tucker for *Rhythm Country and Blues* (US MCA 10969, 1994)

Jimmy Lewis

Hold On To What You've Got for Jimmy Lewis' *Soul-Gasm* (US Mardi Gras MB 4004, 1997)

Solomon Burke

Everybody's Got a Game from 1997 US *The Definition of Soul* Point Blank 7243 8 42557 2 5, 1996)

APPENDIX 2

Cover Versions

All these songs were recorded by Little Richard. An asterisk indicates that Richard had a writing credit.

'All Around the World' – Earl Preston & the T.T.'s, Shakers (aka Kingsize Taylor & the Dominoes)

'Baby Face' – Eddie Cantor (best known version before Little Richard), Bobby Darin (US No. 42, 1962), Benny Davis (original hit, 1926), Sammy Kaye (1948), Art Mooney (1948), Whispering Jack Smith, Wing & A Prayer Fife & Drums Corp (US No.14, 1976), Johnny Worth

*'Bama Lama Bama Loo' – Deejays, Tom Jones (higher key than Little Richard)

'By the Light of the Silvery Moon' – Freddie and the Dreamers, Lillian Lorraine (*Ziegfeld Follies of 1909*), Jackie Wilson, Johnny Worth

*'Can't Believe You Wanna Leave' – Doug Sahm

*'Directly from My Heart' – Frank Zappa with Don 'Sugarcane' Harris

'Get Down with It' – Slade (UK No.16, 1971), Derry Wilkie (last recorded performance)

'Heeby-Jeebies' - Fourmost, Kingsize Taylor & the Dominoes

'The Girl Can't Help It' – Animals, Wayne Fontana & the Mindbenders, Fourmost (with Sounds Inc), Renegades, Cliff Richard (slowed-down arrangement)

'Good Golly Miss Molly' – Bobby Brant & the Poe-Cats, Jaybirds, Jerry Lee Lewis (UK No.31, 1963), Little Bo Pete & the Rock'n'Roll Janitors, (1974 single from Oscar Tobin Jr), Hal Munro, Pete MacLaine & the Clan (Decca 45, unreleased as Swingin' Blue Jeans beat them to it), Nilsson (1971 outtake crossed with 'Lucille'), Mitch Ryder (US No.4, 1966 as part of medley), Denny Seyton & the Sabres, Tony Sheridan, Swinging Blue Jeans (UK No.11, 1964: new version with Colin Manley, 1988), Kingsize Taylor, Valiants (original), Gene Vincent & the Shouts

*'Hey Hey Hey Hey' – Beatles, Howie Casey & the Seniors, Downliners Sect, Tammy St John, Undertakers

*'Jenny Jenny' – Flash Cadillac & the Continental Kids (in 'Jenny Take a Ride'), Fleetwood Mac, Bill Haley, Carl Perkins, Mitch Ryder (in 'Jenny Take a Ride', US 10 UK 33), Searchers (in 'Jenny Take a Ride')

Kansas City – Beatles, Freddy Cannon, Dion, Fats Domino, Everly Brothers, Billy Fury, Bill Haley, Wilbert Harrison, Herman's Hermits, Wanda Jackson, Brenda Lee, Willie Nelson, Muddy Waters and many, many more

*Keep A-Knockin' – original by James Wiggins (1928) and then recorded by Bob Wills and Louis Jordan. Everly Brothers, Flamin' Groovies, Lindisfarne, Outlaws, Alan Price, Suzie Quatro, Johnny Rivers, Scorpions, Shakin' Stevens, Trashmen. Also included in 'Santa and the Satellite' by Buchanan and Goodman

*'Long Tall Sally' – Atlanta Rhythm Section, Beatles, Blue C, Pat Boone (US No.8, 1956), Chimbo's Revival (Copenhagen), Eddie Cochran, Deans (early demo by Merseybeat group), Dave Grohl, Isley Brothers, Kinks, Koppykats, Merseybeats, Migil 5, Cark Perkins, Elvis Presley, Roadrunners, Marty Robbins, Sam the Sham and the Pharaohs (first LP), Swinging Blue Jeans, Vince Taylor & his Playboys (label says 'Lone Tall Sally'), Kingsize Taylor, Tornados, Gene Vincent

*'Lucille' – Animals, Beatles, Deep Purple, Everly Brothers (US No.21, 1960), Fireballs, Bill Haley, Johnny Hallyday, Hollies, Waylon Jennings, Tom Jones, Little Bo Pete & the Rock'n'Roll Janitors (1974 single from Oscar Tobin Jr), Marauders, John Mayall, Nilsson (1971 outtake with 'Good Golly Miss Molly'), Orion, Peter & Gordon, Paul McCartney, Otis Redding, Renegades, Shadows, Status Quo, Bobby Vee & the Crickets, Ventures, Johnny Winters. Despite their reputation as prog rock band, Procol Harum would knock out Little Richard classics like 'Lucille' from time to time. 'Sometimes it was too cold to play anything slow,' recalled Gary Brooker.

*'Miss Ann' – Kris Ryan & the Questions

*'Ooh! My Soul' – Beatles, Kingsize Taylor, Ritchie Valens (as 'Ooh My Head')

'Ready Teddy' – Johnny Hallyday, Buddy Holly, Carl Perkins, Elvis Presley, Cliff Richard & the Drifters, Searchers, Tony Sheridan, Sounds Inc, Shakin' Stevens, Swinging Blue Jeans (unreleased in 60s), Vince Taylor & Playboys, Tornados, Gene Vincent, plus Cliff Richard & Adam Faith (together on Royal Variety Show, 1960)

'Rip It Up' – Beatles (*Let It Be* sessions), Marc Bolan (1973 demo with 'Gave my baby a black eye'), Commander Cody and his Lost Planet Airmen, Everly Brothers, Gerry & the Pacemakers, Bill Haley (US No.25, 1956), Hanson, Wanda Jackson, Mickie Most, Elvis Presley, Alan Price Set (for German TV), Cliff Richard (at BBC), Roadrunners, Scorpions, Star Combo, Shakin' Stevens, Vince Taylor & Playboys (though from intro, you'd think he was about to do 'Dixieland Rock'), Zombies. In the Australian TV series, *Friday on My Mind,* the Easybeats are told to get a rougher sound so they played 'Rip It Up'.

'Send Me Some Lovin'' – Lloyd Price, Sam Cooke (US No.13, 1963), Freddie & the Dreamers (on London Palladium and on *NME* Pollwinners Concert), Buddy Holly, Sherry Holly, John Lennon, Crispian St Peters, Otis Redding

*'She's Got It''– Johnny Guitar & Paul Murphy (1957 demo), Jimmy & the Rackets

*'Slippin' And Slidin'' – The Band, Bill Black's Combo, Blues Band, Billy 'Crash' Craddock, Mickey Gilley, Kingsize Taylor & the Dominoes, Gerry & the Pacemakers, Wanda Jackson, John Lennon, Dickie Pride, Shakin' Stevens, Willy & the Poor Boys, Johnny Winter, Roy Young/ The opening words of Bob Dylan's 'One Moe Weekend' are 'Slippin' and a-slidin''.

*'True Fine Mama' – Howie Casey & the Seniors

*'Tutti Frutti' – Pat Boone (US No.12, 1956), Commander Cody & his Lost Planet Airmen, Fleetwood Mac, Four Jones Boys, Dennisons, Sleepy LaBeef, MC5, Art Mooney, Elvis Presley, Queen, Swinging Blue Jeans. (Les Braid of the Swinging Blue Jeans: 'The song is a bit jazzy, a leftover from our old days.')

Bibliography

***The Life and Times of Little Richard: the Quasar of Rock*, Charles White (Pan, 1984)**
Hang onto your hats, as this is the most frenzied and enjoyable of all rock biographies and was updated in 1994 and 2002. Little Richard and his cohorts are quoted verbatim, and the book is full of life. It has been extensively used while I was writing this book because it is the only detailed interview with Little Richard that there is, but are all those anecdotes true? Hopefully, *Send Me Some Lovin'* presents a truer picture but that in no way detracts from this extraordinary document. There is no other rock book like it.

***Frank Tashlin*, edited by Roger Garcia (British Film Institute, 1994)**
Frank Tashlin was a screenwriter and director, mostly associated with Jerry Lewis. He wrote, directed and produced *The Girl Can't Help It*, which was made with much more care than the rock'n'roll quickies. The book is illustrated with his cartoons and scripts and leading critics line up to praise him.

***Rage to Survive: The Etta James Story*, Etta James & David Ritz (Da Capo, 1998)**
Chas White's biography of Little Richard opened the door, and Etta James came tumbling through. Etta has stories on Little Richard (and Larry Williams) which confirm their behaviour.

***Little Richard: the Birth of Rock'n'Roll*, David Kirby (Continuum, 2009)**
According to David Kirby, an English professor at Florida State University, Chas White's famed biography of Little Richard was flawed because White presented him as the world's craziest nut. Well, I thought that's because he was (with dear Chas coming in at No.2). It's an arresting thought and it implies that Kirby is going to demonstrate that Little Richard's career is built on artifice, that he created this public persona and he's not like that at all: he put on his slippers and watched TV all night. It's possible someone could be like that – Tom Waits is a good example – but maintaining that character is hard and you may become the very character you've created.

Kirby repeats himself so much that you will think you're on the wrong page. He says that Little Richard was born with one leg shorter than the other, but to refer to him as 'a cripple' is ridiculous. If you watch his dance routine with John Goodman in *King Ralph* (1991), Little Richard moves with no trouble at all. Len Hutton, with one leg shorter than the other, hit a record 364 against the Australians – was he one too?

***Dirty Bird Blues*, Clarence Major (Penguin Classics, 2022)**
Clarence Major's brilliant novel about life in bars and blues clubs in Chicago and Omaha in the early 1950s is vivid and colourful and the Dirty Bird of the title refers to Old Crow whiskey. Little Richard knew this world and as the main character, Man, remarks, 'Blues done saved as many lives as the church.' Now reissued with informative essays as a Penguin Classic.

Index

www.ingramcontent.com/pod-product-compliance
Ingram Content Group UK Ltd.
Pitfield, Milton Keynes, MK11 3LW, UK
UKHW050940130625
459566UK00004B/40

9 780857 162441